Dangerous matter

DANGEROUS MATTER
English Drama and Politics in 1623/24

JERZY LIMON

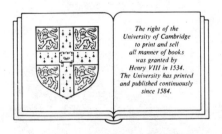

The right of the
University of Cambridge
to print and sell
all manner of books
was granted by
Henry VIII in 1534.
The University has printed
and published continuously
since 1584.

CAMBRIDGE UNIVERSITY PRESS

Cambridge
London   New York   New Rochelle
Melbourne   Sydney

Published by the Press Syndicate of the University of Cambridge
The Pitt Building, Trumpington Street, Cambridge CB2 1RP
32 East 57th Street, New York, NY 10022, USA
10 Stamford Road, Oakleigh, Melbourne 3166, Australia

First published 1986

Printed in Great Britain at
the University Press, Cambridge

British Library Cataloguing in Publication Data
Limon, Jerzy
Dangerous matter: English drama and politics
in 1623/4.
1. English drama – Early modern and Elizabethan,
1500–1600 – History and criticism 2. Politics
in literature
I. Title
822'.3'09358   PR658.P65

Library of Congress Cataloguing in Publication Data
Limon, Jerzy, 1950–
Dangerous matter.
Bibliography: p.
Includes index.
1. English drama – 17th century – History and
criticism. 2. Politics in literature. 3. Great Britain
– Politics and government – 1603–1625. 4. Theater –
England – History – 17th century. 5. Politics and
literature – Great Britain. I. Title.
PR678.P65L54   1986   822'.3'09358   85-29127

ISBN 0 521 30664 7

Contents

Acknowledgements

I would like to thank the British Council for awarding me a grant that enabled me to compile materials for this book in England. Dr Richard Proudfoot's critical comments were of enormous help. And special thanks to Judith Landry, who devoted her precious time to polish my English.

J.L.

Introduction

Owing to its mimetic qualities and the ability to pretend to be a 'mirror up to nature', to be an objective and unambiguous 'reflection' of the empirical world, a dramatic text reveals through its seeming 'objectivity' an enormous persuasive power, and may with ease function as an efficient instrument of propaganda. The understanding of this potentiality has always tempted those in power to take full administrative control of the dissemination of drama. This was particularly the case in societies – like that of James I – where the majority of people were illiterate. That dramatic texts could become useful tools in political struggle, or a means of persuasion that was capable of influencing wide circles of society, had already been fully recognized during the reign of the early Tudors. David Bevington's *Tudor Drama and Politics*[1] provides an impressive amount of evidence for that. However, in most of the examples he provides, particular performances of politically engaged plays, reflecting the ideology of particular court factions, had in fact limited court audiences and took place on single occasions only. It was not until the last years of James I's reign that, for the first time, dramatic texts were disseminated on a wide scale for basically political purposes; they were not confined to court, nor even to London itself, nor were they limited to single performances. During the period of several months, starting in November 1623, thousands of people had an opportunity to see or read dozens of plays, a number of which raised important political issues of the day, and dealt with topics of great importance to the entire nation and to what seemed to be the future of Protestantism.

This book will concentrate on the extant plays and masques that were circulated in England, both in print and in theatrical performances, during the period immediately following the return of Prince Charles and the Duke of Buckingham from Spain in October 1623. Their return was the result of the failure of the marriage negotiations through which James I had hoped to bring peace to Europe, and also marked the beginning of a new phase in English foreign policy. These dramatic texts have one thing in common: when staged, or circulated in print in 1623/24, they served an important political purpose, which this book will aim to reveal. Because of the unprecedented scale and scope of this particular theatrical season, it is difficult to avoid an impression that it was not a spontaneous reaction of the dramatists of the period against the mishandling of England's foreign policies

I

by the court, but a consciously contrived campaign, initiated and sponsored by a group of politicians whose goal it was to use all means available to win the support of both nobility and the commons. Unfortunately, in most cases, it is impossible to prove who in particular 'stood behind' a given performance, or publication, just as it may well have been impossible to do so in the period under discussion, but some pieces of evidence and the extant texts of plays and masques strengthen our contention that this was a consciously organized campaign, something that this book will attempt to prove. That a dozen or so plays, printed or staged within one theatrical season only, dealt directly with or alluded to the same political issues, cannot be a matter of mere coincidence. Moreover, the circulation of these plays was concomitant with, and preceded by, a positive flood of pamphlets, ballads, sermons, broadsheets and newsletters of various kinds, which in different forms treated of identical issues. The theatres, it appears, were not isolated in their newly acknowledged function as mass media, but constituted part of a larger propaganda campaign, and their importance lay, among other things, in the fact that theatre performances could appeal to and influence the opinions of the illiterate section of society. The latter purpose was in a way similar to that of sermons, for the pulpit was one of the strongest instruments for shaping public opinion.

The involvement of Jacobean plays in contemporary affairs was indeed amazing, especially in the light of strict censorship and severe punishment for those who tried to neglect the letter of the law. The very fact that new proclamations imposing harsh restrictions upon writers and printers were passed during the early years of James I's reign is significant, for it reveals the monarch's or, more generally, the state's recognition of the impact of the written or spoken word; an impact – it has to be added – detrimental to the interests of the Crown. When, in 1617, James decided to enter into negotiations with Spain over the possible marriage of Prince Charles and the Infanta, Protestants in England were appalled by the prospect of having yet another Catholic Queen. But when the negotiations continued after the outbreak of what was to become the Thirty Years War, and after the hope of The Protestant Union, Frederick, Duke of the Rhenish Palatinate and King of Bohemia, together with his English wife Princess Elizabeth, were forced out of Bohemia by the imperial forces and a Spanish army occupied the Palatinate, the outcry of anger and opposition to James I's line of policy became wide-spread. In consequence, new legal restrictions were introduced. The first drastic proclamation was issued on 24 December 1620, and was aimed at lavish and licentious speech concerning matters of state; it was reissued on 26 July 1621. A campaign against 'disorderly printing' began a little later than the one condemning free speech: on 25 September 1623 a proclamation was published against the printing and selling of books contrary to the laws of the land and the regulations of the Company of

Stationers.[2] Plays of course had their own censor, the Master of the Revels, whose duty it was to suppress any texts that commented critically on the policies or conduct of the court; the presentation on stage of the high-born who were still living; unfavourable presentation of friendly foreign powers or their sovereigns, nobles, or subjects; comment on religious controversy; the use of profanity and oaths and personal satire about influential people.[3]

There is a good deal of evidence that Englishmen's interest in politics, both domestic and foreign, was much intensified after the outbreak of war in Bohemia. Through an accelerating development of events, a local conflict in Bohemia between the Estates and the Emperor, who was also the King of Bohemia, evolved into a clash of two religions, and it was generally anticipated that England would play a major role in the conflict. However, in the early phase of the war, printed sources of news available to the English were very few. The gap between the public interest and what was actually printed could not be filled with royal proclamations and declarations, which were in fact selective and propagandist. Because of the enormous interest of the general public in England in the rapidly developing events on the Continent, the country was soon to experience a revolution in the dissemination of news. This was the appearance of the first newspapers in the English language, the earliest extant copies of which were printed in the Netherlands in 1620 and 1621. At this stage, each issue – of what was to become known as corantos – consisted of one leaf in small folio with the text in two columns on each side of the leaf.[4] That the Netherlands became the site of the press for various publications in English is of little surprise: it was in The Hague that Frederick and Elizabeth found refuge, and in fact the city began to be considered the capital of the Protestant party on the Continent. It certainly lay within the most relevant interests of the Elector's court that public opinion in England should be appropriately informed about events of great significance to an endangered Protestantism. It seems that these first newspapers became quite popular, for already in 1621 a series of news publications was printed in London by Thomas Archer (none of these, however, is extant), and in September of the same year another book-seller, 'N.B.', obtained a privilege to publish corantos, or which several numbers have survived.[5] It is interesting to note that home news was forbidden to be printed (this could only be done, and was done, abroad), and the first English newspapers published in England were devoted entirely to foreign affairs, with Bohemia and the Palatinate figuring as the most salient countries. With an expanding reading audience, these early prints appeared insufficient to cover the whole variety of news coming from the war-torn Continent. Thus, in about the middle of 1622, Thomas Archer and Nicholas Bourne became partners and started publishing news in small quarto volumes, the so-called books-of-news, or newsbooks. In the autumn of the same year several other stationers entered the field and a sort of news syndicate was formed and their newsbooks were published in a numbered series.[6] Even a brief look through the extant copies reveals an interesting fact, namely, that the focus of particular issues rested almost entirely on issues essential to the interests of Frederick and his supporters. The actions of both sides involved in the conflict were described in minute detail and the speed with which items of news reached printing presses in London was amazing. Thus, the English could follow all the recent developments on the Continent and relate them to what was publicly known or gossiped about James's policies. According to a detailed study by Folke Dahl, the number of copies of the different number printed was no less than 400,[7] and there is no doubt that particular copies were read by or to a number of people.

We have enough evidence available for the claim that in the period under discussion there were constant attempts to use drama and theatres as a means of disseminating news. Let us give some examples to illustrate how newsbooks, ballads, sermons and other publications, and theatres, were in fact treated as complementary means of such dissemination, strikingly reminiscent of today's mass media. When news of the massacre of English merchants at Amboyna reached London by mid 1624 it was first embodied in a ballad, entitled 'News out of East India: of the cruell and bloody usage of our English merchants and others at Amboyna, by the Netherlandish Governour and Councell there'.[8] It was then related in another publication, *Cruel and barbarous tortures and execucons Done upon English at Ambo[y]na in the East Indies by the Du[t]ch*[9]. Soon afterwards, a contemporary source tells us that:

The East India Company have ordered Greenburg, a painter, to paint a detailed picture of all the tortures inflicted on the English at Amboyna, and would have had it all acted in a play, but the Council was appealed to by the Dutch ministers, and stopped it, for fear of disturbance this Shrovetide.[10]

This is confirmed by the well-known letter-writer of the period, John Chamberlain, who on 26 February wrote to Carleton,

the Dutch have lost their friends here. Wilkinson has printed a sermon, with a bitter preface against them, and a play is written on the Amboyna, and also a large picture of it is made for the East India Company, but both are suppressed by Council.[11]

For our purposes here it is important to note that almost immediately after the news of the massacre had reached London, the merchants of the East India Company found it appropriate to order a play and have it presented to the general public. Some Dutch ministers, having learnt about the whole enterprise before the play had been completed, decided to make an official complaint to the Privy Council which, in turn, suppressed the play not only to satisfy the demands of the Dutch, but also for fear of public disorder. It was feared that a single performance of the play could in fact provoke public disturbances. In current terms, the Company had ordered a 'documentary' on the subject, hired a 'production team', and was planning to stir public opinion against the Dutch – their great competitors in trade, it may be added. By so doing, the merchants revealed full understanding of the enormous power of theatre to influence public opinion, and this power was equally acknowledged by the politicians of that period.

It is also important to note that in the case described above, it was not the Master of the Revels (the King's official censor) who decided whether or not the play should be licensed. The example provided illustrates clearly that the Privy Council had the power to suppress a play or, when needed, to influence the Master of the Revels' decision or even allow a company of actors to play without a licence. For instance, when the news of the fall of the great Dutch statesman, John of Barneveld, attracted enormous interest in England, a ballad on the subject was instantaneously composed, which was followed by a play. A contemporary letter informs us that:

The Players heere were bringing of Barnavelt upon the stage, and had bestowed a great deal of money to prepare all things for the purpose, but at the instant were prohibited by my Lo. of London [i.e. John King, the Bishop of London].[12]

The reason for the suppression of the play was certainly political: Barneveld was suddenly arrested and accused of high treason for plotting against his lord, Maurice of Nassau, Prince of Orange (who was Frederick of Bohemia's uncle and a great supporter of his cause). He was said to have been in the pay of the Spanish, and, as an influential and trusted politician, carried out treacherous schemes to the detriment of his country and of Protestants in general. Thus, to present his activity on stage would provide the spectators with an example and a warning against the dangers of 'Spanish practices', and would without doubt have evoked obvious associations with certain English personages, commonly acclaimed as the King's evil advisers; that is, with those who were said to have formed the Spanish faction at court and were in fact in the pay of the Spanish ambassador, Gondomar. That Barneveld was considered a Spanish-paid traitor may be illustrated by a passage from a treatise entitled *A Narrative of the wicked Plots carried on by Seignior Gondamore, for advancing the Popish Religion and Spanish Faction*, in which Gondomar informs the nuncio and other Spanish nobles that 'we have received late and sad news of the apprehension of our trusty and able pensioner Barnevelt, and of discovery of other our intendments'. In the play Barneveld is presented as a proud, ambitious man, jealous of the governor and Calvinist Prince Maurice of Nassau who, to achieve his goals, accepts Spanish help and organizes an armed mutiny against the state, eventually to be defeated with the aid of the English garrisons in the Low Countries.

The suppression of the play by the Bishop of London did not, however, stop the players from trying to find the support of even more influential peers and, after a fortnight, on 27 August 1619, the same man penned another letter, in which he stated that:

Our players have found the meanes to goe through with the play of Barnavelt and it hath had many spectators and received applause.[13]

Thus, 'finding the meanes' was an important part of London's theatrical life in this period of severe censorship. The Office Book of Sir Henry Herbert includes several conspicuous examples of his interventions. For instance, in August 1623, he recorded the following:

For the Company at the Curtaine; A Tragedy of the Plantation of Virginia [another 'documentary', it seems]; the profaneness to be left out, otherwise not tolerated.[14]

The legal basis for the Master of the Revels' power to licence plays was the Royal Commission of 1581, which was reissued in 1603 and in 1622, and which included the following clause:

in case any of them, whatsoever they be, will obstinately refuse upon warning unto them given . . . to accomplish and obey our commandment in this behalf, then it shall be lawful to . . . Master of the Revels . . ., or his sufficient deputy, to attack the party or parties so offending, and him or them to commit to ward, to remain without bail or mainprise until such time as the same . . . Master of the Revels, or his sufficient deputy, shall think the time of his or their imprisonment to be punished for his or their said offences in that behalf.[15]

The consequences of neglecting the Master of the Revels' decisions were serious. But this happened every now and then to the extent that sometimes plays were staged without being licensed at all. We learn about such an incident in 1624, when the players apologized to Sir Henry for staging a play called *The Spanish Viceroy*.[16]

Because the interests of various court factions were often different from those of James I, the Master of the Revels experienced at times difficult situations, when he had to take into account the pressures of equally influential sides. He could fall into disgrace for licensing a play, or for the opposite. In the summer of 1624, for instance, he licensed Thomas Middleton's play, *A Game at Chesse*, by which he caused the King's fury, but also, on the other hand, fully satisfied Prince Charles and the Duke of Buckingham. This will be discussed in detail in chapter 4. So, to keep his position, the Master of the Revels had to balance carefully between the often contradictory demands of his superiors, the most important of whom was, of course, the King, with his genuine interest in the theatre.

Sometimes, the Master of the Revels received complaints from ordinary people and requests to suppress a play that they found offensive. But in these cases his decisions seem to have been totally arbitrary. For instance when, in the summer of 1624, rumours spread about a play being written on one of the recent events that occurred in London,[17] an official complaint was made by one Anne Elsden, who was the victim of a cunning plot against her life and prosperity, and who was also the heroine-to-be of the play, claiming that

libellous and scandallous enterlude & play . . . being thus contriued & made . . . to scandalize & disgrace Anne Elsden & make her ridiculous to the world, cause & procure the . . . play or enterlude to be seuerall tymes acted & played at the playhouse called the Bull at Clarkenwell on the Countye of Middlesex by the players there.[18]

Nevertheless, the play was licensed in September 1624, and when it was first acted at the Red Bull, Anne Elsden made another attempt to suppress it, and sent her son-in-law to the Deputy Master of the Revels with a petition to him to prohibit the performance. The Deputy Master of the Revels accepted a bribe of twenty shillings and promised to forbid the play, which he never did. Thus, the only result of the petition was to double the fees of the Office of the Revels.[19]

Most of the examples given above inform us that plays were talked about not only after they had been acted, but also while they were being written. This in itself proves the important role played by theatre in the life of London. Like newsbooks, plays were in a way expected to deal with contemporary matters, and this undoubtedly excited people's interest to see a particular play that was the 'talk of the town'. Rumours and gossiping also served the function of an advertising campaign, and may have in fact been spread by the players themselves. All of this heightened people's desire to see the 'forbidden fruit of politics' displayed on the theatre stage. This desire was also stimulated by other forms of disseminating the news, which were usually written and printed before the playwrights rendered the same, or similar, plots into dramas. All these non-dramatic publications prepared the ground, as it were, for attracting the attention of theatrical audiences, who went to see plays expecting events known to them from elsewhere to come 'alive', and were certainly capable of understanding all the allusions the players made to events or people they were not allowed to show directly in theatre. Moreover, plays often circulated in manuscript copies, some of which survive today in different transcriptions.[20] The players in Philip Massinger's *The Roman Actor* are attacked in a conspicuous way:

> You are they
> That search into the secrets of the time,
> And, under feigned names, on the stage, present
> Actions not to be touched at; and traduce
> Persons of rank and quality of both sexes,
> And, with satirical and bitter jests,
> Make even the senators ridiculous
> To the plebeians   (i.iii)

The actors' defence is also worth quoting, for it must have been frequent around the time the play was written:

> ... And, for traducing such
> That are above us, publishing to the world
> Their secret crimes, we are as innocent
> As such as are born dumb.   (i.iii)

Thus, revealing the 'secret crimes' of those 'above' to the general public was seen as one of functions of the theatre.

Plays were only a part, undoubtedly a very important one, of a campaign of political propaganda, carried out on an unprecedented scale and initiated in the last months of 1623. Apart from sundry 'legal' publications, printed in London, the country was flooded by various tracts and pamphlets in English printed abroad, which – dealing directly with domestic matters – had to be smuggled into England. The consequences of this, or of un-licensed printing of political literature, were very serious. For instance, in 1623 one William Philips was committed for translating a French pamphlet and sentenced to death.[21] John Reynolds was sent to prison and fined £1000 in 1624 for printing without a licence *Votivae Anglia*.[22] Even though George Hakewill, Prince Charles's chaplain, did not publish the treatise he had written against the match with Spain, but simply passed it over in manuscript to the Prince's tutor, and to Charles himself, he was nevertheless imprisoned for his 'bald interference' and dismissed from the chaplaincy.[23] These publications were persistent, often shrewd and openly critical of James I, with a frequent touch of personal satire and ridicule, and their influence can be measured by the extent to which they aroused public opinion. When, for instance, Thomas Scott's *Vox Populi* was published anonymously in 1620 (it had four editions in that year alone), the Venetian ambassador noted in his report to the Doge and Senate, dated 4 December, that the book

severely castigates the Spanish ambassador here [i.e. Count of Gondomar], who therefore foams with wrath in every direction and it is said that he has sent it to the King to make complaint. This has transpired and given rise to much comment.[24]

The serious political consequences of Scott's book were also described about the same time and in greater detail by Sir Simond D'Ewes in his journal, where he commented:

But the King himself, hoping to get the Prince Elector, his son-in-law, to be restored to the Palatinate by an amicable treaty, was much incensed at the sight of it [i.e. of *Vox Populi*], as being published at an unseasonable time ... There was, therefore, so much and so speady search made for the author of it, as he scarcely escaped the hands of the persuivants, who had they taken him, he had certainly tasted of a sharp censure: for the Spanish Ambassador himself did at this time suppose and fear the people's eyes to be opened so far with the perusal of this book and their hearts to be so extremely irritated with that discovery of his villainous practices, as he caused his house for a while to be secured in Holborn by a guard of men, it being the Bishop of Ely's house, at the lower end of Holborn.[25]

That Scott was able to escape severe punishment may be readily accounted for by the fact that he had been a chaplain to William Herbert, Earl of Pembroke, and his anti-Spanish stand coincided with that of his patron. Scott was by no means an isolated example, and although James made constant attempts to silence the militant clergy, they continued to meddle in state matters and preached against Spain.[26] For example, John Everard, reader at St Martin-in-the-Fields, was imprisoned at least twice for sermons against the Spanish marriage of Prince Charles; and when John Knights of Oxford concluded in his sermon that 'if kings grow unruly and tyrannical they may be corrected and brought into order by their subjects', King James threatened 'to have the copy of it publicly burnt by the hangman as heretical'.[27] Even pictures and caricatures were used by James's opponents, and we know of a minister at Ipswich imprisoned upon Gondomar's complaint for rendering a picture of the Gunpowder Plot, depicting the Pope sitting in a council with a cardinal on one hand and the devil on the other.[28] And the same Thomas Scott, in another treatise entitled *Vox Coeli, or News from Heaven*, mentions in his address to the Parliament of 1624 that he 'sawe Allureds honest letter [Thomas Allured was Lord Ever's secretary, and was the author of a letter against the Spanish match, for which he incurred the Duke of Buckingham's displeasure], Scots loyal Vox Populi, D. Whiting, D. Everard, and Claytons zealous Sermons, and others suppressed and silenced; as also Wards Faithful picture'.[29]

The suppression of freedom of speech and printing, and the prosecution of writers generally acclaimed as patriotic, were certainly difficult to comprehend for the majority of people. The discrepancy between what they viewed to be the vital interests of the country and the King's unpopular stand seemed to have no rational explanation, unless someone dared to accuse James of high treason. The blame was placed, therefore, if not on James directly, then on either his 'evil' councillors, representing the so-called Spanish faction,[30] or on the Spaniards themselves, who – it was thought – through the machiavellian practices of Gondomar and others, managed to dupe the King by false promises. For instance, in another tract that Scott wrote, entitled *A Narrative of the wicked Plots carried on by Seignior Gondamore, for advancing the Popish Religion and Spanish Faction*, written c. 1623/24, Gondomar himself – who appears in a dispute with the Papal nuncio and other Spanish nobles – admits that

both in England and Scotland, all, for the most part . . . oppose this match to the utmost, by prayers, counsels, speeches, and wishes; but, if one be found longer-tongued than his fellows, we have still means to charm their sauciness, to silence them, to expel them [from?] the court; to disgrace them . . . For instance . . . a doctor of theirs, and a chaplain in ordinary to the King, gave many reasons in a letter, against this marriage . . . which I understanding, so wrought underhand, that the doctor was committed.[31]

It may be added that this was at times also the fate of English peers who had the courage to speak openly against James's policy. For instance, when in 1621 the Earl of Oxford spoke over his wine against Popery and the Spanish match, and this was reported to the King, he was imprisoned in the Tower.[32] Although he was soon released, Oxford had not learnt his lesson and fell into disgrace again in 1622, this time for saying that England had a King who had placed his ecclesiastical supremacy in the hands of the Pope, and his temporal supremacy in the hands of the King of Spain and thus he was nothing better than Philip's viceroy. This also was reported to the King and the Earl was immediately sent back to the Tower, and James talked of bringing him to trial for high treason, and of cutting off his head.³³ Oxford remained in confinement until the early months of 1624.

Therefore, if dramatic literature was to become involved in the politics of the day, to face strict censorship and the severe consequences of neglecting the latter, playwrights and players had to find a means of conveying political messages in such a way as would not endanger their personal freedom. In the majority of cases discussed in the subsequent chapters of this book, the extant plays and masques are often strongly biased against the line of James I's foreign policy, and constitute in fact its conspicuous criticism, so one may suspect that, in spite of all the risk involved, the players and playwrights felt secure enough to engage themselves in what seemed to be an anti-royal campaign initiated by the new court party of Prince Charles and the Duke of Buckingham. If they had not been supported by their influential patrons, they would undoubtedly either have abstained from provocative political comment, or suffered its serious consequences. The latter factor was widely acknowledged by theatre people. In the Prologue to Wentworth Smith's play *The Hector of Germanie, or the Palsgrave, Prime Elector*, published in 1615, we read the following lines:

> Our Authour for himselfe, this bad me say,
> Although the Palsgraue be the name of th'Play,
> Tis not that Prince, which in this Kingdome late,
> Marryed the Mayden glory of our state;
> What Pen dares be so bold in this strict age,
> To bring him while he lives upon the Stage?
> And though he would, Authorities sterne brow
> Such a presumptuous deed will not allow:
> And he must not offend Authoritie ...   (A₂ᵛ)

These lines could actually serve as an epigraph to this book, for they reveal the author's consciousness of the restrictions imposed upon him as the playwright, and of the spectators' or readers' ability to associate the protagonist of this pseudo-historical play with Frederick, the Duke of the Rhenish Palatinate who had recently married James's daughter, Elizabeth. This ability of both theatre and reading audiences to associate dramatic characters, either historical or fictitious, with their contemporary 'equivalents', and also to grasp the underlying meaning and the allusiveness of seemingly non-political plots, to 'read between the lines', is in fact a characteristic feature of the entire period under discussion. It enabled playwrights to create pseudo-historical and pseudo-mythological, or allegorical, texts which had the potential ability to evoke predictable and desired associations in both spectators and readers.

This ability characterized of course the 'other side' too, that is, those whose duty it was to protect the interests of the King, like the Master of the Revels and his deputy and informers, and it also characterized James himself. His sensitivity to plays, and his grasp of the underlying 'message' or – in fact –

his over-sensitivity and his tendency to read into a text an interpretation of his own, may be illustrated by the following example. When Prince Charles's company performed at court in the Christmas season of 1619/20, and presented an uncensored play, the players were seriously reprimanded by the King, who was disturbed by what he interpreted as an allusion in the play to the recurrent rumours accusing him of the responsibility for Prince Henry's death. This is how the affair is described by the Venetian ambassador, in a letter of 10 January 1620:

In connection with the subject of comedians, I ought not conceal the following event from your Serenity [i.e. the Doge and Senate], owing to the mistery that it involves. The comedians of the prince, in the presence of the King his father, played a drama the other day in which a king with his two sons has one of them put to death, simply upon suspicion that he wished to deprive him of his crown, and the other son actually did deprive him of it afterwards. This moved the king in an extraordinary manner, both inwardly and outwardly.[34]

It is difficult to avoid the impression that Prince Charles was responsible for the staging of that particular play at court, but it is impossible to determine to what extent he realized that his father might find the play offensive. If he did, then this would appear to have been either a practical joke played on James by the Prince, or a performance of the 'mouse-trap' type we find in Shakespeare's *Hamlet*. On another occasion, we learn about the King acting as the 'High Censor' himself. During the preparations for the masque to be staged on 6 January 1624, the same Venetian ambassador informs us that 'the usual verses written for the masque containing some rather free remarks against the Spaniards, they were altered by his [i.e. James's] command'.[35]

That the stage may be a valuable means of propaganda was also argued by Thomas Scott:

We see sometimes Kings are content in plays and masks to be admonished of divers things ... And might I not borrow a Spanish name or two, as well as French or Italian, to grace this comedy with stately actors? Or must they only be reserved for kingly tragedies? Why not Gondomar as well as Hieronymo or Duke d'Alva? And why not Philip as well as Peter, or Alfonso, or Caesar? Or might I not make as bold with them, as they with our Black Prince, or Henry the Eighth, or Edward the Sixth, or Queen Elizabeth, or King James, or the King and Queen of Bohemia? If this be censurable for being a fiction, it is surely for lack of a fool, which, they say, comedies should not be without, and for need, this witty objector may supply the place.[36]

As will be shown in the following chapters, all the contemporary personages mentioned in the list above actually appeared in plays staged in 1624, Gondomar and Philip and James in Middleton's *A Game at Chesse*, and the King and Queen of Bohemia in Thomas Drue's *The Life of the Duchess of Suffolk*.

Of the four companies of players active in London in 1623, the most appropriate to take theatrical arms against Spain and James I's policies were those of Elizabeth, that is, the Lady Elizabeth Company, and of Frederick, that is, the Palsgrave's Company. Scholars have already noticed that the latter company's repertory in that particular season was characterized by an unprecedented number of plays. Moreover, most of these plays were written by members of this company, like Richard Gunnell and Samuel Rowley. Rowley's sudden appearance in London's theatrical life after a period of ten years' absence, added to other evidence, indicates that in 1623 some of the companies were reorganized in preparation for what seems to have been a minutely calculated theatrical campaign. A company which would appear useful in carrying out a political scheme had to be composed of trustworthy and reliable players who would be prepared to undertake the considerable risk involved. It is around this period that we find attacks against Catholic players,[37] and there are also signs that the reorganization of companies was concomitant with the appearance of new playwrights, ready to take orders for new plays. Moreover, some extant pieces of evidence indicate that it was Prince Charles himself who stood behind at least some of the changes and preparations that were made for the forthcoming season of 1623/24. We know, for instance, that towards the end of his stay in Madrid, Prince Charles ordered one George Vincent to bring some English players and musicians from the Continent. Vincent had a reputation as an actor–manager; in 1617 he had organized a company of players in London for service at the Prince of Poland's court in Warsaw.[38] In 1622 he was recorded as a manager of a company of his own in England.[39] And from the documents of 1623 and 1624 we learn that three English actors and musicians who had been temporarily employed at the court of Philip Julius, the Duke of Pomerania, in Wolgast, received a letter from George Vincent towards the end of August 1623, asking them 'for urgent reasons' to go to England.[40] From another document of 1624 we learn that it was the Prince of Wales who expressed a desire to employ these players in England, promising to pay them so much that it 'would suffice till the end of their lives'. Whether Prince Charles was reorganizing his own company, his sister's, or his brother-in-law's remains uncertain, but undoubtedly he took a personal interest in theatrical matters in London even before his return from Madrid.

In the political situation briefly described above, a number of plays and masques appeared, all of which had one thing in common: they alluded to major political issues of the day. These issues and consequently the surviving plays and masques may be roughly divided into several groups, which will be the subject of corresponding chapters of this book.

1. The first issue was Prince Charles's safe return from Madrid without the Infanta, an event that was widely celebrated in prose and verse and in drama. For instance, we know of a masque written by a courtier, John Maynard, which was staged on 17 November 1623; a contemporary account tells us that the masque had as its subject Prince Charles's return and that it offended the Spanish ambassadors. We also know that the performance was sponsored and financed by the Duke of Buckingham. Another masque

dealing with the same topic is Ben Jonson's *Neptune's Triumph for Albion's Return*, which was to be staged on 6 January 1624, but was cancelled owing to a diplomatic dispute over precedence. In this pseudo-mythological piece, Neptune's court is celebrating the triumph of Albion's return from abroad, from the court of Oceanos, where Albion had experienced many formidable dangers from which he narrowly escaped. The analogy to the recent return of Prince Charles is fairly obvious in this text.

2. Second was the issue of Bohemia and the Palatinate. The Winter King and Queen had not only lost their kingdom, but also their hereditary duchy. There was little hope for a peaceful settlement of this problem as Frederick was also deprived of the title of Elector. The miserable situation of Frederick and Elizabeth, who had found temporary refuge in The Hague, was widely acknowledged in England and elaborated upon in sundry pamphlets, sermons, poems, ballads, tracts and – of course – in plays. As an example of the latter, one play may readily be mentioned: Thomas Drue's *The Life of the Duchess of Suffolk*, licensed for the public stage on 2 January 1624.

3. The third issue of the day, closely linked with the previous one, was that of war – England's obligation to declare war against Spain for the restitution of the Palatinate in particular, and against the Catholic Antichrist in general. This strong determination of a number of Englishmen to take part in the conflict on the Continent is a recurrent motif in the literature of the period, especially in the early months of 1624, when it was expected that the summoning of Parliament would consequently provide sufficient funds for the maintenance of the army and the navy. In this context two plays will be discussed, Philip Massinger's *The Bondman* and Dekker and Ford's *The Sun's Darling*, both licensed in March 1624.

4. The fourth issue was of Spain in general. For some odd reasons, the English associated Spain and Spaniards with all the evils at home, on the Continent and in the colonies. The cause of all the calamities that had befallen Frederick and Elizabeth, England and Protestantism in general, was Spain, commonly associated with the Antichrist. This led to the belief that a victorious war against Spain would not only recover the Palatinate and Bohemia for their rightful owners, but would also be the victory of God's people, the elect, over the evil forces of the Antichrist. Consequently, in the literature of the period, Spaniards are presented as a treacherous nation, filled with ambition to conquer the world, as bloodthirsty Catholics indefatigable in their attempts to destroy true Christian religion. And the best-known play on the subject is Thomas Middleton's *A Game at Chesse*, licensed and staged in the summer of 1624, which also marks the end of this peculiar theatrical season.

Before we proceed to discuss particular plays of the 1623/24 season, it is necessary to explain what our critical approach will be. In the vast majority of essays and books on a similar subject, that is, on the relationship between literature and politics, the aim of a critic usually seems to be to track down the 'political meaning' of a given literary text, as if this 'meaning' were an intrinsic feature of the latter. This approach, characteristic for Elizabethan and Jacobean drama studies, leads to endless disputes about whether a given text is or is not political, about topical allusions, or about what the author 'had in mind' when writing a given text. From our point of view, a writer's 'intentions' are irrelevant to a critical analysis of a literary text. In our opinion, a literary text has no other 'political meaning' than that in its own created world. This should be distinguished from a political function that any literary work may acquire in its social circulation. We may talk about political function whenever some of the elements of the created world of the text evoke in readers or spectators certain responses and associations with the extra-textual political reality known to them. In this case, however, the 'intentions' of the author, or of any other person (or people) responsible for the dissemination of a given work, may be taken into account, for they tell us what sort of response in readers or spectators was initially anticipated, and may also be useful in determining the extent to which this anticipation found appropriate response. It may be noted in passing that this is exactly the area of censors' activity, for their concern with political plays, or with any other texts, is strictly connected with a censor's anticipation of a political function a given text may acquire in its social circulation. Thus, in countries where censorship is in operation, a political play may receive a licence for publication, or staging, as long as a censor does not anticipate the text's ability to acquire a political function detrimental to the interests of those whom he or she represents. In other words, a political text may, but does not have to, acquire a political function in the communicational process. The 'politics' of a play are confined to its autonomous created world, and thus form an invariant feature of the text, whereas a political function is variable owing to its topical, often accidental, temporal and circumstantial nature. This also explains why a non-political text may acquire this function: when circulated in a particular historical period, and in a given society, certain elements of the created world may evoke in readers or spectators certain associations with the politics of the day, or of the past. It may be said that the political function of a literary text, acquired within the particular context in which the communicational process takes place, is independent both of the author's 'intentions' and of the autonomous meaning of the text.

To illustrate a play's ability to evoke certain responses and associations in spectators or readers, incongruous with what have traditionally been labelled 'author's intentions', it may be useful to begin with an example of this phenomenon from a different epoch. When a Polish gentleman, Karol Sienkiewicz, visited London in the summer of 1820, he went to see several plays there, all of which he described in his *Diary*. On 8 July he went to Covent Garden and he recorded that 'Mr Garrick's *The Clandestine*

Marriage was played ... Second was the farce, of which I understood nothing, because I had no book. With the exception of when an actor said: "the Queen will order you to throw down your arms", people began to clap their hands, because now the word "Queen" moves everybody here.' On 17 August, Sienkiewicz went to the Drury Lane theatre, where he saw *Hamlet* with Edmund Kean playing the leading role, and among other things he recorded in his *Diary* the following: 'After the tragedy and before the comedy began, there were shouts "long live the Queen" and applause. And in *Hamlet*, when the King and Queen were seated on the throne, somebody shouted that this was Mr Brougham and the Queen.' And on 28 August, he saw a performance of *Othello*, a scene of which he described in the following terms: 'Emilia, Iago's wife, not knowing about the crime of her husband, clears Desdemona of accusations before him and speaks the words which seem to have been deliberately written for today's circumstances. Therefore, this raised such a noise as I have never heard in a theatre. These are the words:

> I will be hang'd, if some eternal villain
> Some cogging cozening slave, to get some office,
> Have not devis'd this slander; I'll be hang'd else

and then:

> Oh, heaven, that such companions thoud'st unfold;
> And put in every honest hand a whip,
> To lash the rascal naked through the world!

Everybody started to shout, to wave hats and handkerchiefs over their heads.'

The quoted excerpts from Sienkiewicz's *Diary* may serve as an example of how a single word, a sentence, or a single scene, may at times become of great significance to the spectators or readers of a play and evoke responses in them that bear no relation to the created world of a performance, or to a literary text. To shout and wave hats and handkerchiefs as a reaction to a serious scene is odd to say the least, but to associate Claudius with one 'Mr Brougham' seems simply preposterous to us, living in a different epoch. The awkward behaviour of spectators in the instances described above, equally inappropriate to the farce and the tragedies, can be fully comprehended only when an additional piece of information is given, namely, that these peculiar performances took place during the infamous trial of the Queen, who was accused of adultery, and whose barrister was Henry Brougham. This trial stirred public opinion and became the greatest political issue of the day. It would undoubtedly be ridiculous to assume that the London spectators of 1820 did not understand what *Hamlet* and *Othello* 'were about' and interpreted the plays, falsely, as being about 'their' Queen, but their cognition of the performance seems to have been interrupted by sudden associations, evoked by apparently single words or scenes, with some extratheatrical reality known to them.

The above example has further implications. Since what we have just labelled the 'extra-theatrical reality' is variable, owing to the complex social, political and cultural changes within a given society, so the reception of the same dramatic text also varies. Only internal features of a literary text remain invariant. Thus, a political play, that is, a play creating an autonomous world with explicit political content, does not necessarily have to function as a political piece in its social circulation. This is the case in particular when at a given time and in a given society, the political issues created by the text no longer bear any relation to the extra-textual reality. A suitable example of a play of this kind would be Thomas Middleton's *A Game at Chesse*, the most successful 'political' play of 1624. Today, the political message of the text is totally lost, because the conflicts and issues presented have no relation whatsoever to today's politics. One cannot, of course, exclude the possibility that some time in the future Middleton's play may once again acquire a political function.

On the other hand, a number of plays, written in the past as non-political pieces, may acquire a temporary political significance, owing to the resemblance of the created world, or some of its elements, to the political context at the time when the text is circulated. For instance, *The Merchant of Venice* was hardly a political play in Shakespeare's England, whereas it was consciously used as a political propaganda piece in Nazi Germany. Another Shakespearean example would be *The Winter's Tale*, a play seemingly innocent of political implication, and yet, when staged at the Royal Court in spring 1624 it acquired, albeit for one evening only, political significance by evoking a Bohemian topic, a very sensitive issue at the time. In both of these examples, the author's 'intentions' are insignificant, and only the 'intentions' of those responsible for circulating the plays in that particular context may be taken into account, for they may be helpful in determining whether the acquired political function was anticipated, or simply accidental.

Yet another distinction has to be made, namely, between a dramatic text and its theatrical performance, a distinction whose lack can cause confusion, misunderstanding and scholarly controversy. In our understanding, drama is a distinct literary genre, whose meaning is independent of actual theatrical productions. Theatre is a different art form, in which dialogue – or, broadly speaking, verbal means of expression – is only one element, with scenery, lighting, music, acting etc. as other, equally important components in a conglomerate and highly complex structure.

Very often, or course, although not necessarily, a literary text dominates a production, but the way it is presented on stage depends on, and is subordinated to, many factors external to the text proper. Furthermore, a production does not necessarily have to be congruous with the author's 'message': it is in itself an interpretation, creating a message of its own. The coalescence of the two, a dramatic text and its actual staging, may but does not have to form an ideologically consistent unit. When writing *Richard II*,

Shakespeare could not have forseen that this play would be employed for political purposes during his lifetime. The play, with a meaning of its own, when staged on the eve of the Essex rebellion acquired an additional political function, whose significance bore no relation to the author's original intentions. This secondary meaning, as opposed to the primary meaning of the literary text, was of course comprehensible only to informed members of the audience, in this case presumably a handful only. To the remaining spectators at the production of *Richard II* on 7 February 1601, this 'meaning-added play' need have had no extra-theatrical associations of the kind hoped for and anticipated by the conspirators, who had ordered the play to be staged on the eve of their ill-famed mutiny in order to gain the Londoners' support and understanding for their cause. Essex's failure significantly to influence public opinion through this newly recognized propaganda medium confirms our initial assertion that the reception of a given play, or in fact any literary text, does not have to be congruous with the intentions of the people responsible for a particular production, or for the dissemination of a literary text.

In his interesting book *Literature and Propaganda*[41] A.P. Foulkes presents a basic model of communication applicable both to literature and propaganda, a model that will appear useful for our purposes here:

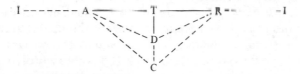

In this model, (A) is the author who produces the text (T) which is received by the reader (R). The text is defined as a 'structure of signs which possess designative values' (D), while 'the designata can themselves possess connotative dimensions' (C). The lines which run from (D) and (C) to both (A) and (R) are broken in order to indicate that the designata and connotations perceived or intended by (A) are not necessarily identical to those perceived by (R). The relationship which obtains between (R) and D/C and (A) and D/C is subject to the controlling influence of (I), the 'interpretants' in the broadest sense, including ultimately the individual experience of the multifarious ideological and social forces which modify, shape and influence our understanding of all signs. If we expand Foulkes's model, we shall obtain one applicable to a theatrical performance. In this case, however, the model of communication will be more complex, for the author's text is adapted for stage by a 'production team' (P) – itself influenced by (I_1), and a theatrical performance creates new signs which possess new designative values (D_1), and the new designata can, of course, possess connotative dimensions (C_1). Furthermore, spectator's, or (S)'s, response is subjected to the influence of (I_1).

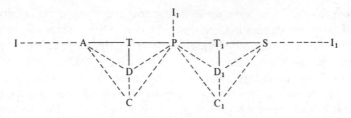

The relationship between D/C and D_1/C_1 is complex, because it depends on (P's) interpretation of (T), which in turn is controlled by (I_1). (P) of course interprets (T) according to his artistic and ideological aims, whether or not he understands D/C, thus producing (T_1), that is, a theatrical performance, creating a D_1/C_1 which may frequently differ considerably from that intended by (A). (P) may of course make an attempt to generate a D_1/C_1 reminiscent, or even very similar to, the D/C in what is sometimes labelled a faithful production. Thus, (S), the spectator, perceives the adapted (T_1) as if through the filter of (P), and (S's) ability to compare the relationship between D/C and D_1/C_1 depends basically on his knowledge of (T). By (T_1) I mean a 'theatrical text' in its broadest sense, that is, incorporating all the elements of a theatrical performance, not only the verbal ones. (P) and (S), who coexist in relation to a given performance, necessarily share the same I (designated I_1).

Since in the case of old plays we do not have enough evidence to discuss all the complexities of (T_1), we have to confine our discussion to the potential ability of (T) to acquire a political function, and to its intrinsic possibility of becoming (T_1) and thus creating (D_1) and (C_1). In other words, by attempting to reconstruct the social and political context on the basis of evidence available, and by relating a dramatic text to it, we should be able to describe the new and particular meaning that the text acquired, or may have acquired, in the communicational process within that very context. Our analysis will therefore focus primarily on a dramatic text and its ability to allude to certain elements of extra-textual reality, from which the text gains a political function, usually ephemeral and confined to a given historical period. Contemporary accounts describing either particular performances, or readers' responses, will only be useful in pointing out whether a given text acquired the political function it was expected to acquire on particular occasions. By focusing on this peculiar potentiality of a dramatic text, we shall be in a position to discuss the political significance of texts, or which we have no evidence of performance. Let us mention one example, which will be discussed in greater detail below, that of Ben Jonson's masque, *Neptune's Triumph*. In spite of the fact that its staging, planned for 6 January 1624, was cancelled, we can still analyse the text's potential political significance, as revealed by the text's relationship to the historical context of that particular play.

To sum up, it may be said that a literary text is capable of functioning as a political piece only in a communicative process during a particular historical period, within a given society and within the social and political context that the given period creates. Out of the context, the text's political function will either be different, or be lost entirely. The same text is therefore capable of acquiring different political significance, or none at all, solely as a consequence of external factors. It is only thus that a play can become 'political'. For this reason, a number of literary works have the potential ability to acquire a political function, whether intended by the author or not, a function which is usually short-lived, because of the pace of social and political changes within the society in which the test is circulated. This political function could also be labelled persuasive, for the ultimate goal of disseminating a text with a recognized potentiality of the kind discussed above is to influence, or generate, the desired responses in wider sections of society.

That was certainly the goal of those who sponsored the appearance of a number of plays in one particular theatrical season in London in 1623/24. These plays were written by a number of different playwrights and belong to different types of dramatic literature, and yet they have one thing in common, namely their ability to acquire in that particular context a significant political function. In our analysis of these plays, apart from reconstructing the political milieu in which they circulated, we shall make an attempt to show what intrinsic elements in the text in question enabled them to acquire this function under severe censorship.

1 The matter of Prince Charles's return

PRINCE Charles's safe return from Madrid, and the fact that he returned without the Infanta, was followed by a number of printed poems, sermons and tracts, describing the welcoming celebrations and the joy of the English people. For instance, John Taylor's *Prince Charles his welcome from Spaine* (1623) includes a poem, in which we read the following:

> The bells proclaimed aloud in every steeple,
> The joyfull acclamations of the people;
> The ordnance thundered with so high a straine,
> As if great Mars they meant to entertain,
> The bonfires blazing, infinite almost,
> Gave such a heart as if the world did roast.
> True mirth and gladnesse was in every place:
> Thus sure I thinke, this sixt day of October,
> Ten thousand men will goe to bed scarce (&c.)
> This was a day a jewell well return'd,
> For whom this kingdom yesterday so mourn'd.
> God length his dayes who is the cause of this,
> And make us thankefull for so greate a blisse.[1]

It is interesting to note that Taylor's description of the celebrations, as well as his poem, do not include any anti-Spanish comments or allusions. Moreover, at one point Taylor mentions that 'Amongst the rest, the Spanish ambassadors, both at Exeter-house in the Strand, and at Ely-house in Holborne, did expresse their loves by their charges and rejoycings'.[2] So Charles's return was not automatically associated with the breach with Spain, or, at least, nor at this time. From what has been said in the Introduction, one would expect publications of the kind quoted above[3] to be followed by plays dealing with similar issues.

Less than a fortnight after Prince Charles's and the Duke of Buckingham's return from Madrid, it became obvious that, apart from costly presents that they received from the King of Spain, the young adventurers brought to England an unconcealed hostility against Spain and the Spaniards. As one of the most experienced diplomats in London, Alvise Valaresso observed in his report to the Doge and Senate of 27 October 1623 (17 October os)

Of the Prince I think I may assert positively that he is quite alienated from the Spaniards and would like to break off all negotiations ... One may rest assured as regards Buckingham of the strongest aversion for the Spaniards. He certainly received many offences, his sharp quarrel with Olivares; his fear for himself if the Infanta should come, and already he has not refrained from speaking strongly against the deceit of the Spaniards ... and he is certainly deeply interested in the rupture of the negotiations and the friendship with Spain.[4]

King James, of course, was still convinced that the marriage negotiations would be happily concluded in the near future. Thus, in order to give the impression that 'nothing has changed', and to contradict the gossips and rumours of the kind quoted above, the King seems to have used all his remaining influence on Buckingham and made the latter invite the Spanish ambassadors to a banquet. This certainly was thought a sign of goodwill to the Spaniards. The same Venetian ambassador reported on 11 November (31 October OS) that

Buckingham is certainly disgusted. He speaks against the Spaniards and almost seems to advertise his new opinions ... In a few days Buckingham is to give a banquet in his own palace to all Spanish ambassadors, though the king ordered it and will bear the expense.[5]

It appears that the Duke refused to organize the banquet out of free will, and yielded to James's demand only on condition that the King would cover the expense and that the latter fact would not be concealed from public knowledge. Buckingham's sole contribution to the entertainment was a masque written by a young courtier and a protégé of his, John Maynard. The masque, unfortunately, is not extant, but from external evidence we know that its aim was to present recent political events in accordance with the Duke's new line of policy. It offended the Spanish ambassadors, as we learn from John Chamberlain's letter of 21 November:

The great feast held at Yorkhouse on Tewsday [sic] night. The King, Prince, and Spanish ambassadors were all present saving the Marques Hynoijosa who wold not abate the least puntillo of his pretensions. I heare litle how matters past there, but only the supreaboundant plentie ... The banquet cost three hundreth pounds; there was a maske of younge Maynards invention, wherof I heare litle or no commendation, but rather that the Spaniards tooke offence at yt: the main argument of yt was a congratulation for the Princes returne.[6]

The same is described by the Venetian ambassador in the following terms:

On Wednesday [sic] night Buckingham entertained the Ambassadors Mendoza, Colonna and Messia at his own house. Inoiosa was not present as he never leaves the house with Mendoza because of the question of precedence. The expense was royal, and borne by the royal purse. There was a sumptuous banquet finely set out; a masque with various intermezzi, followed by a dance of twelve masked gentlemen; many ladies were present with a show of rich jewels. They professed to celebrate the prince's return ... The feast was made by Buckingham either as a token of reconciliation with the Spaniards or to leave it doubtful whether the king went to that house to honour the ambassadors or Buckingham.[7]

And the documents published by John Orrell prove that it was Buckingham who paid for the masque. Some of the entries in the Duke's household accounts include the following:

Paide to the kinges Musicions that plaide at the Maske when the Spanish Ambassadors
were enterteyned at yorkhouse the 17. Nouember   26. –. –:
Paide another sett of Musick for their attendance at that time   2. –. –:
Giuen to Mountague the dauncer for his prouicion that time by his Lordships order:
           40. –. –:
Paide a bill for Spanish Ruffes &c for the Mask the 20. Nouember   3. 6. –:
Paide another small bill for that Mask, for maskes &c. 18. Nouember   5. 12. –:[8]

For our purposes here it is important to note that for the first time after his
return from Madrid, Buckingham used a theatrical performance, sponsored
and financed by himself, which carried a political message congruous with
his new line of policy. It was not the fact that the masque 'celebrated' the
Prince's return that offended the Spanish ambassadors. They themselves
took part in the nationwide celebrations, and did that, as the Venetian
ambassador put it,

to celebrate the prince's return as the brother-in-law designate of their king, and such is the
delusive power of their arts, that a large portion of the English, blinded by seeing so many
things upside down, firmly believe in the marriage.[9]

Therefore, it must have been the motive behind these celebrations, as implied
by the masque, that offended the ambassadors. There must have been
expression of the common belief (and Buckingham's hoped-for goal) that the
Prince's return without the Infanta meant that the negotiations with Spain
were broken off and that England had turned away from that commonly
resented alliance.

Subject-matter similar to that of John Maynard's masque was employed
by Ben Jonson in his masque, to be staged at court on 6 January 1624.[10] The
first mention of the preparations made for this traditional entertainment is
found in a report of the Venetian ambassador in England, Alvise Valaresso,
addressed to the Doge and Senate and dated 22 December 1623 (12 December
os):

The prince is preparing a masque, to which the Spanish ambassadors will probably be
invited, as they did not attend the one last year.[11]

A couple of days later, on 18 December (os), Sir Edward Conway wrote to the
Earl of Bristol, mentioning in passing that

The King has been indisposed, but is better, the Prince and the Duke [of Buckingham] are
well, and practise the maske diligently every day.[12]

The same Venetian ambassador gives a further piece of information in his
report of 12 January 1624 (2 January os):

The prince's usual masque will soon be performed, and I hope to be invited, with some of
the other ambassadors.[13]

On the following day, John Chamberlain wrote to Carleton mentioning that

here is much practising against maske on Twelfth Night and many meetings at noblemens
houses in the afternoones.[14]

And on 19 January (9 January OS) the same Alvise Valaresso informed the Doge and Senate that:

As regards his [i.e. James's] instability or rather his stability in evil, I need only mention that the usual verses written for the masque containing some rather free remarks against the Spaniards, they were altered by his command, and while in others this might be the result of prudence, in him it is nothing but the fear of offending the Spaniards ... The masque is delayed. I had word from the Chamberlain that I was to be invited ... They had almost decided to invite the Spanish ambassadors this year, it being their turn, in the course of the usual alternation, but France protested that he desired his place, otherwise his country would not be friendly, and so everything remains in suspense and no one knows what will happen.[15]

Chamberlain describes the same in a slightly different manner:

the maske for twelfth night was put of, by reason of the k⁵ indisposition, as was pretended, but the true cause is thought to be the competition of the French and Spanish ambassadors, which could not be accomodated in presence, and whethersoever of them were absent yt wold sound to his disgrace, and so much the Spanish ambassadors did intimate upon notice that the French was first invited, and forbare not to say that (among many other) they shold take this for the most notorious affront.[16]

That the masque was in fact prepared by Prince Charles and the Duke of Buckingham is also confirmed by Sir John Finett.[17] But for our purposes here the most important piece of information is that provided by the Venetian ambassador in his report of 19 January (9 January OS), by which we are informed that the King had read the masque before its scheduled performance and, finding it anti-Spanish, ordered the text to be altered. James's prudence may have had its roots in the unexpected embarrassment he certainly experienced on the occasion of the staging of John Maynard's masque.[18] This can also serve as an example of the importance attached in those days to theatrical performances at court, with James fulfilling the function of the 'high censor', and also of a widely acknowledged fact that a dramatic text had the potential to become a political instrument of propaganda. Because no further evidence is available, we are not in a position to establish the relationship between the extant printed version of *Neptune's Triumph* and the author's original. However, the very fact that the King in person expunged the text of what he considered to be anti-Spanish elements implies that at this point, at the turn of 1623 and 1624, he still firmly believed in the successful conclusion of his political schemes. On the other hand, this also proves that people who had ordered Jonson to write the masque, that is, Prince Charles and the Duke of Buckingham, had nothing against the anti-Spanish elements in the text, and we may even assume that the author was instructed in detail what his masque should include. It is difficult to imagine Jonson writing a text which would deal with delicate political issues solely from his own inspiration, without having consulted his sponsors about details.

Before we turn to *Neptune's Triumph*, it may be added that this was not the first time during James I's reign that the staging of a masque at court had been the cause of a diplomatic row over precedence. The fundamental reason for these recurrent incidents was that ambassadors of warring countries, or countries with relations frozen by an on-going cold war, could not attend public meetings or festivities together. For example, from the documents uncovered by John Orrell,[19] we learn about a similar occurrence in January 1609:

The French ambassador wishes to see the queen's masque but the ambassador extraordinary from Spain . . . who has precedence over the ordinary Spanish ambassador, let it be known that he was more than equal to the French ambassador and told their Majesties that he had come expressly to see the queen's masque. It has been announced that the masque is not ready and has been postponed until February.[20]

And when the staging of Jonson's *Mercury Vindicated* was scheduled for 6 January 1615, the Spanish ambassador, having arrived at court, would not watch the masque because the ambassador of the United Provinces was present. As the result of the Spanish ambassador's demonstration

The Lord Chamberlain went to-and-fro between him and the King, but he stayed in a little room until the King ordered both the ambassadors to go home.[21]

Consequently, the masque was repeated two days later, and no ambassador was invited.

But James's prudence early in January 1624 may be accounted for by the general state of affairs in Anglo-Spanish relations. By this time the Spanish court had been sufficiently offended by the English to allow the King to add an insult to an injury. This was occasioned by the increasing political activity of the Prince and the Duke of Buckingham, who seemed to be forming a party within the court, and were in fact undertaking actions that were undermining James's policy.[22] For example, on 13 November letters were dispatched to the English ambassador in Madrid, including a request for the King of Spain to outline in writing the aid he was willing to give toward the restoration of the Palatinate, and a new proxy, valid until March. But, two days later, the Prince sent letters to the Earl of Bristol depriving him of any power regarding the delivery of the procuration.[23] On the same day, the Spanish ambassadors had an audience with James, and the King had to admit in public that the restitution of the Palatinate had never been considered a condition of the Spanish match and that it was unreasonable to expect Philip IV to take arms against his close relative, the Emperor.[24] James was still determined to achieve a peaceful settlement of the Palatinate question with the support of Spain. Prince Charles and Buckingham, on the other hand, tried to promote their idea that the restoration of the Palatinate was possible only through military action. For the present, most of the Privy Councillors were still inclined to favour their monarch's policy.[25] About this time a letter arrived from the Earl of Bristol, announcing that the Pope's dispensation was expected hourly in Madrid, which meant that the marriage might be solemnized before the new instructions deferring the delivery of the proxy could reach the ambassador. It was not until mid-December that the anxiety of the English was relieved when the news reached London that the marriage had been prevented virtually on the eve of its celebration.[26] Consequently, the Spaniards were highly offended. As John Chamberlain put it in a letter to Sir Dudley Carleton, dated 20 December 1623, both of the messengers relate that

they came in goode time, for the match was in great forwardness and redy to be solemnised, for the scaffolds and other publike preparations were set up and in order, so that their comming was taken for a great affront, as yf yt had ben a point nommé to forbid the banes.[27]

The date fixed for the marriage was 29 November, and Bristol received his dispatches on the 26th. In face of such an insult, the Infanta ceased to be addressed as the Princess of England, she abandoned her English lessons, and the Prince's letters were no longer delivered to her, but were returned, sealed, to the sender.[28]

In view of the facts set out above, it is by no means surprising that, while preparations for the masque of 6 January 1624 were being made, the King took the trouble to check whether the text had anything detrimental to his policy. Having confirmed his suspicions, he ordered the text to be expurgated of all the apparent anti-Spanish elements. Therefore, the extant text of *Neptune's Triumph for the Return of Albion* is a censored version of the author's original. Nevertheless, we shall make an attempt to establish the political function the masque would have played had it been staged on 6 January 1624. We shall also try to show how the text would fail to create a meaningful world of its own if devoid of its very specific and particular historical and political context.

One of the curious features of *Neptune's Triumph for the Return of Albion* is the first stage direction:

His Matie being set, and the loud Musique ceasing. All, that is discouered of a Scene, are two erected Pillars, dedicated to Neptune, with this inscription vpon the one,

(a) NEP. RED.

on the other,

(b) SEC. IOV.

The POET entring on the STAGE, to disperse the Argument, is cald to by the Master-Cooke.

And in the margin of the Quarto edition of 1624, we find the following notes:

(a) In the m⟨o⟩neys of Vespasi⟨an⟩ and Adrian, w⟨c⟩ find this put fo⟨r⟩ NEPTVNO REDVCI, vnd⟨er⟩ Neptunalia, F⟨e⟩riae. vi. NEP. dicatae.
(b) That is, S⟨e⟩cundo IOV⟨I.⟩ for so Neptune ⟨is⟩ cald by Statiu⟨s⟩ in Achil⟨l⟩eid.1. Secundus IVPITER, De⟨x⟩–tramq; secund⟨i⟩, Quod superest, complexa Iouis⟨,⟩ as PLVTO is cald IVPITER tertiu⟨s.⟩

The first sentence of the above stage direction seems to suggest that 'His Matie' is one of the characters in the masque. His active role in the implied performance, however, ends with the instruction given in that particular sentence. The performance begins with 'His Majesty's' appearance: his

25

entrance and his being seated function as a signal for the 'loud music' to cease and for a 'scene' to be 'discouered'. The King's physical presence is indicated in the text, and in fact the performance cannot begin without it, unless the stage direction is neglected, or – in other words – violated. This causal relationship between King and performance indicates that the latter is subordinated to the monarch's physical presence and actually – anticipating evidence provided below – we may ascertain that the King plays the function of the Spectator: the masque is addressed to him, and only 'through' him to other spectators or readers.[29] The created world of the masque thereby incorporates the 'world of James I' and creates its meaning only through the relation to the latter.

As J. Goldberg put it, in Jonson's masques:

Text and monarch stood in the same relationship to the performance onstage; at the masque, there was another silent text, the king himself. As much as Jonson's invention, he was the soul of the masque. Silent, uncostumed, offstage, no part of the visible design, yet there would be no design without him. All the words, all the spectacle aim at him. He is the permanent form of the masque . . . The invention of the masque is translated into the flesh of the king.[30]

And one can only agree with Goldberg's comment that Jonson 'writes into the masque the king's role as nonparticipating spectator', and that the King's arrival and his 'setting' are 'recorded in the text to become part of the poet's device'.[31] *Neptune's Triumph* is no exception in this respect: the 'setting' of the King opens a number of his other masques, for instance, *The Masque of Queens* (1609), *Love Freed from Ignorance and Folly* (1611), *The Irish Masque at Court* (1613) and *The Fortunate Isles* (1625); James's presence is also noted at the opening of *For the Honour of Wales* (1618).

From the conversation of the two characters that appear on stage, the Poet and the Master Cook, we learn that a 'representation' of a masque is going to take place 'anon'. The Master Cook objects to this, claiming that that is his 'roome, and region too, the banquetting-house! And in matter of feast, and solemnitie, nothing is to be presented here, but with my acqaintance, and allowance to it.' Thus, the location is defined precisely: the masque is being staged in the Banqueting Hall, the famous building designed by Inigo Jones. And the action begins 'now', that is, it takes place in the present moment, after the King had taken his seat, and the music had ceased. From the stage direction we know that the Poet had appeared on the stage 'to disperse the Argument', which implies that his conversation with the Master Cook is not taking place sometime earlier, before the masque had begun: there is no gap between the time in the created world of the masque and the physical time of the King-the-Spectator watching it. This unity of time and space in the created world with the implied location and time of its staging is a curious example of a dramatic text, although not unknown in the period under discussion. In a way, the entire opening scene of the masque, with the Cook and the Poet involved in a discussion on the relationship between cookery and poetry, is reminiscent of inductions to full-length plays of the period. One of the usual features of the latter, which are in themselves miniature examples of drama-within-drama, is the physical unity of time and space in the world they create and in that of the implied staging and its audience. This temporal and locational unity characterizes, of course, practically all the masques by Ben Jonson. As Stephen Orgel points out, it enabled the author to 'allegorize the audience and setting along with the event'; as the action develops, 'we are no longer in the Banqueting House of Whitehall, but in Neptune's court ... not only is the king addressed as Neptune, but the whole court becomes involved in the transformation'.[32]

This physical coalescence of created world and the implied location of its staging is further underlined in our play by the Poet and the Cook, who identify themselves as the King's servants. And it is made clear later in the text that they are not servants of a king, but of a particular King who is the Spectator of the masque, that is, James I.

POET

You are not his Maiesties Confectioner? Are you?

COOKE

No, but one that has as good title to the roome [i.e. the Banqueting Hall], his Master-Cooke. What are you, Sir?

POET

The most vnprofitable of his seruants, I, Sir, the Poet. A kind of Christmas Ingine; one, that is vsed, as least once a yeare, for trifling instrument, of wit, or so. (28 36)

The only boundary that separates the two worlds is a theatrical convention, by which the Poet and the Cook pretend not to notice the Spectator, that is, the King, and by so doing they become dramatic characters, although it may have been the actual poet and cook of the royal household on stage. By employing this simple convention, any servant or courtier of the King would instantaneously become an actor impersonating himself. The text of *Neptune's Triumph* incorporates the King into itself, yet makes his presence unnoticeable to the other characters. Without the King, the theatrical implication of the text would be lost in this scene. This implies that the text addresses itself to James I, thus indicating the precise context in which it can be fully comprehended. Without this context, the text becomes, or rather remains, little more than meaningless.

After the Cook's praise of his own 'art', the Poet at last has a chance to begin reading the 'argument' of the masque. We learn that

> The mightie Neptune, mightie in his styles,
> And large command of waters, and of Isles,
> Not, as the Lord and Souerainge of the Seas,
> But, Chief in the art of riding, late did please
> To send his Albion forth, the most his owne,
> Vpon discouery, to themselues best knowne,
> Through Celtiberia ... (130–6)

The 'argument' of the masque, then, seems to take us back to mythological times, in accordance with the title and the names of Neptune and Albion. Neptune, as described here, has all the attributes of his Greek predecessor Poseidon who, apart from being the god of the sea, was also said to have created the horse, and was believed to have taught men the art of managing horses by the bridle. (Albion was in fact Poseidon's son, not Neptune's, but the confusion of the two gods was frequent in the Renaissance.) Neptune, acting not as the 'lord and sovereign of the seas', but as the 'chief in the art of riding' sent Albion to 'Celtiberia' in order to discover something 'to themselues best knowne'. Albion, therefore, did not sail to 'Celtiberia', but went there on horseback. 'Celtiberia' is a curious word, but since at the time the masque was written, 'Celt' and 'Celtic' could mean anything 'old' or 'ancient', and 'Iberia' denoted Spain, or Portugal, or both, the most likely meaning of this neologism is 'ancient Spain'. The Poet states that Albion's mission took place 'late', that is, 'recently', or 'not long ago' and, since the point of reference of 'now' is the moment when he reads the 'argument', that is, 6 January 1624, the text contradicts the facts as they are presented in mythology and becomes allegorical, in the sense that it employs mythological characters to impersonate individuals living in the contemporary world. Because there are no further text references to indicate that the action is taking place in the mythological past, and also because we know of no mythological tale describing Neptune sending Albion on horseback to Celtiberia, it is clear that the mythological attributes and names employed are only a disguise for a non-mythological level of meaning.

Since the masque is addressed to the Spectator, King James, and only through him is addressed to other implied spectators or readers,[33] it is only in this 'royal context' that the mythological disguise can be remarked. James himself has often been identified by his contemporaries with Neptune, an English god of the sea,[34] and if we accept that identification as valid in the created world of the masque, the latter becomes in fact 'James's Triumph for the Return of Charles', and it tells us the 'story' of the Prince's journey to Spain (which was, historically, undertaken on horseback), and of his triumphant return. All of these were 'recent' events, recent in reference to the time of the masque, as they took place between February and October 1623. Moreover, the text itself identifies Neptune with the King who appears in the opening stage direction, for Neptune himself does not appear as a character in the masque, in spite of the fact that he is constantly referred to. The title states clearly that it is Neptune's triumph, not somebody else's, and the fact that he does not appear among the *dramatis personae* may be accounted for only by his identification with the King-the-Spectator. As will be shown below, the masque in fact identifies Neptune's court, both as a physical building and as an institution, with the actual court of James I.

Let us return to the Poet's 'argument' for further corroboration of the above comments:

> and, to assist his course,
> Gaue him his powerfull (ᶜ) MANAGER of Horse,
> With diuine Proteus, Father of disguise,
> To waite vpon them with his counsels wise
> In all extremes.   (136–40)

Note (ᶜ) reads as follows: 'A power of NEPTVNES by which he is cald Hippius or Damaeus, and conferd on a person of speciall honour, in the Allegory, as by office, vid. infra.' Again, we shall not find a mythological tale describing a journey to Celtiberia undertaken by Albion, Hippius and Proteus. And to conscientious spectators or readers this would immediately appear as a mythological blunder, which would prove either the author's ignorance or his conscious alteration of mythological facts to create a second, non-mythological level of meaning. Since the text identifies Neptune with King James, by which it alludes to the recent Spanish adventure of Prince Charles, both Hippius and Proteus may be identified with Charles's companions in his journey to Spain. Thus, Hippius, or the 'Manager of Horse', may easily be identified with the Duke of Buckingham, who was in fact James's Master of the Horse, and was certainly 'powerful', and Proteus impersonates Sir Francis Cottington, who was the Prince's private secretary and an expert in Spanish affairs. Proteus was said to have the ability to change shape, hence he is labelled 'father of disguise' in the quoted passage, which may allude to Cottington's 'ability' to be taken for a Spaniard (owing to his impeccable command of Spanish), or – what is even more likely – it makes Cottington responsible for the idea that both Charles and Buckingham should begin their clandestine journey in disguise. The historical fact is that the young adventurers started their journey on 18 February 1623 disguised with false beards and under the names of Tom and John Smith. They joined Cottington at Dover and sailed together to France, then, via Paris they travelled on horseback to Spain.[35]

> His [i.e. Neptune's] great commands being done,
> And he desirous to review his Sonne,
> He doth dispatch a floting Ile, from hence,
> Vnto the Hesperian shores, to waft him thence.
> Where, what the arts were, vsde to make him stay,
> And how the Syrens woo'd him, by the way,
> What Monsters he encountered on the coast,
> How neare our generall Ioy was to be lost,
> Is not our subiect now: (140–8)

When Albion had completed the mission assigned to him by Neptune, the father desired to have him back at court, and for this reason 'dispatch[ed] a floting Ile' towards the 'Hesperian' [i.e. Western], shores 'to waft him thence', which for various reasons proved to be not an easy task. It is worth pointing out that the Poet describes the 'Ile' being dispatched 'from hence', meaning 'from here', and the reference point of 'here' in the masque is the

Banqueting Hall, *ergo* London, *ergo* England. Hence Neptune's court is identified with that of James's, and the 'Hesperian' shores with the shores of Spain. What is even more important to the masque's relationship to the politics of the day is the fact, clearly stressed by the text, that Albion's journey to Spain was inspired by Neptune, who 'late did please' to send his son abroad for reasons 'to themselues best knowne', and it was Neptune's 'commands' that Albion had fulfilled there.[36] However, the many obstacles that Albion faced in Celtiberia made his immediate return impossible. Somebody not precisely defined used 'arts', meaning 'tricks', to make the Prince stay and the Sirens lured him as with their sweet songs they lured Odysseus (in both cases, it appears, without apparent success); not to mention the 'Monsters he encountered on the coast'. These put Albion in great danger, and his safe return was not at all certain. But, since all the perils of Albion's journey belong to the past now, they make:

> The present gladnesse greater, for their sake.
> But what the triumphs are, the feast, the sport,
> And proud solemnities of Neptunes Court,
> Now he is safe, and Fame's not heard in vaine,
> But we behold our happie pledge againe.
> That with him, loyall HIPPIVS is returnd,
> Who for it, vnder so much envie, burnd
> With his owne brightnes, till her steru'd snakes saw
> What Neptune did impose, to him was law. (149–57)

The last four verses refer to the Duke of Buckingham as 'loyall Hippius', but they do not explain what caused the 'envie' and what or who exactly were the 'steru'd snakes' that eventually realized that Neptune's orders were 'law' to the loyal Master of the Horse. This would imply that Hippius was 'enviously' accused of disloyalty and disobedience to Neptune, which is an obvious allusion to the recurrent attacks against Buckingham for exposing Prince Charles to the dangers connected with his journey to Spain and with his stay there. As one historian put it, when the news of Charles and Buckingham's departure spread in London:

Especially loud was the outcry against Buckingham. Great Lords, who were not afraid to say what they meant, declared their opinion that he had been guilty of high treason in carrying the Prince out of the realm, and that he would one day have to answer in Parliament for what he had done. Even James began to hesitate, and seemed inclined to cast the blame from his own shoulders upon those of his favourite and his son.[37]

And by presenting Neptune as a loving father, who misses his son and sends a 'floting Ile' to speed his return home, the masque in turn clears James of the recurrent accusations of his being an 'unnatural father' to both Frederick and Elizabeth, and to Charles. The following excerpt from *The Court and Character of King James* is a conspicuous example of contemporary rumours:

Now the folly of this voyage plotted onely by greene heads, began to appeare, many shewing much sorrow, many smiling at their follies (and in truth glad in their hearts) and however the King was a cunning dissembler, and shewed much outward sorrow ... yet something was discerned, which made his Court beleeve little griefe came neare his heart, for that hatred he bare to Buckingham long ... and his adoring the rising sun, not looking after the sun setting, made the world beleeve hee would thinke it no ill bargain to loose his son, so Buckingham might bee lost also, for had hee not been weary of Buckingham, he would never have adventured him in such a journey, all his Courties knew that very well.[38]

At this point, then, the masque clears Buckingham of all blame: he was only carrying out the King's orders, which in fact were 'law' to him; and it also clears James of the accusation of being an 'unnatural father'.

The solemnities, mentioned in the text, celebrating Charles's arrival were amazing indeed, and by no means confined to the royal court: this was a nation-wide rejoicing, as we are informed by numerous contemporary accounts. The Venetian ambassador in England, Alvise Valaresso, reported to the Doge and Senate on 10 October 1623 that:

The news of the prince's arrival ... reached the city about midnight and set the bells ringing and that aroused the citizens. All of them, irrespective of rank, being filled with boundless joy, immediately lighted large and numerous bonfires. During the day they kept the shops closed and dispensed wine about the streets and when night fell they again lighted their bonfires in immense numbers ... Such a concourse of people collected at Buckingham's house during the short time that the prince stayed there, that his coach could hardly pass through the street and seemed to be carried on men's shoulders.[39]

And the same is described by John Chamberlain in his letter of 11 October to Sir Dudley Carleton:

I have not heard of more demonstrations of public joy then were here and every where from the highest to the lowest, such spreading of tables in the streets with all manner of provisions, setting out whole hoggesheads of wine and butts of sacke, but specially such number of bonfires both here and all along as he went ... as is almost incredible.[40]

Charles's return was also widely described in printed sermons, pamphlets and poems;[41] a church was even founded to commemorate the great event.

To return to the last-quoted line from our play: the Poet's 'argument' is interrupted by the Cook who wants to know why the masque had not been written earlier; the Poet answers that

It was not time,
To mixe this Musick with the vulgars chime.
Stay, till th'abortiue, and extemporall dinne
Of balladry, were vnderstood a sinne,
Minerua cry'd: that, what tumultuous verse,
Or prose could make, or steale, they might reherse,
And euery Songster had sung out his fit;
That all the Countrey, and the Citie-wit,
Of bels, and bonfires, and good cheere was spent,
And Neptunes Guard had drunke al that they meant;

31

> That all the tales and stories now were old
> Of the Sea-Monster Archy, or growne cold:
> For Muses then might venter, vndeterr'd,
> For they loue, then, to sing, when they are heard.   (161–74)

The 'Sea-Monster Archy' has been identified as Archibald Armstrong, the court jester, who had joined the Prince in Spain and had become quite a popular figure at the Spanish court. An Englishman's letter from Madrid tells us that

> Our cousin Archy hath more privileges than any, for he often goes with his fool's coat where the Infanta is with her meninas [maids] and ladies of honour, and keeps a'blowing and blustering among them, and blurts out what he lists.[42]

Archy is also known for courage with which he goaded Buckingham, when in Madrid, with taunts and sneers, until the Duke threatened to have him hanged.[43] We also know that Archy quarrelled with some other courtiers, as we learn from Chamberlain's letter of 11 October 1623:

> Tobie Mathew is come home with the Prince, and we heare of some incounters twixt him and Archie in Spaine wherwith he was so much distasted that once at a dinner he was faine to forsake the table.[44]

We may therefore suspect that after his return from Madrid, the big-mouthed jester did not hesitate to present his own interpretation of the events in Spain, thus providing source-material for gossip and rumour. We shall return to him below, when in the masque he is elevated to the position of the chief court gossip.

Having heard the Poet's explanation, the Cook now wants to know how the Poet is going to present his masque, 'In a fine Island, say you?' (178), to which he receives an answer, 'Yes, a Delos'. It may be recalled here that Delos is one of the Aegean islands, mentioned in Greek mythology as the birthplace of Apollo and Artemis, the children of Leto (Latona) and Zeus.

> Such, as when faire Latona fell in trauaile,
> Great Neptune made emergent.   (181–2)

According to some of the later myths, Latona was not allowed to give birth on land, and Poseidon, or Neptune, helped her to the island where it was permitted, because it floated and was washed by the waves. It is important to note that the island in question is not the mythological Delos, but is referred to as 'a Delos: such as . . .' And when the Cook expresses his disappointment with what he sees on stage: 'Ha' you nothing, / But a bare Island?' (192–3), the Poet explains to him: 'Yes, we haue a tree too, / Which we doe call the Tree of Harmonie' (195–6). This, however, is a very special tree:

> And is the same with (g) what we read, the Sunne
> Brought forth in the Indian Musicana first,
> And thus it growes. The goodly bole, being got
> To certaine cubic height, from euery side

> The boughes decline, which taking roote afresh,
> Spring up new boles, & those spring new, & newer,
> Till the whole tree become a Porticus,
> Or arched Arbour, able to receiue
> A numberous troupe, such as our Albion,   (197–205)
> [(ᵍ) Vid. Strab.Geogr.lib.15.]⁴⁵

Thus Delos is identified literally with England. The word 'harmony' as used here seems to indicate one of the possible seventeenth-century meanings: 'peaceableness', or 'concord' (def. 2, *OED*). Thus, the most important attribute of Delos–England is the 'Tree of Harmony', or the tree of peace, which spreads out to form an 'arched arbour' large enough to accommodate a whole country. This metaphor would, of course, be very pleasing to King James, for he saw himself as the peace-maker of Europe.

When the Cook finds out that there will be no 'antimasque', he announces that he had prepared a dish of that sort himself: this is a 'metaphorical dish' that 'will take the present palates', in which 'persons' will appear representing 'the meats', that is, the ingredients of 'Olla Podrida'. They are the characters of the forthcoming antimasque, but before they appear from the pot, or cauldron, to present their parts, they are described by the Cook as people who

> ... relish nothing, but di stato,
> (But in another fashion, then you dreame of)
> Know all things the wrong way, talke of the affaires,
> The clouds, the cortines, and the mysteries
> That are afoot, and, from what hands they haue 'hem
> (The master of the Elephant, or the Camels)
> What correspondences are held; the Posts
> That go, & come, and know, almost, their minutes,
> All but their businesse: Therein, they are fishes.
> But ha' their garlick, as the Prouerb sayes,
> They are our Quest of enquiry, after newes.   (245–55)

It is obvious that the court gossips are alluded to in the passage above and, as we learn from the Cook's Child, 'Amphibion Archy is the chiefe' (261). Thus, the earlier reference to Archy is expounded here and the court fool becomes the leader of the court gossips who 'know all things the wrong way', for their sources are as well informed as 'the master of the Elephant, or the Camels'. The latter seems to be an allusion to the recent sensational events in London: as we learn from John Chamberlain's letter of 12 July 1623

The king of Spaine hath sent hither five camells and an elephant, which going thorough the towne this day sevenight after midnight could not yet passe unsene.⁴⁶

And in the newly uncovered Revels documents of Sir Henry Herbert, we find the following entry:

A license to Mʳ. John Williams with foure more to make showe of an Elephant for a yeare after the date hereof 20 Augᵗ. 1623.⁴⁷

The court gossips are compared to fishes (253), for they are as mute as fishes in matters of the true state of affairs, and the gossip and rumour that they spread poison the truth as garlic poisons fresh air. This is the reason why the Cook asks the Child whether he had put Archy into the pot 'for Garlick' (265). In the conversation that follows the remaining ingredients of this 'metaphorical dish' are mentioned. Thus, we have 'a brace of Dwarfes' for partridge, 'a fine lac'd Mutton, or two' – that is, prostitutes – for mutton;[48] 'M\u02b3. Ambler, Newes-master of Poules' stands for capon, and 'Captain Buz' for turkey, a 'gentleman of the Forrest' represents a pheasant, whereas a 'plump pulterer's wife in Grace's street' plays 'hen with egges i' the belly' and finally, 'Hogrel the butcher, and the Sow his wife' are meant to represent bacon. Since all of these ingredients are 'rotten boyld', the Cook asks the Child to 'poure 'hem out' (323–5). This is followed by the next stage direction:

The Antimaske is daunc'd by the persons describ'd, comming out of the pot. (330–1.)

And the antimasque dance marks the end of the scene preceding the masque proper, and the function of this scene was

(a) to identify Neptune and his court with James I and his court;

(b) to present the argument of the masque as a true version of recent political events, connected with Prince Charles's journey to Spain, with his stay there and subsequent return, and

(c) to invalidate all other versions of the same events by uncovering their irresponsible and gossipy character.

The masque proper begins with the following stage direction:

The Iland is discouered, the Masquers sitting in their seuerall sieges. The heauens opening, and Apollo, with Mercury, some Muses, the Goddesse Harmony, make the musique, the while the Iland moues forward, Proteus sitting below, and APOLLO sings.   (334–9)

Apollo's song is addressed to Proteus, who is asked to inform Neptune that his Albion, 'Prince of all his Isles', 'is home returned well' (345–7). This is followed by a speech, or song, by Chorus, in which we find significant lines:

> And all the Heau'ns consent,
> With Harmony, to tune their notes,
> In answer to the publike votes,
> That, for it, up were sent.   (351–4)

Thus, the Heavens with Harmony 'tuned their notes' in answer to the common desire of the people and their prayers. 'It' in the last line quoted stands, of course, for the Prince's safe return from Spain. In other words, God had listened to the voice of his people and conducted the Prince's voyage home, thus ending the danger of the Spanish match, which was seen as a serious, if not calamitous, threat to the country and to the 'true' religion.

A question immediately arises, why was the Prince sent to Spain in the first place? Was it not the King's serious mistake that endangered the future of his people, and also the Prince's life? This was precisely the issue much discussed in the period after Charles's return. As Chamberlain observed in his letter of 8 November:

The daunger of the Princes journy into Spaine is dayly apprehended more then yt was at first, insomuch that even wise men mervaile how he got so easilie thence, but the conclusion is that ... he might thancke God he was come safe.[49]

As we have noted above, Ben Jonson's masque makes an attempt to free the King from all the blame, and this is what the Chorus has to say in that respect:

> It was no enuious Stepdames rage;
> Or Tyrans malice of the age,
> That did employ him forth.
> But such a Wisdome, that would proue,
> By sending him, their hearts, and loue,
> That else might feare his worth.   (355–60)

Thus, James's political scheme was not a 'Stepdames rage', nor 'Tyrans malice', but it was, in fact, 'Wisdome', a sort of clever way of testing the Spaniards' true nature: by sending Prince Charles there, their true intentions could be discovered, the real facet of their 'hearts and loue'. What follows is that the King is not to be blamed, just the opposite: it was his wisdom that revealed the cunning falsehood of the seeming friends. This is further confirmed by Proteus who sings:

> I! now the Pompe of Neptunes triumph shines!
> And all the glories of his great designes
> Are read, reflected, in his sonnes returne!   (368–70)

The text makes it obvious to spectators or readers that it was not a complete fiasco for the King; on the contrary, Prince Charles's return to England without the Infanta reflected the 'glories' of James's 'great designes', and, consequently, 'the Pompe of Neptunes triumph shines'. It is worth pointing out that according to the stage direction, Proteus sings his song 'to the State' (362–3), that is, directly to James seated in his throne. This in turn leaves no doubt whose triumph it is. As the title suggests, Albion's home-coming is not his triumph, but Neptune's; correspondingly, Charles's return is celebrated in the masque not as his triumph, but the triumph of the King and his political wisdom. And in this way, James's foreign policy satisfies the hopes of his people.

PORTVNVS
How all the eyes, the lookes, the hearts here, burne
At his ariuall!
SARON
These are the true fires,
Are made of ioyes!
PROTEVS
Of longings!

35

PORTVNVS
Of desires!

SARON
Of hopes!

PROTEVS
Of feares!

PORTVNVS
Not intermitted blocks.

SARON
But pure affections, and from odorous stocks! (371–88)

Furthermore, the desired conclusion of the King's political scheme contributes to his fame as a wise politician:

PROTEVS
My King lookes higher, as he scorned the warres
Of windes, and with his trident touchd the starres.
There is no wrinkle, in his brow, or frowne (392–5)

Had it not been for his wisdom, he would not have avoided being 'drowned' in a trap set to catch him and the 'youths':

But, as his cares he would in nectar drowne,
And all the siluer-footed Nymphs were drest,
To waite vpon him, to the Oceans feast.

PORTVNVS
Or, here in rowes vpon the bankes were set,
And had their seuerall hayres made into net
To catch the youths in, as they came on shore. (396–402)

Similarly, 'Haliclyon', or the Duke of Buckingham,[50] was in great danger, for the sirens made attempts to entrap him. The brave Duke managed to escape:

Though they no practise, nor no arts forgot,
That might haue wonne him, or by charme, or song.

PROTEVS
Or laying forth their tresses all along
Vpon the glassie waues;

PORTVNVS
Then diuing:

PROTEVS
Then,
Vp with their heads, as they were mad of men.

SARON
And there, the highest-going billowes crowne,
Vntill some lustie Sea-god pull'd them downe. (416–28)

Rejoicing reaches its peak at Albion's and Haliclyon's entrance: songs are sung and the masquers dance, after which the palace of Oceanus is 'discovered with loud music'. This undoubtedly is the same Oceanus at whose feast the Nymphs wanted to ensnare the King (see the quotation above, lines 396–8). The discovery of the palace is not welcomed at all, as clearly stated by the Poet:

> Behold the Palace of Oceanus!
> Hayle, Reuerend structures! Boast no more to vs
> Thy being able, all the Gods to feast;
> We haue seene enough: our Albion was thy guest.   (458–61)

These lines leave no doubt that Oceanus is meant to be identified with Philip IV, and the palace of the former with the royal palace in Madrid, where Charles was the guest of honour for several months. Then, the scene changes and 'the second prospect of the Sea is showne'; this is to contrast the palace of Oceanus, as is apparent from the Poet's comment:

> Nowe turne and view the wonders of the deepe,
> Where Proteus heards, & Neptunes Orkes doe keep,
> Where all is plough'd, yet still the pasture's greene,
> The wayes are found, and yet no path is seene.   (466–9)

As a political metaphor, the last two lines of the quoted passage seem to indicate a certain degree of uncertainty as to the future of James's policy: a new phase had begun and the ground is 'ploughed', or prepared, and yet the crop is impossible to identify, because the 'pasture's greene'; 'the wayes are found', that is, the matter is debated, and yet none of the suggested solutions has been accepted and therefore 'no path is seene'.

This is followed by a song to the Ladies, after which 'the fleete is discouered' (505). Again, the Poet's words are significant:

> 'Tis time, your eyes should be refresh'd at length
> With something new, a part of Neptunes strength.
> See, yond', his fleete, ready to goe, or come,
> Or fetch the riches of the Ocean home,
> So to secure him both in peace, and warres,
> Till not one ship alone, but all be starres.   (508–13)

At this point, the text clearly suggests a solution to the current political situation in England, taking the side of one of the parties involved in the ongoing controversy. King James was reluctant to make use of England's greatest power, the navy, favouring instead, if necessary, a limited military involvement on land. Both the Prince and the Duke were ardent advocates of a different concept, the aim of which was to attack Spain at sea, and through fetching 'the riches of the Ocean [read: Spanish] home', weaken the enemy to the point where Spain would not be able to cover the expenses of its large army; consequently, there would be a mutiny of soldiers for want of pay. This is clearly the 'message' of the quoted lines.

The last songs of Proteus, Portunus and Saron prove our earlier assertion that Neptune is to be identified with King James: they address 'Neptune' directly:

37

[PROTEUS] Yet now, great Lord of waters, and of Isles,
Giue Proteus leaue to turne vnto his wiles:
PORTVNVS
And, whilst young Albion doth thy labours ease,
Dispatch Portunus to thy Ports,
SARON
And Saron to thy Seas: (539–45)

and yet we know that there is no Neptune among the *dramatis personae*; the only king present is James I. And the final words of the Chorus are also addressed to him:

And may thy Subiects hearts be all on < e > flame:
Whilst thou dost keepe the earth in firme estate,
And, 'mongst the winds, dost suffer no debate.
But bothe at sea, and land, our powers increase,
With health, and all the golden gifts of peace.   (550–4)

The 'message' of these lines is clear: what needs to be done to guarantee peace is to increase England's power on land and sea.

The above comments were detailed enough to show that, when isolated from the contemporary political context, the masque fails in its ability to create a meaningful and non-contradictory composition. The pseudo-mythological elements are mixed with the non-mythological without any consistency and 'reason'. The plot, if there is one, hardly makes any sense: we are presented with a sequence of dialogues, mixed with songs and dances, celebrating the return of Neptune's son, Albion, from the court of Oceanus in Celtiberia. The goal of Albion's mission is not clearly explained, and we only learn that he had encountered numerous obstacles which made his earlier return impossible. This mission has given rise to various rumours at Neptune's court, all of which the text condemns as not true. Albion's return is for some reason considered Neptune's great 'victory' and a proof of his wisdom. In conclusion, Neptune is reminded that in order to guarantee peace, he has to maintain a strong navy and army. Moreover, most of the events in the masque are not developed through a dramatic action, but are narrated in dialogue form. Because of their highly allusive and metaphorical character, their comprehension rests entirely on the spectators' or readers' knowledge of the events alluded to. This technique of creating meaning is characteristic for a modern political cabaret, and in fact *Neptune's Triumph* may be treated as an interesting, early example of this 'genre'. On the other hand, the masque is a conspicuous example of a text which has no autonomous meaning by itself and therefore does not fulfil the basic requirement of a literary work. When isolated from the system of meaning external to the text, to which it constantly alludes, and, moreover, with which it identifies itself, the masque becomes a conglomerate mixture of loosely connected or totally unconnected scenes that cannot form a compositional unity. *Neptune's Triumph* was meant to acquire meaning through its staging before the King; the physical presence of James I was therefore fundamental. This play, then, is an example of a text that creates meaning *only* through its relationship to a section of an extra-textual reality, and it can be understood *only* through the 'prism' of this reality. As pointed out by L.S. Marcus, we are 'beginning to discover that the "present occasion" of Jonson's masques usually went beyond general praise of king, queen, and courtiers to commemorate important events in the life of court and nation', and 'for some of Jonson's masques, the present occasion is so crucial that without discovering it we cannot understand their argument or perceive their artistic unity'.[51]

2 The matter of the King and Queen of Bohemia

THE anonymous text of *The Life of the Duchess of Suffolk* was printed in London in 1631, being the first known and only edition of the play.[1] Its authorship and possible date may be established on the basis of indirect evidence, for the play in question was mentioned in Sir Henry Herbert's Office Book:

[2 January] For the Palsgrave's Company; The History of the Dutchess of Suffolk; which being full of dangerous matter was much reformed by me; I had two pounds for my pains: Written by Mr. Drew.[2]

On the basis of the above piece of evidence, we may claim with certainty that the play was written by a minor dramatist of the period, Thomas Drue, who is also said to have been the author of another extant play, *The Bloody Banquet* (1620).[3] Since *The Life of the Duchess of Suffolk* was licensed on 2 January 1624, we may ascertain that the play must have been written during, or before, 1623, with the former possibility being more likely. That the play was actually staged in a theatre we learn from the title-page of the 1631 edition:

As it hath beene divers and sundry times acted, with good applause.

As is apparent from Sir Henry's note, he would have read the play when the manuscript had to be licensed for staging by the Palsgrave's Company. Because the play was – in his words – 'full of dangerous matter', it 'was much reformed' by the censorious Master of the Revels[4] and, undoubtedly, the extant text differs substantially from the author's original version.

In earlier criticism of *The Life of the Duchess of Suffolk* it is acknowledged that its primary source was one of the chapters in John Foxe's *Acts and Monuments*, first published in 1563 and better known as *The Book of Martyrs*. This assertion is not invalidated by John Payne Collier's hypothesis that Thomas Drue's play is a revised version of a lost play by William Haughton, *The English Fugitives*, which is mentioned in the diary of Philip Henslowe under the date April 1600.[5] Even if this was true, it is beyond doubt that Haughton had based his play on *The Book of Martyrs*. Foxe's account of Katherine's fortunes was also used by Holinshed in his *Chronicles*.[6] A secondary source of the play usually referred to in the criticism is a ballad by Thomas Deloney, *The Dutchesse of Suffolkes Calamitie* (1602),[7] which, in turn, is also based, with minor deviations, on Foxe's account of the Duchess of Suffolk's 'martyrdom'. In fact, Thomas Drue has taken only one episode from the ballad and used it in one of the scenes in Act III. Yet two other sources of the play, hitherto unnoticed by critics, may be suggested; these are: (1) certain facts from Anglo-Polish relations in the middle of the sixteenth century, and (2) contemporary political events on the Continent, especially those connected with the outbreak of the Thirty Years War and the role played in it by the Elector of the Rhenish Palatinate, Frederick V (1596–1632), and his wife, the English Princess Elizabeth, the only daughter of James I of England. In the latter case, it is difficult, if not impossible, to point out any definite text, or texts, which supplied the author with various pieces of information connected with the events on the Continent, but these events were closely followed in England and were in fact described in sundry pamphlets and newsbooks, and it may be taken for granted that they were commonly known.[8]

To sum up the above preliminary observations, we may say that the main plot of the play is primarily based on Foxe's work, both in the selection of *dramatis personae* and of particular episodes, and in the chronology and sequence of the action proper. In the play, however, there are numerous deviations from the major source, changes and additions which at first glance may indicate the author's ignorance of history, but it may be proved that these striking alterations were inserted into the text on purpose in order to create a second level of meaning, to achieve a second perspective for a broader interpretation of the play. By making use of a historical plot and setting, the 1550s, Thomas Drue arranged his historical material in such a way that the play may be interpreted as a drama dealing, by analogy, with contemporary events, that is, the 1620s. The latter, of course, could occur only if the created world of the play evoked particular associations in implied readers, or spectators, with certain elements of the extra-textual reality known to them. If the play managed to evoke these associations, *The Life of the Duchess of Suffolk* may, therefore, be considered on two planes: one, as a historical, or biographical drama, and two, through underlying references and allusions, as a propaganda piece, constituting – when staged or read in early 1624 – severe criticism of James I's foreign policy and one of the voices in the wide-spread campaign for the salvation of endangered Protestantism and its new martyrs.

It may be noted at this point that Thomas Drue was not the first dramatist of the period to make this peculiar use of history. As J.D. Spikes pointed out:

Samuel Rowley's *startling rearrangement* [my italics] of the events of the reign of Henry VIII in the first Jacobean history play, *When You See Me You Know Me*, creates a faithful dramatic reflection of Foxe's historical interpretation of the reign, and also suggests a parallel with the court of James in 1604, the year the play was probably performed.[9]

Similarly, another example of an early Jacobean historical play alluding strongly to contemporary matters would be Dekker and Webster's *Famous*

History of Sir Thomas Wyat (*c.* 1604).[10] Thus, *The Life of the Duchess of Suffolk* is not an isolated example of a historical play which revealed its ability to function in a particular political context as a text alluding to contemporary events; it belongs in fact to an earlier tradition.

Let us begin our analysis of the play with some basic historical facts. Katherine, later the Dowager Duchess of Suffolk, was born in 1520, the only child of Lord William Willoughby and Maria de Salines – Katherine of Aragon's relative. After the death of her father in 1526, Katherine inherited his title and fortune, but remained under the wardship of Charles Brandon, the Duke of Suffolk, one of England's greatest peers, whose fourth wife she became at the age of fourteen. Her husband died in 1545, and their two sons died on the same day during the plague of 1551. By the end of 1552 Katherine had married one Richard Bertie, a learned courtier, without, however, any noble title. About this time the Dowager Duchess of Suffolk was active in the field of disseminating Protestantism and, among other things, she financially supported Hugh Latimer (who also appears in the play), one of the leading and best-known reformers of the entire period.[11] After the accession of Mary Tudor in 1553, Katherine was forced to leave England with her family and remained in exile until the succession of Elizabeth I. She died in 1580. These are, more or less, the basic facts about the Duchess provided by *The Dictionary of National Biography*.

Although the dramatists of the period did not hesitate to expand the time frame of their works to include decades, or even whole generations, Thomas Drue – contrary to the title, *The Life of the Duchess of Suffolk*, which suggests a broad time frame – restricted the time of presented events to only a few years, strictly speaking to the period between 1553 and 1558, during which the Duchess was persecuted and forced to wander with her family on the Continent. This reflects, with minor – but significant – deviations, the time frame of Foxe's account of Katherine's peregrinations. Because the details of Foxe's work are not widely known today, it is worthwhile for the sake of clarity to begin with a brief recollection of those parts of *The Book of Martyrs* which are devoted to Katherine's vicissitudes.[12]

Foxe's account of the Duchess' 'martyrdom' begins soon after the accession of Mary Tudor. The newly nominated Bishop of Winchester, the devout enemy of Protestants, Stephen Gardiner, who also appears in the play, summons Richard Bertie, the Duchess's husband, to his palace on the pretext of discussing some old debts, but in fact to interrogate him in matters of religion. Seeing through the Bishop's evil intentions, Bertie returns home and informs the Duchess of the danger; eventually, they decide to leave the country. Through a cunning trick, Bertie deceives the Bishop and in the beginning of June 1553 receives a passport to go 'beyond the seas' and sails for the Continent to await his beloved wife and little daughter. All this is also presented in Drue's play: the described events in the third scene of Act I, supplemented with a melodramatic farewell scene opening Act II. In accordance with their secret plan, on 2 January 1554, Katherine leaves her house, The Barbican, to join her husband on the Continent. Her flight is, of course, illegal and takes place in great secrecy. Foxe tells us that the Duchess was accompanied by one Robert Cranwell (who is also one of the *dramatis personae*), her one-year-old daughter, four servants (including the court fool!) and three waiting-women. The flight was, naturally, abundant in adventures of various kinds, skilfully used by Thomas Drue in his play, and making up the three middle acts. As Foxe's account has it, having experienced sundry adventures, the separated couple reunite on the Continent. However, their happiness is short-lived, for they are warned by a well-wishing English ambassador in the Netherlands[13] that they are being chased, and that

the Duke of Brunswick was shortly with ten ensigns to pass by Wesell, for the service of the house of Austria against the French king, the said duchess and her husband should with the same charge and company be intercepted.

Having escaped from the threat of the Duke of Brunswick, the Duchess and her husband found themselves in Windsheim in Germany, a town under the jurisdiction of the Duke Palatine. They stayed there for some time, but did not enjoy the Duke's support for they fell into serious financial problems there, facing humiliating poverty. Rescue from this destitution came suddenly and from the least expected part of the world:

there came suddenly letters from the palatine of Wilna, and the King of Poland (being instructed of their hard estate by a baron, named John Alasco, that was sometime in England), offering them large courtesy.

Although delighted with the unexpected offer, Katherine and Bertie were not without a certain degree of scepticism and even suspicion ('it's too good to be true'), and therefore they sent one Barlow, the former Bishop of Chichester, as their envoy to Poland, to ensure that there was no double-dealing behind the offer. After Barlow's return, equipped with the King of Poland's letters of assurance, in April 1557, the fugitives left Windsheim for Poland. Once again their journey was abundant in adventures and even in mortal danger. However, everything ends well:

And thus master Bertie and his wife, escaping the danger, proceeded in their journey toward Poland, where in conclusion they were quietly entertained of the king, and placed honourably in the earldom of the said king of Poland, in Sanogelia, called Crozan,[14] where master Berty with the duchess, having the king's absolute power of government over the said earldom, continued in great quietness and honour, till the death of queen Mary.

These are in fact Foxe's last words in the chapter devoted to Katherine, the Duchess of Suffolk. Around the events described in *The Book of Martyrs*, Thomas Drue constructed the plot of *The Life of the Duchess of Suffolk*.

It should be stressed here that in those times, *The Book of Martyrs* was, next to the Bible, the most popular and widely read book in England. As we learn from William Haller's notable book,[15] by the close of the seventeenth century something like 10 000 copies of the work had been set in circulation in English print, more than any other book of similar scope except the Bible. Much earlier even than that, in 1577, as we learn from William Harrison, 'every office at court had either a Bible or book of the acts and monuments of the church of England, or both'.[16] Thus, we may assume that the details of the lives of particular martyrs of the new faith were commonly known. Katherine, the Duchess of Suffolk, was no exception in this respect, and her adventurous peregrinations on the Continent were additionally popularized by Holinshed and by Deloney's ballad of 1602.[17] And a couple of months after Thomas Drue had written his play, the Duchess's life was described by another contemporary author:

after the death of the Duke of Suffolke, this Lady Katherine his Duchesse maryed with Bartue, by whom shee had a sonne (borne beyond the Seas) which she called Peregrine, and was in her right Lord Willoughby of Eresby. To tell the Storie of this great Duchesse life, how worthily, Religiously, and bountifully shee liued here in England; how malitiously, cruelly, and treacherously shee was hunted, and pursued for her life, ouer all Christendome, by an whole Kennel of the Popes worst deuouring Woolues: to tell the dangers shee escaped, the magnanimitie she vsed, the extremities shee was put to; to tell the snares that were laid to intrap her; and the pretty fleights, her sweetnesse vsed to escape them; to see how busie the Deuill was to vndermine her, and how strong God was to protect her, would raise vp amazement, euen in stones, and make the Earth cry out, *O Dea certe*![18]

Bearing this in mind, a question may be raised: if Thomas Drue's play really was – as most critics see it[19] – only a recollection of the martyrdom of the first generation of Protestants in England, then one can but wonder why this particular source has been chosen at all by the author. Undoubtedly, this is a story full of adventures, but at the same time it stands in no relation to the tragic fates of the true martyrs of the new faith, who often paid the highest price possible for their activity. In the play under discussion there is no sign of true martyrdom, as there is no sign of it in the corresponding chapter of *The Book of Martyrs*. Although Thomas Drue is at pains to present scenes of 'horror' and great tension to his spectators, or readers, by expanding and accumulating the sensational scenes based on Foxe's account and Deloney's ballad, by exaggerating the dangers and by stressing the misery and humiliation of the protagonists, yet he does not go beyond the bounderies of farce or melodrama. Having escaped by means of some ingenious trick from one source of oppression, the fugitives immediately fall prey to another, equally perilous. And this continues, practically without interval, for the duration of the three middle acts. Let us give some examples.

It may be observed that most of the adventures are of the same kind, that of the conventional 'hide-and-seek' type. Thus, we have a secret escape in disguise (II.iii–v), culminating in out-witting the chase and, at the end, one of the oppressors is thrown into a well (III.i). There are, of course, highwaymen in the play, who, apart from her riches, desire to sample the Duchess's charms: she is rescued from rape at the last moment by Bertie (III.ii). In the meantime, the Nurse abandons the baby in the forest, and only by miraculous chance is the child found (III.iii). On the way to a peaceful place, a storm breaks out, it is snowing and it thunders (sic!). And then, in such horrible conditions, the Duchess feels the pangs of child-birth; the only quiet place they can find is a church porch. Fortunately, they are miraculously saved once again; this time the adventitious aid comes from no other than Erasmus of Rotterdam in person, who for no reason whatever appeared in that isolated place to converse with the Duchess and Bertie in Latin (III.iii).[20] Soon after the birth of a son (which is a historical fact: their son, Peregrine, was born in Wesel in Germany on 12 October 1555),[21] a new danger appears in the form of the Duke of Brunswick. Once again, a crafty trick saves them from being caught (IV.i–ii). If this were not enough, an accidental brawl with a Captain of the Polish army brings new deadly danger to the Duchess and Bertie. However, everything ends well, when the fugitives, arrested, are brought before an old friend of theirs, the King of Poland (V.i). In addition, the children, who have been lost yet again, are brought to the court too, and the family reunion is crowned with the happy news of Queen Mary's death and the accession of Elizabeth I (V.i). A decision is made to return home immediately, and the play ends with a scene in London, where their erstwhile oppressors were already under arrest, the confiscated property is returned to the rightful owners, Bertie is nominated as Secretary of State, and the faithful servants are appropriately rewarded. This last scene is Thomas Drue's addition, for there is no mention of any of these events in *The Book of Martyrs*. However, it may be added that after his return to England, Bertie was in fact offered some sort of public office by Sir William Cecil, and he also sat in Parliament in the 1560s.[22]

Thus, one has to agree that there is not much of true 'martyrdom' in the play, and, moreover, the accumulated dangers and peripeteia seldom have any direct relation to religious persecution. This makes the interpretation of Drue's play additionally difficult. Clearly, this cannot be treated as an attempt to present Katherine as a 'Protestant saint', as the martyr of the new faith. As such, the drama is a complete failure, for the significance of religious motifs is trivial, to say the least. How, then, can this surprising choice of that particular historical character as protagonist of the play be convincingly explained? As has been pointed out above, Thomas Drue's play is not merely a 'theatrical' version of John Foxe's account of the Duchess of Suffolk's Continental wanderings. There are certain changes, omissions and additions in the play, and these deviations from the basic source and their function in the text will be investigated in this chapter. The results should provide an answer to the question raised above.

As has already been indicated, the time frame of the play is not fully

congruous with Foxe's narrative. The beginning of Act I is set during the lifetime of King Edward VI, and it is in the middle of scene ii that we learn about
his death and Mary's accession to the throne. This part of the play may be
treated as conventional exposition. Apart from the apparently idealized
Katherine, Bertie also appears, still as the Duchess's courtier. Interestingly,
Foxe, that is, the future author of *The Book of Martyrs*, is one of the servants
in the Duchess's household. His appearance in the play, and his praiseworthy
role throughout the action, seem to serve at least two functions. The first is to
inform the spectators, or readers, that the major source of the play is Foxe's
account of the events, included in his *Acts and Monuments*. The second is to
heighten both the play's verisimilitude, and Foxe's 'later' account. Therefore, the story of the Duchess's Continental travels as described in *The Book
of Martyrs*, and as presented in the play, becomes, as it were, 'more true'; by
presenting Foxe as the eye-witness of events, Drue makes him more
trustworthy as the author. It may be added that the historical John Foxe also
spent several years in exile.

The title of the play, taken together with the appearance of Foxe in the first
scene, serves the important function of a signal to the spectators or readers,
and makes identification of the major source of the text almost immediately
possible. Of course, the author's message would appeal only to those
spectators, or readers, who were acquainted with *The Book of Martyrs*. At
this point, when writing the play, the author had at least two possibilities for
handling his material: he could follow strictly Foxe's account, thus
producing a dramatized version of one of the chapters in *The Book of
Martyrs*, or he could expand the available story with new episodes, or alter
those at hand in such a way as to achieve his artistic aim. Our basic
assumption is that in the case of *The Life of the Duchess of Suffolk*, this
artistic goal was to create a second layer of meaning, which would allude to
contemporary events and thus make the play 'contemporary'. To achieve
this, the available material had to be altered in such a way that the changes
would be noticed and understood by the aware spectators or readers.

The first major deviation from the primary source occurs as early as Act I,
scene i, in which the Duchess receives a letter from King Edward VI,
recommending the Duke Palatine as a suitor for her hand. The Duchess's
immediate reaction is negative:

> My Widdowes tears are scarce wipt from my cheeke   (I.i.16)[23]

She becomes involved in a long conversation with Bertie, discussing the
matter of marriage. In this scene Bertie is still only her courtier and adviser.
And it is in fact Bertie who tries to convince the Duchess to accept the
Palatine's unexpected offer of marriage. He describes the Duke in the
following words:

> His spirit like ensign doth display
> The worthinesse of his heroicke birth,
> His more concealed vertues varnish that,
> To make his comet [merit] wondered at,
> Nature in moulding of his lyneaments
> Has sham'd the cunning workemanship of Arte   (1.i.98–103)

Their dialogue slowly turns to flirtatious banter, apparently initiated by the Duchess, which is interrupted by the appearance of the Duke, who – to everybody's surprise – turns out to be the newly elected King of Poland.[24] The King greets Katherine with the following:

> Madam, my latest service comes to bring
> An old affection from a new made king   (1.i.145–6)

He is followed by the appearance at court of rival suitors, and the Duchess has to announce her choice: once again to everybody's surprise, she chooses Bertie for her husband, a man with no title, but, at the same time with no vices. And with this ends the exposition, apparently different from the major source of the play.

The chief deviation seems to be the introduction of the King of Poland as a suitor for Katherine's hand. There is no mention of this in Foxe's *Book of Martyrs*. However, as has already been indicated, the dramatic time of the play does not correspond fully to the time of the source: the play begins 'earlier'. Thomas Drue may have therefore based this particular episode on another source, as yet unidentified in the criticism of the play. Another significant aberration from historical truth is that, in his drama, Drue has crowned the Duke Palatine with Poland's crown. It may be recalled here that the Duke is referred to in *The Book of Martyrs*, but only as a ruler of his duchy, where Katherine and her family found temporary refuge, apparently not under the Elector's protection: it was in the Palatinate that they suffered distress and misery, which was eventually relieved by the invitation from the King of Poland and the Duke of Lithuania. Furthermore, Foxe included several details, which Drue totally neglected in his play, such as the fact that both the King (Sigismund Augustus) and the Duke (Nicholas Radziwiłł) had been informed about Katherine's difficult situation by Jan Łaski, known in England as John Alasco.[25] Drue has also omitted Barlow's mission, the aim of which was to obtain the royal guarantees. Although in the play, the fugitives eventually reach the Polish court (v.i), this court is located in Windsheim in the Rhenish Palatinate. It may even be said that never in history were the boundaries of Poland moved so far westwards! Moreover, as indicated by Foxe, the King of Poland placed Katherine and her family 'in the earldom . . . in Sanogelia, called Crozan', where the English lived 'in great quietness and honour, till the death of queen Mary'. 'Sanogelia' is, of course, a corrupted form of 'Samogetia' (Pol. Żmudź), one of the north-eastern Polish provinces (now in the USSR), and 'Crozan' is a Latinized version of Polish 'Kroże', a town not far away from Wilno (the capital of the Grand Duchy of Lithuania). Neither of these two is mentioned in Drue's play. Actually, not a single Polish town or province is mentioned in the play, and the protagonists do not in fact cross the boundaries of historical Poland, but of a fictitious country ruled by a fictitious monarch. Thus, a careful spectator or reader would immediately reach the conclusion that the play is not a faithful account of Katherine's and Bertie's exile, but an altered version, and perhaps even more than that. A further conclusion would be that this deviation from the commonly known story was caused either by the author's ignorance, or by his conscious handling of the available material which would direct the attention of the spectator/reader to some extra-textual reality. In order to determine which of the two possibilities governs the created world of the play and in order to identify precisely the reality alluded to, the text had to convey additional pieces of information. It may be added here that the historical Duchess stayed in Poland for approximately two years, and returned to England in the summer of 1559,[26] whereas in the drama Katherine returns to England immediately she receives the news of Queen Mary's death.

How does all this relate to the historical facts? We have to take them into account in order to determine whether Thomas Drue has used other sources for his play, perhaps more authoritative sources than Foxe's narrative. Let us begin with the following problem: did the contemporary King of Poland, Sigismund Augustus, really seek the hand of Katherine? This in fact would have been possible only after the death of his first wife, Elizabeth of Austria, in June 1545, or after the death of his second wife, Barbara Radziwiłł, in 1551. Strangely enough, the first of these dates coincides with the death of Katherine's first husband, the Duke of Suffolk, Charles Brandon, whereas the second one coincides with the death of her sons. Family legend of the Dukes of Suffolk (today it is the family of the late Earl of Ancaster), which has survived to our times,[27] claims that Sigismund Augustus did in fact ask for Katherine's hand. It is known historically that after the death of his first wife Sigismund Augustus sent an envoy, Stanislaus Lasota, to several European courts with a secret mission. Lasota reached London in February 1546 and was received by Henry VIII and his sixth wife, Katherine Parr, with the honour and dignity proper to ambassadors.[28] Most probably going beyond his authority, Lasota officially announced the royal offer of marriage with Princess Mary. This is contained in a report of one Van der Delft, sent in February 1546 to the Emperor, Charles V:

I can discover nothing about the Polish ambassador. It is publicly asserted that he has come about a marriage for his master with Lady Mary, whom the Queen has twitted about it. The King knighted the Ambassador, and placed a golden collar around his neck.[29]

From the same document we learn about the court gossip connected with the alleged new matrimonial plans of Henry VIII and that 'Madame Suffolke is much talked about'.[30] For our purposes, it is significant to note Katherine's presence at the royal court during the Polish envoy's visit. Owing to the fact that in the case of Mary Lasota's scheme misfired, it is plausible, although by no means certain, that he was looking for yet another appropriate candidate, and beautiful Katherine may have caught his eye, especially in view of his lord's weakness for beautiful women. Although no direct evidence is available, we may suspect that Lasota once again went beyond the limits of his authority and carried out semi-official talks with the young widow. In this way, Thomas Drue's play would be the reflection of an otherwise unconfirmed legend.

Even if Katherine was really taken into consideration in the matrimonial plans of the King of Poland, this king was the last member of the Jagiellonian dynasty, Sigismund Augustus, and not the then Elector of the Rhenish Palatinate, Frederick II (1482–1556). It may be added that this same Frederick actually paid a visit to England during the last years of Henry VIII's reign, and was received, among others, by the Duke of Suffolk, Katherine's first husband, and would have met the Duchess. Nothing is known, however, about Frederick's matrimonial plans in connection with Katherine. It seems hardly possible that Thomas Drue could mistake Frederick for Sigismund Augustus, and the Rhenish Palatinate for the Kingdom of Poland. First, he made use of Foxe's work, where the distinction between the two men and between the two countries is very clear, and, secondly, even if Poland was an unknown land to Thomas Drue, the contemporary political events on the Continent placed the Palatinate firmly in the English consciousness. Basic facts concerning the Duchy's history and its geographical location were commonly known, and yet, in his play, Drue seems to have fused together two independent historical facts: Frederick II's visit to England in the early 1540s, and the alleged offer of marriage brought to England by the Polish envoy in February 1546. Is this merely a blunder on Drue's part? The answer of course is yes, but a conscious one, and its function in the play is of great significance, for it is one of the means used by the author to direct the attention of spectators or readers to the second layer of the play's meaning. It seems that in the political situation of the 1620s an explanation may be found for the astonishing distortion of historical facts in the play, which, in turn, may serve as a characteristic example of dramatic techniques applied by dramatists of the period in what may be labelled 'not-only-historical plays', that is, plays in which historical material would be selected and altered in such a way that the created world of the play would bear resemblance to some elements of the extra-textual reality. By so doing, the spectator/reader could be made aware of the contemporary relevance of an 'historical' drama.

We might recall here that in 1612 a very important event took place in London: the betrothal followed by the marriage of Elizabeth, James I's only daughter, and the young Duke of the Rhenish Palatinate, Frederick V. The

Duke, or Palsgrave, almost instantaneously became one of the most popular persons in England, due not only to his widely acknowledged charm, manners and splendid education, but also – perhaps, above all – for political and religious reasons, which at that time were inseparable. It has to be stressed that Frederick, as one of three Protestant Electors (out of the total of seven), was the great hope of what might be broadly termed the Protestant party on the Continent – although the anti-Habsburg coalition did later actually include some Catholic countries (e.g. France). The marriage, then, was widely celebrated in England. Antony Nixon, among others, claimed that

> By it great Brittaine, and the Palsgraues Land,
> Shall check the Popish pride with fierce Alarme,
> And make it in much trepidation stand.[31]

And Thomas Heywood called his countrymen to

> Behold that Prince, the Empires prince Elector,
> Of the religious Protestants protector.[32]

A pseudo-historical play was written by Wentworth Smith, the title of which is meaningful: *The Hector of Germanie, or The Palsgrave, Prime Elector* (printed in London in 1615). This curious piece is characterized on the one hand by 'the absolute inaccuracy of every historic statement, character, or situation', on the other the play

is interesting in its romance and patriotic appeal. Englishmen, great by the power of their successes, are everywhere the fear of their enemies and toast of their friends. Spaniards and Frenchmen are scoffed and derided, while the Germans are lauded to the skies.[33]

Similarly, Elizabeth was praised as the champion of the true religion, and because God's Church, of which the Calvinists in Germany were members, was endangered by the Catholic Antichrist, she and her husband were seen as the future conquerors of the new 'Armada', and in this sense she was associated with her great namesake – Queen Elizabeth I.[34] For England, the newly married couple meant even more: in the event of Prince Charles's death, Elizabeth and Frederick guaranteed succession.[35] Therefore, they were looked upon as the future King and Queen of England, and their fortunes on the Continent were followed with great attention by the English.

Let us now move to a different part of Europe, 'skipping' several years on the way there. In August 1619, a very important decision was made, the consequences of which were of great significance to almost the whole of Europe: the Estates of Bohemia deposed the Emperor Ferdinand II as the King of Bohemia and, several days later, on 26 August, elected Frederick V, the Elector of the Rhenish Palatinate. This converted a local conflict into the greatest calamity of the seventeenth century: the Thirty Years War.[36] Before, however, any military actions were undertaken on a wider scale, on 4 November 1619, Frederick and Elizabeth were crowned in Prague as the

King and Queen of Bohemia. Even their journeying into Prague was treated by Englishmen as a 'crusade' against Catholicism, and one of the writers, describing the departure of Elizabeth and Frederick from the Palatinate, expressed his belligerent views in the following way:

And shall we suffer our sweete Princess, our royall infanta, the only daughter of our soveraigne lord and king, to goe before us into the field and not follow after her?[37]

Their marriage was widely celebrated all over England: the enthusiastic Londoners attempted to stage illuminations in the new King's honour, and Protestants throughout the whole country began to collect money to help Frederick in his actions against the Catholic League.[38] The famous letter-writer of the period, John Chamberlain, wrote in April 1620 to Sir Dudley Carleton, indicating that the City officials were 'about some course to provide monie for Bohemia' and 'there is a collection likewise among the Clergie, whereof divers have under-written bountifully and cheerefully'. And we also learn from the same letter that the Earl of Dorset had contributed £1000 and promised to give the sum annually for the next four years.[39] Others volunteered and took arms to fight for the Protestant cause under the command of Sir Andrew Gray, who in March 1620 recruited 1000 men in England and 1000 more in Scotland. And John Taylor composed a poem entitled 'A Friendly Farevel to all the noble Souldiers that goe out of Great Britaine unto Bohemia'.[40] And he also went to Bohemia himself, for a brief visit which he later described in *Taylor his Travels: From the Citty of London in England, to the Citty of Prague in Bohemia,*[41] giving a full account of the architecture of the city, local customs, cost of living and the preparations for war.

All of this, however, did not significantly change Frederick's weak situations on the Continent;[42] before long imperial troops marched into the rebellious country and the royal couple, with their new-born son had to flee from the capital, never to return there. For this reason, Frederick is known in history as the Winter King. Even in such a critical situation, Frederick's father-in-law, James I of England, did not cease to deplore and discountenance his son-in-law's policy, and – to the astonishment and disappointment of the exasperated Protestant party – did hardly anything to rescue him from both military and political disaster.

James's reaction was in fact characteristic of the 'peace-maker' he considered himself to be. After the news of Frederick's election had reached him early in September 1619, the King summoned his Council on the 12th of that month to debate upon its legality. He informed Frederick's envoy, Dolma, that unless convincing proof of the election's legality were provided, the King of Bohemia (in fact, James refused to use this title) could not expect any assistance from England.[43] Moreover, at every European court, the English ambassador was obliged to protest James's neutrality and innocence of his son-in-law's irresponsible actions. In the way very appropriate to a learned monarch, James decided to study the laws and constitutions of Bohemia himself in order to determine whose claims were just and honourable. Eventually, by February 1620 the King had reached the conclusion that the Emperor's claim of hereditary right to Bohemia was groundless, but he still had to consider whether the deposition of an elected King was constitutionally valid. This legalistic approach of course determined James's actions, which confused and dismayed the majority of the English people. For instance, in this period even the clergy were not allowed to pray for Frederick and Elizabeth under the titles of King and Queen of Bohemia. Similarly, until March 1620 James had been refusing to give leave to levy a regiment for service in Bohemia, nor would he grant his permission for the City loan of £100 000 sought by Frederick's envoy.[44]

Therefore, when in November 1620 the imperial troops won a great victory in the battle of White Hill and consequently captured Prague with ease, the English Protestants reacted hysterically. The fact that in August of the same year the hated Spanish troops under General Spinola had entered the Palatinate and, finding little resistance, had occupied it as far as the Rhine only fuelled the flames. Deprived of the possibility of returning home, the Elector and King of Bohemia was forced, together with his entire downtrodden family, into a humiliating exile: through Silesia and Brandenburg they eventually reached the Netherlands, where at last they found refuge in The Hague, supported by Frederick's uncle Maurice of Nassau, the Prince of Orange. In England, meanwhile a big campaign was initiated to raise funds and other means of support for Frederick and Elizabeth. Petitions were sent to James I, the Parliament of 1621 debated on this matter,[45] everything possible was done to persuade the King to effective action for the sake of his daughter and son-in-law, who had even been deprived of their hereditary duchy. It was also demanded of the King that war against Spain should be declared immediately; a demand which was justified, among other things, by what was considered to be the unwarranted conquest of the Palatinate.

But James would have betrayed himself as the 'peace-maker' had he not tried to find a peaceful solution of the conflict. His firm belief was that the Continental turmoil could be ended by new dynastic ties: he wished to negotiate a marriage between Prince Charles and the Spanish Infanta and through this union, the Palatinate would be returned to its rightful owners; further, he desired to see a betrothal of his eldest grandson (i.e. Frederick's and Elizabeth's first son) with the Emperor's daughter, which would provide grounds for bargaining for Bohemia.[46] And this was the consistent line of James I's foreign policy before and during 1623, and in that year – to make things worse for Frederick and his supporters – the King withdrew the English garrison from Frederick's last stronghold in Germany, the fortress of Frankenthal, as a sign to the Catholics of his goodwill.[47] The reaction this latter move evoked in England needs no explanation here. As if there was no end to the sequence of calamities, in the summer of 1623, one of the few supporters of Frederick, the Duke of Brunswick, Christian I (1599–1626), was severely defeated in the battle with imperial troops at Stadtlohn.[48] Three weeks later, Frederick – who by this time had already been deprived of his Electorship by the force of the Emperor's decree – temporarily abandoned his political schemes and endeavours to reconquer Bohemia and the Palatinate, and – yielding to the promptings of his father-in-law – signed an armistice with the Emperor.

In the meantime, the Prince of Wales had gone to Spain to fetch his Infanta, a mission that turned out to be a political and personal disaster. This is described in detail in other chapters of this book. For our purposes here it is sufficient to recall that having returned from Madrid in October 1623, Prince Charles and the Duke of Buckingham formed a court 'party' of their own in strong opposition to James's handling of foreign policy. The restitution of the Palatinate was the *sine qua non* of this party's policy, to be achieved at all costs.[49] In order to win popular support a propaganda campaign was initiated, the aim of which was to deplore James's line of policy, to reveal the treachery of Catholics in general and Spain in particular and to stress the humiliation and destitution of Frederick and Elizabeth as sufficient reason for England to enter the war against the Catholic League.

In such a political situation as briefly described above, Thomas Drue wrote his *Life of the Duchess of Suffolk*. Because the war against the Habsburgs was not treated by the majority of the English – at least not in the first phase of the Thirty Years War – as a dynastic war, that is, a struggle for succession to the Bohemian throne, but primarily as a religious war, a crusade as it were against the Catholic Antichrist (in which the Protestants saw their mission), a certain analogy may be found between the vicissitudes of the Duchess of Suffolk and her family as presented in Thomas Drue's play and contemporary events on the Continent. In both cases calamities fall on Protestant aristocrats from the hands of ruthless and blood-thirsty Catholics. In both, a courageous flight prevents them from persecution and imprisonment, if not from death; in both, the heroes suffer the confiscation of their fortune, undergo numerous formidable dangers, and eventually find refuge in a friendly country, supported by a praiseworthy nobleman. To make this comparison clear let us recall briefly basic facts connected with Elizabeth's flight from Prague, which – like Katherine in the play – she had to undertake on her own.[50] This started on 10 November 1620, with a slow-moving procession of 300 heavily laden vehicles. By the time they had reached the mountains on the border with Silesia, it had begun to snow heavily, blocking the roads. Some unfaithful servants used the opportunity to plunder Elizabeth's baggage-wagons. The Queen had to dismount into snow and was then carried on horseback behind an English volunteer.[51] And this was the period of her late pregnancy, for Elizabeth was known to be expecting a child around Christmas. On 5 December, the Queen reached Frankfurt-on-Oder in Brandenburg. However, the Elector of Brandenburg was not at all delighted with the news of Elizabeth's arrival, although he was married to Frederick's sister. Eventually, he offered shelter at the castle of Cüstrin, which was in a miserable state: neither food nor fuel were available.[52] Letters were sent to the Duke of Brunswick asking for help, but the Duke replied that although he would be willing to be her host, he could not make the decision without consulting his mother, who happened to be away. Thus, the Queen had to stay in extremely uncomfortable conditions at Cüstrin where, on 6 January 1621, she gave birth to her fifth child, christened Maurice. In the meantime, her host received an imperial mandate 'requiring him not to harbour the King in his dominions, nor to suffer the Queen to stay in them longer than he could truly excuse it upon her Majestie's inability to go on'.[53] Georg Wilhelm could not, of course, get rid of the royal guest so, instead, he complained about the amount of food consumed at Cüstrin, and he provided a meticulous list in support of his complaint, which even included the geese, hens and eggs which had been the diet of the invalid Queen.[54] In consequence, the Queen left as soon as she could, and was eventually reunited with her husband in Upper Westphalia in mid-March, having left the baby in Berlin in the nursery of her sister-in-law.[55] It was only then that they received a kind invitation from Frederick's uncle, Maurice of Nassau, the Prince of Orange, to establish themselves in The Hague, which turned out to be Elizabeth's home for the next forty years.

To continue with our comparison of Katherine's and Elizabeth's vicissitudes: it may be observed that both of these courageous women are pregnant during their flight, and give birth to their sons in most unfavourable conditions. During the flight each of them loses her baby, which is found by miraculous chance.[56] In addition, both the King of Poland in the play, and the historical Maurice of Nassau, Prince of Orange, had been suitors to Katherine and Elizabeth respectively. Both were rejected,[57] and yet these noble men, one in the play, and the other in real life, did not hesitate to bring help and relief not only to the women whom they desired as their wives, but also to their families. The humiliation of the high-born, who are exposed to various dangers and often left at the mercy of strangers, makes the parallel situations even more conspicuous. That this analogy is not accidental is proved by the text of the play. When one of the chief persecutors of the Duchess, Bonner, is anxiously waiting for the news whether the fugitives had been caught (this scene takes place in Act IV), the second 'villain', Gardiner, describes his nightmare to him:

> I dreamt my Lord, that Bertie and the Dutches,
> Were both advanc't vpon a regall throne,
> And had their temples wreath'd with glittering gold   (IV.iii.5–7)

The consternation and fury of the leaders of the Catholic League at the news of Frederick's election to the Bohemian throne must have reached nightmare proportions. The allusion conveyed by the lines quoted above to contemporary events is irrefutable.

Thomas Drue's play, being a recollection of the vicissitudes of Katherine and Bertie, full not so much of martyrdom as of fortitude and determination in overcoming 'the sea of troubles', alludes at the same time to the equally heroic exile of Frederick and Elizabeth. And, through this second layer of meaning – if understood by contemporaries – the play could function as a strong criticism of James I's foreign policy, denouncing the monarch who, according to public opinion, did nothing to help the homeless wanderers. We are told how a praiseworthy ruler should behave in a similar situation by one of the characters in Drue's play. This is Atkinson, Queen Elizabeth's envoy, who was sent with a rescue mission on the Continent immediately after she had been advanced to the English throne. When received by the King of Poland, Atkinson gives a speech (Drue's own invention), in which, among other things, we read the following:

> My Sovereigne hearing, that the Lady Katherine,
> The Suffolke Dutches, her allie in blood,
> Did live obscurely in these Provinces,
> In want, in misery, in great distresse,
> Sends to repeale both her, and all her friends.   (v.i.98–102)

It was commonly known in England that Frederick and Elizabeth were in a tremendously difficult financial situation; in fact, they suffered poverty and hardship,[58] and were truly 'In want, in misery, in great distresse'. It may also be pointed out that Atkinson refers to Poland in a curious way: 'these Provinces'. Although the OED acknowledges a seventeenth-century meaning of the word 'province' as a 'country', the plural form used by Atkinson finds little justification. 'These Provinces' may also be understood as 'in this region', but the association with 'The United Provinces', that is, with the Netherlands, is rather obvious. We should remember that, not long before the play was written, the King and Queen of Bohemia had found refuge in The Hague, a fact commonly known in England. Thus, Atkinson is telling us how James I should have reacted to the misfortunes of his 'allies in blood' had he been a monarch of Elizabeth's dimension.[59] Otherwise, he remains an 'unnatural father'. The latter accusation recurs in the political literature of the period, as in the following example:

They, that take the affaires of your [i.e. James's] children abroad most to hearts, not being able to discerne the compassion of your bowels, but judging thinges by the exterior of your actions, will hardlie be perswaded, that you are their father; because they see, the lamentable estate, whereto you suffer things to run, comes nearer to destruction than the nature of fatherly correction ... In your Majesties owne taverns, for one healthe that is begun to your selfe, there are ten drunke to the Princes, your forraygn children.[60]

However, the reasons for James's attitude towards Frederick and Elizabeth were complex. Apart from his uncertainty as to the legality of Frederick's election, briefly discussed above, and his consistent attempts to find a peaceful settlement of the conflict, James was also reluctant to invite his 'children' to England. In the Spanish ambassador's words, the King feared that the Palsgrave would 'come here with his children and form a party with the Calvinists of his own particular sect'.[61] This, in a way, is confirmed by a modern historian:

[James] was more concerned with peace than the victory of militant Protestantism over the papal anti-Christ. He was also conscious of the dishonour of his daughter being married to a penniless 'elected' king, and he was unenthusiastic about the prospect of having these two quixotic wanderers showing up in England one day to become figureheads of an ultra-Protestant war party.[62]

An attempt has been made to give a plausible answer to the question raised above, why in *The Life of the Duchess of Suffolk* Frederick V's ancestor was presented as the King of Poland, quite contrary to historical facts. A claim that Thomas Drue was ignorant in historical matters is without much validity. It has already been mentioned on several occasions that Drue used *The Book of Martyrs* as his primary source, and he seems to have been well acquainted with other historical sources and with the contemporary situation in international politics. The distortion of historical facts must have been done consciously to achieve a certain goal that he had in mind. With perhaps one exception there is no historical analogy or precedent for this curious distortion of history. The analogy here is that both the dukes, the one in Drue's play and the historical Frederick II, are elected kings of neighbouring countries, Poland and Bohemia. It seems to be without much relevance that both of these are Slavic countries and that they are situated in the same part of Europe. What really counts is the fictitious precedent: Thomas Drue's play suggests that there is nothing extraordinary, or awkward, in the fact that the Duke of the Rhenish Palatinate has been elected King of Bohemia, since one of his ancestors was also elected King of Poland; an election to a foreign throne lies, as it were, in the family tradition and, besides, the seventeenth-century Frederick is of royal descent.

The latter argument was of particular importance and constitutes Thomas Drue's contribution to the general discussion of the legality of Frederick's election. This was the fundamental propaganda issue for both sides involved in the conflict. Frederick and those who supported him argued that, in spite of the fact that the Emperor had been elected King of Bohemia in the past, his deposition declared by the Estates was an equally legal act, for Bohemia, being an independent unit of the Empire, was not under the direct rule of the Emperor. In other words, the Bohemian crown was wrested not from the Emperor, but only from the Austrian Archduke, Ferdinand Habsburg.[63] And it was only the Archduke who had in the past been elected King, and was later dethroned. The fact that he happened to be the Emperor of the Holy Roman Empire of the German Nation at the same time did not impair the legality of the Bohemian Estates' decision. On the basis of the above argument,

Frederick claimed that by accepting the Bohemian crown he was not breaking the imperial peace. This view is also reflected in numerous political treatises that circulated in England, many of which appeared about the time *The Life of the Duchess of Suffolk* was being performed in the Fortune.[64] Naturally, the Emperor and his allies were of a different opinion in the matter. The decision of the Bohemian Estates was interpreted as an illegal act declared by a group of rebels; hence, the dethronement had no legal grounds, and Frederick was a usurper. The problem of the legal status of the Kingdom of Bohemia was solved in March 1620 at a meeting at Mühlhausen, where it was pronounced that Bohemia was an integral part of the Empire.[65] Frederick had therefore broken the imperial peace and laid himself open to the direct penalties of law. He was summoned to withdraw from Bohemia before 1 June 1620; in case of felony this would be regarded as a declaration of war. Adamant, Frederick did not of course obey this ultimatum, and consequently from 1 June every loyal subject of the Empire was obliged to take arms against the usurper.[66] (The latter consequence may also explain the Elector of Brandenburg's awkward behaviour as host at Elizabeth's arrival in his duchy).

In view of all this, Thomas Drue's play appears to be one of the voices in the political controversy. Frederick's ancestor in the play is elected the King of Poland, whose legality is not questioned at all, and he is also presented as a man of honour and a just monarch. This is particularly clear in the first scene of Act V, where he greets Katherine and Bertie, offering support, oblivious of his past disappointment as a suitor for Katherine's hand. At this point he could have been easily associated by readers, or spectators, with his contemporary 'equivalent', Maurice of Nassau, who had been a (rejected) suitor to Elizabeth's hand and yet nobly offered her support in 1621, a fact commonly praised in England. Therefore, through the presentation of an honourable and great ancestor, and by stressing Frederick's royal heritage and descent, Drue's play served a propaganda function, supporting the court faction led by Charles and the Duke of Buckingham and, in broader terms, the Protestant cause on the Continent. This function would have been considerably weakened if – in congruity with historical fact – Thomas Drue had presented in his play the true King of Poland, Sigismund Augustus of the Catholic Jagiellonian dynasty. Why, then, do we have a Catholic King of Poland included in the play at all? In answer, it may be pointed out that in the play there is not one reference made to the Catholicism of the King; just the opposite: Poland turns out to be situated somewhere in Germany and to be a Protestant country ruled by a Protestant monarch. Thus, the attributes of the King, as presented in the play, are contradictory and belong to two different historical characters: Sigismund Augustus of Poland and Maurice of Nassau, Prince of Orange. In addition, the very title of the King of Poland used in the play did not necessarily have to evoke negative associations early in 1624:

during the Thirty Years War Poland remained neutral, and the relations between the two countries remained friendly throughout the entire period.

It has been widely acknowledged by scholars that the drama of the Stuart period was linked even more with the royal court than was the case in the Elizabethan era, and the plays of this period often reflected struggles between particular political factions. There is enough evidence available for the claim that after Frederick's and Elizabeth's flight from Prague, and especially after the failure of the marriage negotiations with Spain, there was a faction of that sort at the royal court of England, whose major goal it was to oppose the foreign policy of the King and to try to persuade him that no peaceful settlement was possible and, consequently, the solution to the Continental conflict was a military one. Precisely for this reason, the staging of Thomas Drue's play early in January 1624 could not have been accidental. In view of the sudden appearance of political literature dealing with very similar issues, it appears to have been one of the elements of a political campaign carried out on a wider scale. Equally significant was the fact that the play was staged in the Fortune theatre at Cripplegate. It may be pointed out that during his first visit to London in 1612/13, Frederick presented himself as a great admirer of theatre and, following the death of Prince Henry in January 1613, the Elector took under his personal patronage one of the leading London acting companies, the former Prince Henry's Men, permanently performing in the Fortune.[67] Ever since then the company carried the name of the Palsgrave's Company, and it was for this particular troupe that Thomas Drue wrote his play, as is apparent from Sir Henry Herbert's note quoted above, and this in fact is the only extant piece of the repertory list of these players of the 1623/24 season.[68] Undoubtedly, theatre was a fully recognized medium for the political propaganda campaign initiated by Charles and Buckingham and it was certainly appropriate to have a play supporting Frederick and Elizabeth staged by the Palsgrave's own company of players. Curiously enough, The Barbican, often mentioned both in the play and in Foxe's account, had actually been the historical dukes of Suffolk's estate for over 200 years. This was one of the largest houses at Cripplegate, not far away from the actual location of the Fortune, in which the Life of the Duchess of Suffolk was staged in 1624. Moreover, Thomas Deloney, the author of the ballad The Duchess of Suffolkes Calamitie, also lived near Cripplegate. As if there were not enough 'neighbourhood' links of that kind, it may be added that John Foxe, the author of The Book of Martyrs, lived at Grub Street, close to Cripplegate.[69]

To conclude, let us return to Sir Henry Herbert's abstruse note, quoted above, in which he, surprisingly, indicated that Thomas Drue's play was 'full of dangerous matter' and that therefore the text had been 'much reformed' by him. This has of course puzzled the critics of the play. What could be 'dangerous' in a text, which is full of unambiguous praise for the Protestant cause, in a country where little was done to show any respect for the religious feelings of the Catholic minority? Certainly, Sir Henry would not have expunged anti-Catholic lines from the text, had they been only religious in character.[70] In view of our analysis of the play's political milieu, it may be said that the Master of the Revels simply fulfilled his duty as the King's official and, taking into consideration royal interests, he unmistakably caught the underlying meaning of the play as an open criticism of James I's foreign policy. Only this criticism could appear 'dangerous' to a censor.

It may be said, then, that Thomas Drue's play belongs to a significant group of English history plays (and history plays in general) which, in accordance with the ancient maxim 'Historia est magistra vitae', sought examples from the historical past, true or fictitious, in order to speak – by analogy – about the present. In the vast majority of cases, English history plays retained their autonomy as literary texts, and may satisfactorily be scrutinized as such in isolation from their historical and political 'context' but, simultaneously, in their social circulation they acquired an additional function of politically 'involved' dramas. With a conscious attempt to write a history play of that sort, that is, a play equipped with a 'double meaning', a dramatist had to solve certain technical problems in order to make his project comprehensible to his audience. First, he had to assume a certain degree of knowledge of both history and contemporary politics among his spectators or readers. Without this knowledge, any attempt of that kind would be fruitless. Secondly, having at his disposal particular historical material, he had to work on it in such a way that, on the one hand, it would be adjusted to the demands of the genre and, on the other, it would include certain meaningful elements which would direct the involved spectator or reader to an extra-textual reality known to him. That was absolutely necessary, because the historical material available to the writer could almost never be unequivocally related to any contemporary reality or code of meaning. A conscious selection of the material was unavoidable for strictly dramatic purposes and this was usually accompanied by certain alterations and additions, the variety and the number of which depended on the artistic aim of the playwright. It is therefore worthwhile to point out a significant feature of history plays of the kind under discussion, and here *The Life of the Duchess of Suffolk* may serve as a conspicuous example; namely, that the peculiar use of the sources is characteristic, or even more than that: it is in fact an intrinsic and essential element of history plays which reveals their potential ability to function as political drama. Through a tendentious selection of available and commonly known material, or through conscious alterations of historical facts, the author indicated that the created world of a play may be related – by analogy, or contrast – to a certain extra-textual reality known to the spectator or reader. The initial 'signal' was of particular importance and had to be conveyed either by title, by the play's scenes, or both, for it would determine the spectators' or readers' comprehension of the underlying meaning. In order to make this signal clear, and so that nobody would be mislead as far as the identification of the implied extra-textual reality was concerned, the author usually included some commonly known attributes of that reality into his text, expecting that they would be identified by his audience.

For example, in *The Life of the Duchess of Suffolk*, and in spite of the fact that the most obvious 'identification factors' had been expunged by the censor, a significant attribute of the extra-textual reality commonly known to contemporary audiences may be found in the episode, quoted above, in which Gardiner describes his nightmare: the coronation of an Englishwoman as Queen of a foreign country. Of course, there were numerous technical means for including certain attributes of an extra-textual reality into the text of a play. It could be done, for instance, by evoking in spectators or readers certain associations through the similarity of names of particular *dramatis personae* with their contemporary 'equivalents' (e.g. the Duke Palatine), through their common features, situational similarities, or by purely verbal means (e.g. by imitating somebody's manner of speech, as may be the case with Polonius in *Hamlet*). The scope of the present inquiry does not allow us to consider all the possibilities inherent in staging, scenery, acting etc.

Clearly, the degree of comprehensibility of a text belonging to the type under discussion varied from one play to another,[71] but in the case of Thomas Drue's drama its potential ability to evoke predictable associations in its audience was apparently too obvious to escape the censor's intervention. A further step in making use of historical material was an attempt to create a play which, while it remained an autonomous literary text, would not only direct the spectator or reader to a particular extra-textual reality, but would also function as the latter's commentary and, occasionally as a political extrapolation. At this stage, when the identity of the implied extra-textual reality is definite then, along with analogy, contrast plays an important role, being of course a specific type of commentary. In the case of Thomas Drue's play, an example of a typical 'reference-analogy' is the description of the Duke Palatine, quoted above. This is spoken by Bertie early in the play and is, in fact, the first significant 'signal', or 'message', indicating the existence of the second level of meaning in the text. Although the person described is the sixteenth-century Duke, his qualities as described by Bertie are equally applicable to the seventeenth-century Frederick V, the Duke Palatine and King of Bohemia. An example of contrast, on the other hand, may readily be provided by recalling Atkinson's speech, also quoted above, which again may be interpreted on two levels, historically and politically, the latter being an obvious criticism of James I's inaction. Characteristically, Atkinson's speech is delivered in Act V and the determined actions of Queen Elizabeth to rescue Katherine and Bertie may have been contrasted with and interpreted as a counter-balance of sluggish moves by James I only because, earlier in the text, the second perspective of cognition had already been signalled, directing the spectator or reader to the particular extra-textual reality.

3 The matter of war

WE are fortunate in being able to date *The Bondman* with unusual precision – Sir Henry Herbert licensed the text for performance on 3 December 1623:

For the Queen of Bohemia's Company; The Noble Bondman: Written by Philip Messenger, gent.[1]

And on 27 December of the same year, Herbert recorded in his Office-Book that

Upon St. John's night, the prince only being there, The Bondman, by the queen [of Bohemia's] company [was performed]. Att Whitehall.[2]

Internal evidence in the play proves that the earliest date for the completion of the manuscript was after the middle of November 1623. The date is accounted for by a topical allusion in v.iii.248–52:

> Let but a Chappell fall, or a street be fir'd,
> A foolish louer hang himself for pure loue,
> Or any such like accident, and before
> They are cold in their graves, some damn'd Dittie's made
> Which makes their ghosts walke.[3]

The 'fall of the chapel' took place in London on 26 October 1623, when a clandestine Catholic service was celebrated at Hunston House, the French ambassador's house in Blackfriars, and the floor of the building collapsed. The event was widely talked and written about. The firing of the street has been identified as the burning of a house in Broad Street on 12 November, when three neighbouring houses caught fire and were also destroyed. The unfortunate lover who hung himself 'for pure love' was a barrister called Needham, who committed suicide on 14 November of the same year. All of these events were described by Chamberlain in his letters to Sir Dudley Carleton, dated 8 and 15 November 1623.[4] We may assume, therefore, that during the second half of November Massinger completed his manuscript and passed it to Herbert to obtain the licence.

Detailed studies have shown that the manuscript copy of *The Bondman* used by the printer (Edward Allde) appears to have been prepared for publication by Massinger himself. His peculiar spellings are preserved, the stage directions are full and 'literary', describing what would be, or was, seen on stage, and there is an absence of directions for music and flourishes, which may serve as evidence against stage-annotation of the manuscript. It may be added that the extant copy in the Folger Library is in Massinger's own hand and with his own extensive corrections.[5]

The major plot of *The Bondman: An Ancient Story*, as summarized by Philip Edwards, is as follows:

In his suit to Cleora of Syracuse, Pisander, a noble Theban, is spurned and dismissed by the girl's arrogant brother, Timagoras. He returns to her service disguised as a slave. The Syracusans, a wealthy and decadent lot, are threatened by Carthage, and on their plea for help to Corinth, Timoleon is sent over to lead them. He organizes an expeditionary force, and with it goes Leosthenes, suitor to Cleora, a self-distrusting and jealous man. To reassure him, Cleora binds her eyes and promises neither to look at nor speak to anyone in his absence. Pisander now incites the slaves to rebellion, and ostentatiously protects Cleora from the violence which he has aroused; he wins her notice and perhaps her affection; still concealing his identity, he makes it clear that he loves her and that he was born no slave. The re-entry of the victorious Syracusans is opposed by the slaves, but when their masters approach them with whips, they crumble in panic. Leosthenes cannot believe that Cleora is still a virgin; when they are told how she has been looked after he and Timagoras treat Pisander with derision and suspicion, and have him imprisoned. Cleora rejects Leosthenes at this, and chooses her slave, who then reveals himself as the noble Theban.[6]

The sources for this story have already been established. The basic source for the slaves' rebellion in Sicily, as presented in *The Bondman*, is the account in Diodorus Siculus (Book XXIV) of the Servile Wars in Sicily of 135–132 BC. However, in this book there is no mention of Timoleon, nor of his military expedition against the Carthaginians, nor – as a matter of fact – is there any mention of the war against Carthage. Moreover, the summoning of Timoleon to Syracuse is described by Diodorus in Book XVI of his work, but the history takes us back to 345–336 BC! It may be added that the latter events were also described by Plutarch in his Life of Timoleon – another source that Massinger may have used.[7] However, from a strictly historical point of view, the first act of *The Bondman* takes place at least two hundred years before the second act begins. This and other peculiarities in Massinger's use of his sources were accounted for in the following terms by Philip Edwards:

Since Massinger was not writing an historical play, but grafting one historical incident on to the second to provide a satisfactory plot for a romantic moral play, there is little point in going into detail of his alterations of the history he found in Diodorus and Plutarch. He ignored the whole preceding history of the tyrant Dionysus and the struggles of Dion, the fact that Corinth was Syracuse's mother-city, the fact that Timoleon did not get Syracuse without fighting – and all that happened after he arrived; there was no rising of the slaves with Timoleon (though he put down a mercenary revolt in 341 B.C.). All Massinger needed was the helplessness of the Sicilians, and a figure of true worth to set against them.[8]

All of this would be true if 'grafting one historical incident on to the second' provided a satisfactory unity of plot for a 'romantic moral play'. But in critical terms Act I fails as an exposition; the exposition in fact begins in Act

II. Furthermore, it does not fall into the characteristic pattern of the composition of Massinger's plays, as established by T.A. Dunn: 'the first act covers the exposition and leads to the initial situation, dilemma, or dramatic paradox from which the rest of the play evolves'. The first act of *The Bondman* can hardly be treated as an exposition and neither the initial situation, nor the issues raised within it, lead to a 'situation, dilemma, or dramatic paradox from which the rest of the play evolves'.[9] The very loose connection of Act I with the major plot of the play cannot therefore be accounted for by Massinger's arbitrary handling of his sources. Even in moral terms the unity of both parts is practically non-existent, for the sacrifice of the Sicilians who offer their wealth and their lives for the good of their country is rather inadequately rewarded with the slaves' mutiny, the ravishing of their wives and daughters and the destruction of the peace and justice of the city by the mob. And Act I would have certainly provided such an experienced playwright as Massinger with an excellent opportunity to give a convincing justification, moral or political, for the slaves' rebellion. In the very source that he used, we are told the mutiny actually came about through the excessive cruelty of one Damophilus and his wife; and that rich and demoralized Sicilians treated their slaves like animals, imposing upon them severe punishment for trifling reasons, or for no reason at all, all of which would have provided Massinger with abundant information had he wanted to write 'a romantic moral play'. In addition, the motives for the war with Carthage are not really expounded in the play. Instead, Act I concentrates on two basic issues, unrelated to what is to follow: the Senator's acceptance of a foreigner to take command of their army, and the necessary sacrifice of the rich to provide means for the maintenance of the troops. To find verifiable reasons for the historical and compositional incongruity between Act I and the rest of the text, let us begin with quoting, once again, from Philip Edward's article:

A study of Massinger at work on his sources in this play shows a man taking a good deal of trouble to fashion a strong dramatic image of weakness and nobility in society and private conduct. If some critics find that the image reflects particular problems of Massinger's day, it is a commendation of the play's breadth, but not an explanation of the play's function.[10]

In our opinion, only through an explanation of the play's function during its circulation in London in March–April 1624 can we account for Massinger's curious use of his sources and for the incongruities mentioned above.

All the information connected with the date, licensing and sources of *The Bondman*, shown above, has been known to scholars for years. However, an attempt will be made to prove that before the manuscript reached the press, Massinger not only corrected the original version, but also – with the possible help of some newly published tracts – rewrote Act I, significantly changing its meaning. This must have taken place no later than March 1624, for the play was entered in the Stationers' Register on 12 March, and presumably printed a couple of weeks later:

m^r Harrison Edw. Blackmore Entred for their Copie vnder the hands of Sr Henry Herbert m^r of the Revell and m^r cole warden A play called the Bondman by Phill: Messenger.[11]

Since the calendar year in England changed on Lady Day, that is, on 25 March, *The Bondman*, carrying the date 1624, must have been issued after that date. The above entry would also imply that Herbert licensed the play again, this time for its printing. Since this was not the usual thing for him to do, at least not in the early years of his activity as the Master of the Revels, a plausible explanation would be that owing to the significant changes made by the author the copy prepared for print in March 1624 differed substantially from the one licensed for staging in December 1623.

In support of this initial assertion, several political tracts will have to be considered, for their subject-matter bears significant resemblance to the issues raised in Act I of the play. All these tracts were written by one man, Thomas Scott, and they were printed on the Continent early in 1624, before the opening of the English Parliament (the latter fact is determined by internal evidence). They are *The Spaniards Perpetvall Designes to an Vniversall Monarchie*, and the two most important for our purposes are *Vox Coeli, or News from Heaven* and *Robert Earl of Essex His Ghost*. Comparing these tracts with the subject-matter of *The Bondman*'s Act I, one is tempted to assume that Massinger must have been acquainted with them when preparing his play for print. Because these tracts show a deep involvement with contemporary political matters, it would be logical to suspect that the alterations made by Massinger in or shortly before March 1624 were of a similar nature. This, however, brings us to a highly controversial issue in criticism, and for this reason we shall make our approach clear once again: an attempt will be made not to 'read into' the text contemporary political issues, but – fully recognizing the autonomous character of the created world of the play – to analyse its function in a particular historical context and without treating this function as a permanent and invariable feature of a literary text. In other words, we shall not claim that *The Bondman* is *about* contemporary English politics, but we shall attempt to prove that certain elements of the play's created world may have been associated – by analogy, contrast, or both – by contemporary spectators or readers with certain elements of the political reality known to them. And by evoking these associations the play also gained a persuasive power and may have influenced public opinion on some of the relevant issues of the day. With the change of the state of affairs, of course, this function ceased to exist. Nevertheless, as is always the case, the text has preserved the potential ability of regaining this function, whenever the political context in which the play circulates is similar to that of spring 1624. An example of this may readily be provided: a broadsheet published by J. Hatchard in 1803, when an invasion of Napoleon's forces was feared, was in fact a lengthy excerpt from Massinger's *Bondman* (I.iii.213–368), and its appeal in that particular context was again thoroughly political and patriotic.

Ever since S.R. Gardiner published his influential, although today widely criticised, essay 'The Political Element in Massinger',[12] *The Bondman*'s 'political message' has been widely discussed. Gardiner's basic assumption is that Act I of the play alludes to contemporary English politics, and Massinger's standpoint is the standpoint of the Herberts, one of the most influential families of the entire period, especially that of William Herbert, Earl of Pembroke:

Buckingham and the Prince had returned from Madrid, and wanted James to declare war with Spain as soon as possible. Pembroke had never been in favour of the Spanish alliance, but he distrusted Buckingham as a leader, and he thought that Buckingham was behaving shabbily in advocating the breach of engagements of which he had been himself the strongest advocate. In these weeks of Pembroke's opposition "The Bondman" was written.[13]

To prove his point, Gardiner quotes several passages from the play that are seemingly critical of Buckingham. His views were followed by B.T. Spencer,[14] who saw the play as an allusion to the politics of the day, with Sicily representing England, Carthage representing Spain, Corinth representing Holland and Timoleon representing Maurice of Nassau; on the basis of these correspondences, Spencer interpreted the play as an appeal to the King and Parliament to take arms against Spain in support of Frederick and Elizabeth. In passing, we may raise the question, to which we shall later return, of how Massinger could make an appeal to Parliament when in November, after completing the play, nobody knew that a parliament would be summoned at all? The above and similar attempts of critics to track down the 'political meaning' and the anti-Stuart bias in *The Bondman* have been strongly refuted by A. Gross and, more recently, by Philip Edwards, who stated:

If one tries to follow the political allegory out, there are many contradictions, and one may feel dubious about Massinger's urging his monarch on to action in a tragi-comedy at the Cockpit.[15]

Our attempt will be to show that there are no contradictions involved, and that the implied addressee of Act I is not James I, but Parliament, or, strictly speaking, the House of Commons.

Without going into details of critical controversies, let us concentrate on the part of the text which seems to have been altered by Massinger in March 1624. The basic reasons for the alterations were the rapidly changing political situation in England and the author's awareness of his text's potential ability to evoke particular associations in his spectators or readers. To write a play urging the King to war against Spain in November 1623 would involve the risk of prosecution and imprisonment;[16] moreover, any attempt of this sort would undoubtedly have caught the eye of the captious censor that Herbert certainly was. In November, and even later, James was still convinced that the difficult marriage negotiations with Spain would eventually reach their happy end and the thought of going to war with what he considered to be a friendly state had not occurred to him. However he was pressed unremittingly by the newly formed 'opposition party', that is, Prince Charles and the Duke of Buckingham, for the assembly of a Parliament. James yielded to their demands, and the decision to summon Parliament had been reached by the end of December.[17] With Parliament commencing on 19 February 1624, both Charles and Buckingham believed strongly that the new House of Commons would be staunchly Protestant, anti-Spanish, and ready to raise sufficient money for the war. After Buckingham's parliamentary speech of 24 February giving reasons why the marriage negotiations had been broken off, in which he elaborated on the treachery of the Spaniards and on their threat to England, the Commons first considered the subject on 1 March. The debate that followed looked

as if a highly organized team of the Duke's supporters were leading the Commons into discovering that they had given support for a war before they had faced the implications of what they were doing. If men spoke against war, the Duke's supporters said they should discuss the breach of the treaties, not war. If men spoke against the burden of supplies, the Duke's supporters said that the breach of the treaties necessarily implied war.[18]

However, as the debate continued in March, Charles and Buckingham discovered, much to their chagrin, that the Commons, with a few exceptions, were almost as reluctant as James to start a war. The money needed was of course the basic obstacle in evoking MPs' enthusiasm for the enterprise. The subsidies voted for in March were barely sufficient to cover the expenses of a mercenary expedition to the Palatinate, and even this would be conditional on the support of the Dutch and the French. In the meantime, a German general, Ernst von Mansfeld, announced his readiness to accept service in England and to command the English expeditionary force on the Continent. Until this time, Mansfeld had fought for Frederick and Elizabeth against the Catholic League and had a dubious reputation as a soldier of fortune, but his military talents were widely acknowledged. Since he was the general of the King and Queen of Bohemia, his popularity in England was enormous. Therefore, when in March 1624 Charles and Buckingham were vainly attempting to urge the Commons to raise sufficient funds for a 'real war', Mansfeld's arrival to England, expected in April, was seen to be of major advantage to the 'war party', as it would convince the suspicious Commons of the sincerity of their adversaries. In this briefly outlined context, let us have a 'fresh' look at Philip Massinger's play, Act I in particular.

The text of *The Bondman* creates a political world in itself, starting with the opening scene. Leosthenes assures young Timagoras that

> The dreadful voice of warre that shakes the City;
> The thundering threates of Carthage; nor their Army
> Raisde to make good those threats, affright not me   (I.i.8–10)

And when Leosthenes asks: 'Who commands / The Carthagenian Fleet?' (I.i.43), Timagoras explains:

> Gisco's their Admirall,
> And tis our happinesse: a rawe young fellow,
> One neuer traind in Armes, but rather fashiond
> To tilt with Ladyes lips, then cracke a Launce,
> Rauish a Feather from a Mistrisse Fanne
> And weare it as a Fauour; a steele Helmet
> Made horrid with glorious Plume, will cracke
> His womans necke.   (I.i.49–56)

This passage has often been interpreted as a satire on the Duke of Buckingham, but for some reason it has been overlooked that Leosthenes's question is about the admiral of the 'Carthagenian Fleet', that is, Sicily's enemy. If we are to associate ancient Carthage with seventeenth-century Spain, then the description of the effeminate admiral would apply only to the contemporary Spanish admiral, and under no circumstances to the Duke of Buckingham. The political situation in the created world of the play is described in greater detail in the dialogue that follows the quoted passage:

> LEOSTHENES. No more of him, the motiues
> That Corinth giues vs ayde?
>   TIMAGORAS. The common danger:
> For Sicily being afire, she is not safe;
> It being apparent that ambitious Carthage,
> That to enlarge her Empire, striues to fasten
> An vniust gripe on vs (that liue free Lords
> Of Syracusa) will not end, till GREECE
> Acknowledge her their Souereigne.
>   LEOSTHENES. I am satisfied.
> What thinke you of our Generall?
>   TIMAGORAS. He is a man
> Of strange and reserude parts; But a great Souldier.
> His Trumpets call vs, I'le forbeare his Character,
> To morrowe in the Senate house at large,
> He will expresse himself.   (I.i.56–63)

In the created world of the play, we have three countries involved in a conflict, Carthage on the one side, and Sicily and Corinth (Greece) in alliance on the other. It is stressed that this alliance is a *sine qua non* of the success, because 'ambitious Carthage, / That to enlarge her Empire, striues to fasten / An vniust gripe on vs (that liue free Lords / Of Syracusa) will not end, till *Greece* / Acknowledge her their Souereigne'. In other words, if we relate these words to England, the country's safety is linked and determined by the safety of the United Provinces. Therefore, an offensive war against the enemy of 'Greece' is in fact a preventive war, protecting the liberty of the Syracusans. This is entirely congruous with the current line of the Duke of Buckingham's policies and is expressed, among other works, in Thomas

Scott's *Robert Earl of Essex His Ghost* (1624), which seems to have been one of Massinger's recent readings:

beware of dis-uniting yourselves from the United States of the Netherlands; for it will be your infinite disadvantage so to do: But rather assist, cherish, and hearten them: They are the best confederates you have ... Since my time on earth, they are increased in men, in munition, in shipping and in wealth; and which should make the knot of unity more strong and fast with you, they were and are of the same true religion.[19]

And later, when the political alliance between England and the United Provinces had been signed, Scott celebrated the event in *Symmachia: Or, A True-Loves Knot. Tyed Betwixt Great Britaine and the Vnited Prouinces, by the wisdom of King Iames* ... (1624).

Carthage is described by the Sicilians as an ambitious Empire trying to conquer the other two countries. The Carthaginians' view of the conflict and of Sicily and Corinth is not presented in the play. The major role in the war, it seems, is to be played by Sicily, for it is Corinth that 'giues vs ayde', and not the other way round. The expected arrival of the general (his name, Timoleon, is given earlier in the text, in line 39) and his appearance in the Senate seem to be of great political importance. Before we go any further in our analysis of the text, it may be asserted at this point that in view of the political situation in England in March–April 1624, it was very likely that Massinger's play evoked associations in spectators or readers with certain aspects of the extra-textual reality known to them. Sicily, as the only island amongst the countries involved in the conflict, could easily have been associated with England, Greece with England's most important ally in that period, the United Provinces, and their common enemy Carthage with Spain. The latter association is strongly supported by the text quoted above, where Carthage is described in terms very similar to those used by contemporary writers in reference to Spain. Let us give a couple of examples.

The very title of Thomas Scott's *The Spaniards Perpetuall Designes to an Vniversall Monarchie* (1624) is suggestive enough, and only a short excerpt from this tract will suffice to illustrate the similarity between the threat of Carthage to Sicily, as described in *The Bondman*, and an Englishman's fear of Spain early in 1624 (*The Spaniards Perpetuall Designes* must have been written before the official announcement of the breach of marriage negotiations i.e. before the end of March 1624):

the negotiations hath giuen the Spaniards time and meanes to subdue the best and greatest part of all Germany [i.e. the Palatinate]: and to push their designes forward; what other thing can be expected from the accomplishment of the marriage, but that in the end we must receiue Law from the Conquerour.[20]

A similar attitude is represented by the author of *Certain Reasons and Argvments of Polecei, Why the King of England should hereafter give over all further Treatie, and enter into warre with the Spaniard* (1624), and by many others, including John Reynolds's *Votiuae Angliae* (1624), Thomas Wood's

An Oration or speech appropriated unto the princes of Christendom (1624) and Thomas Scott's *The Second Part of Vox Populi* (1624) and *A Second Part of Spanish Practices* (1624). The general referred to in scene i of *The Bondman* could be associated in March 1624 only with Ernst von Mansfeld, whose arrival was expected in April. There was no reason whatsoever to associate him with Maurice Duke of Orange. Mansfeld was a 'Dutch' general in the sense that he was in the service of Frederick and Elizabeth who had found temporary refuge in The Hague. Besides, in the play, Timoleon is not presented as a Corinthian: he only arrives in Sicily from Corinth. In the quoted dialogue, he is spoken of as 'a man / Of strange and reserude parts; But a great Souldier.' From other sources we know that Mansfeld's reputation in Europe was slightly tarnished, owing to the notorious destruction spread wherever he went, but he was highly reputed for his knowledge of Germany and his experience in fighting.[21] But at the time of his expected arrival in England, he was looked on as a God-sent commander, who would save England from the Spanish threat by leading the English army to victory over the Catholic League, that is, the forces of Antichrist.[22] Like Timagoras in the play, who seems to know quite a lot about the foreign general and expects to learn more on his arrival, so Londoners were acquainted with Mansfeld's vicissitudes ever since the beginning of the war. His name appears in practically every single issue of newsbooks published in England from 1622, through 1623, until Mansfeld's arrival to England, which is announced in the newsbook of 20 April 1624: '[Mansfeld] went no further than Bologne in France from whence he returned and is lately arriued in England.'[23] This news item is very brief as, by coming to England, Mansfeld had become 'home news', the mention of which was forbidden by law. Books were written about him in English, like *The Appollogie of the Illustrious Prince Ernestus, Earle of Mansfeld, &c. Wherein From His First Entertainment, are layd open the Occasions of his Warres in Bohemia, Austria, and the Palatinate, with his faitful Seruice to the King of Bohemia* (1622).[24] It may also be added that Mansfeld was one of the foreigners whose names were protected by law against libel in England: two London printers, Bourne and Archer, were in serious trouble in the summer of 1622, because they revealed in one of their newsbooks, and without the licenser's knowledge, that Mansfeld had 5000 women of 'easy virtue' in his camp.[25] This revelation, whether true or not, certainly impugned the idealized image of the 'holy' army that fought for 'true religion' against the hellish forces of the Catholics.

In *The Bondman*, the general from Corinth, Timoleon, 'lately arriued in Siracusa', is discussed in the very opening of scene iii. The local nobles seem to be embarrassed by the fact that they have been unable to find a proper commander for their army from among themselves.

> ARCHIDAMUS. So carelesse we haue beene, my noble Lords,
> In the disposing of our owne affaires,

> And ignorant in the Art of gouernment,
> That now we need a stranger to instruct vs. (I.iii.1–4)

This, of course, is reminiscent of Sir Edward Cecil's complaint to the Duke of Buckingham that he intended to retire from the military profession now that 'strangers [i.e. Mansfeld] get the command ... which was never heard of before amongst men of our occupation'.[26] There were, undoubtedly, many people in England who thought exactly in the same way as Massinger's Archidamus, or Buckingham's Cecil. The reasons for this shame and humiliation are given in the dialogue that follows:

> [ARCHIDAMUS] ...
> Yet we are happy, that our neighbour Corinth
> (Pittying the vniust gripe Carthage would lay
> On Siracusa) hath vouchsafed to lend vs
> Her man of men Timoleon to defend
> Our country, and our liberties.
> DIPHILUS. 'Tis a fauour
> We are vnworthy of, and we may blush,
> Necessity compels vs to receive it.
> ARCHIDAMUS. O shame! that we that are a populous Nation,
> Ingag'd to leberall nature, for all blessings
> An Iland can bring forth; we that haue limbs
> And able bodies; Shipping, Armes, and Treasure,
> The sinnewes of the Warre, now we are call'd
> To stand vpon our Guard, cannot produce
> One fit to be our Generall. (I.iii.5–18)

The last speech is reminiscent of a passage found in *An Experimentall Discoverie of Spanish Practices*:

England be well furnished with Armes, men, victuals, and ships, and whatsoever else is necessary for the warres; yet (say I) all this is nothing, when the qualitie and condition is wanting, which giueth form and essence to all enterprises; which is money: which the Kingdome of England, no lesse through the scarcity of Reveneues, as by charge of ordinary expenses is brought unto.[27]

The quotation above was extended to bring about the subject of the economy, which will be important to our further discussion of *The Bondman*. Scarcity of money, referred to in this passage, was in fact the major reason of the economic crisis England suffered in the early 1620s. Parliament had already debated this matter in 1621, but the 'decay of trade' and the 'great depression' could not be accounted for in what we would label today as a rational analysis. As usual, the Spaniards were blamed, or 'Jesuits', but the actual cause for the physical scarcity of money was a series of currency devaluations in the Baltic, which meant that silver fetched a higher price there than in England and, consequently, money was flowing out of the country.[28] The only rational explanation for this otherwise incomprehensible phenomenon found in the 1620s was that the profits in trade were wasted on imports of luxury goods for the rich.

In view of this, there was a danger that when Parliament assembled in March 1624 to debate finances for the war, in spite of their strongly anti-Catholic stand MPs would be reluctant to raise much more than war cries. Thomas Scott expressed clearly what was expected of Parliament in *A Speech Made in the Lower House of Parliament, By Sir Edward Cicell, Colonel* (1624):

The season of the year requireth it, for if we loose the season, which is to be ready with a royall Army, against the beginning of the spring, and so suffer the Spanish side to goe on this yeare as did the last, you [i.e. the MPs] cannot conceiue how it will be in the power of man to keep him from the height of his ambition. Let vs not treat with him, but as I said before with our swords in our hands, his treaties otherwaies are ominous. Let vs ... immediately fal into consultation for the speedy Preparing of mony, armes, munition, and good hearts for the defence of Religion, his Maiestie, his children, and the safety of the Common-wealth, for the prouiding whereof, mony is the first material ... For the same reason then a subsidie is the first thing at this Parliament to be inacted ... freely and presently granted.[29]

However, the MPs mistrusted the King and his sincerity in going to war, and the King mistrusted them and what he thought to be their short-lived enthusiasm for the enterprise, the consequences of which they did not fully understand. As an example of this mutual mistrust, it may be mentioned that for a fortnight, between 5 March and 20 March, nothing could be achieved further to advance Buckingham's plans, because of the controversy over parliamentary procedure. The basic issue was: should the Commons first vote supply, and then James declare war, or should James declare war, and the Commons then vote supply? As a modern historian put it, Buckingham and the MPs were afraid, and reasonably afraid, that

if James were voted supply, he would use it to pay his debts, and declare no war. James was equally reasonably afraid that if he declared war, he would get no sufficient grant of supply, and he would be left committed to a war for which he could not pay.[30]

On 14 March, the King demanded five subsidies (*c.* £350 000) and ten fifteenths (*c.* £300 000) for the war and one subsidy and two fifteenths yearly until his debts were paid.[31] It has to be noted at this point that by 'war' the King meant something different from what was meant by Prince Charles, Buckingham and Parliament. From James's point of view, the only justifiable war would be the one that would lead to the restoration of the illegally occupied Palatinate, the hereditary duchy of Frederick and Elizabeth, now bestowed by the Emperor to the Duke of Bavaria. This did not necessarily mean war against Spain, and although a part of the Palatinate has been conquered and occupied by Spinola and his Spanish army, this was done by order of the Duke of Bavaria and not the King of Spain. In this sense, Spinola was a 'Bavarian' general, not a Spanish one. Thus, to engage in a war against

Spain would be unjustifiable from both a legal and a moral point of view. The other side did not take these legal nuances into account and blamed Spain for all the calamities that had befallen Frederick and Elizabeth and also England.[32] It was naively believed that a successful war against Spain would bring peace and order on the Continent and little attention was paid to the development of events within the Empire. As mentioned above, Buckingham and Parliament had the same goal in mind, but for substantially different reasons. The Duke and his party advocated the war against Spain in order to achieve primarily political goals, whereas the Puritans in Parliament understood war only in religious terms, as the final struggle against the Catholic Antichrist, and in fact they wanted to begin with cleaning the Augean stable at home, by undertaking militant action against recusants. This of course brought about further conflicts between the two sides. In any case, in March 1624 England was slowly moving towards undertaking military action on the Continent. On 20 March the House of Commons granted three subsidies (c. £210 000) and three fifteenths (c. £90 000) after the King's declaration of the utter breach of the treaties with Spain. This means that the King was offered less than a half of what he had asked for, which would hardly be enough to maintain an army of, say 10 000 men for a period longer than a couple of months. Having granted the subsidies, Parliament, now confident of its power, and the King's dependence on its decisions, sent a petition on 3 April demanding the full execution of penal laws against the recusants, with a clause 'that upon no occasion of marriage or treaty, or other request on that behalf from any foreign Prince or State whatsoever', the King 'would take away or slacken the execution of his laws against the Popish Recusants'.[33] James was naturally offended by the Commons giving him conditions, and he immediately ordered a courier (on his way to Madrid with a dispatch announcing the breach of the negotiations) to be overtaken and brought back; as he wrote to Conway, 'Ye know my firm resolution not to make this a war of religion.'[34]

The main reason, however, for James's reaction was the fact that in the meantime, Henry Rich, Viscount Kensington, was sent to Paris with a confidential mission, the aim of which was to discover the disposition of the French court towards a marriage between Charles and the Princess Henrietta Maria, the youngest sister of Louis XIII. Therefore, any actions against the Catholics in England would be detrimental to the future negotiations. Kensington arrived in Paris on 15 February, and was well received there. Both James and Buckingham realized of course that a second attempt to find a Catholic wife for Charles would not strengthen their position in their controversies with Parliament, and for this reason Kensington's mission was clandestine and aimed at achieving yet another target – that of English–French political and military alliance. As S.R. Gardiner put it, 'both James and Buckingham wished this marriage to be at least the seal of an effectual military alliance, and they expected to proceed simultaneously with the two negotiations'.[35] One of the immediate effects of Kensington's mission was that Mansfeld, who had come to France seeking employment (for this was the period of relative quietude in the war), and whom Kensington may have met during his stay in Paris, was advised to go to England in order to persuade James to assist the French in their anti-Spanish actions. Owing to the secrecy surrounding the negotiations with France, it is difficult to determine at which point Mansfeld appeared in their context. He may well have been taken into account as the future commander of English expeditionary forces before Kensington had gone on his mission. And it was Kensington who praised Mansfeld before the French.[36]

By early March, Kensington – who was Buckingham's friend and confidant – was able to report that the French were ready to enter the negotiations.[37] However, the French were still suspicious about James's real intentions, suspecting him of playing 'the French card' in order to extort better terms from the Spaniards. Similarly, there were many MPs who were not thoroughly convinced that James had finally cut the links with Spain. Although on 20 March the initial agreement on the subsidies had been reached, the reading of the actual subsidy bill did not take place until 22 April. Moreover, at the time of Kensington's report of the French side's readiness to enter the negotiations, the King had been in touch with the Spanish ambassadors and seemed to be inclined to return to his former policy of achieving a peaceful settlement.[38] It is about this time that Mansfeld appears on the political horizon of the English court. The political context, provided above, explains why Mansfeld's first initiative in coming to England evoked James's reluctance. It may however, have inspired Buckingham with a new concept of a political manoeuvre, which – if successful – would achieve two aims at once: it would demonstrate both to the French and to Parliament that the court was serious in its new policy, and it would further commit the King to this line. But, before this was achieved, the King of course had to be convinced, which was by no means easy.

As we learn from a report, dated 27 February 1624, of the Venetian ambassador in England to the Doge and Senate, 'Mansfelt has sent a gentleman here to recommend himself to his Majesty's favour'.[39] On 15 March, the same ambassador reported that 'the captain sent by Mansfelt has been to see me, doing so, he said, by special command of his master. He remarked that he had come to ask his Majesty for some ships on which he could take Mansfelt in safety to Italy ... I doubt whether he told me the full context of his commissions.'[40] And on 19 March the same Alvise Valaresso informs us that 'the captain sent by Mansfelt has not yet seen the king and he lingers on awaiting fresh instructions'.[41] James, it seems, refused to see Mansfeld's envoy. The fact that the 'captain' had not shown any intentions of leaving London means that he still had hopes of his mission's success. On

2 April the same writer informs us that 'Mansfelt's captain has received fresh orders, which arrived before Mansfelt went as they say to France, to offer his services to this king and even to ask for 5000 English with a few horses, which he promises will prove useful to his Majesty.'[42] There is little doubt that after a month of the envoy's stay in London, rumours had spread about Mansfeld's offer and the possibility that he might take command of an English army. This, however, had little influence on James as we learn from the same 'well-informed' source:

[16 April] Two days ago the Count of Mansfeld arrived here from Boulogne, after a letter from the constable of France formally forbidding him access to that Court. He sent a person from Boulogne to sound the king about his coming here, and the Secretary Conoval [Conway?] sent word that for various reasons his coming would not be opportune as matters were not yet ripe, and because they had refused Brunswick, though so closely related to the crown. Upon receiving this reply Mansfelt asked if he might not at least come privately with a few followers, with which request his agent approached Sir [Issac] Wake, who advised him to have patience and stop at Boulogne, and in a few days he would cross over and talk with him; but Mansfeld arrived while this answer was on the way. He at once sent to me Captain Rotta to pay his respects and tell me of his arrival. As I knew the whole series of events I felt some hesitation and much astonishment at his decision, recognising that necessity must have driven him and grieving that such a man should be so tossed about, driven from Holland, absolutely refused by France and taking refuge in England against the sovereign's wishes ... and there is no doubt that his coming has displeased everyone, especially the king ... Well, possibly the effect of his coming will not be bad as it will either spur on their resolutions or at least disclose their real intentions. It will be like feeling the king's pulse, as if he puts aside this opportunity it will be most evident that he does not wish to act, and that others can hope for nothing more.[43]

Thus, Mansfeld's arrival created a situation from which James could not back out. His only alternative was either to receive the general's offer of service for England, and by doing so prove to Parliament, to the French and to the 'world' that the King's new policies were not part of a political game and were sincere and irrevocable, or to reject the offer, and by doing so prove to the same quite the opposite. And this is exactly what Buckingham wanted; Mansfeld's physical appearance in London provided the Duke with a trump card he would use in his dealings with James and Parliament. As it turned out, once again James had to yield to Buckingham, which is confirmed by the extraordinarily cordial welcome he eventually gave to Mansfeld, the major intention of which was – as one of the contemporary reports tells us – 'to satisfy the Parliament of the King's resolution'.[44] We shall return to this below.

Therefore, if Massinger's manuscript was complete by 12 March, in the version that reached the press, he must have been informed, or heard allegations about, Mansfeld's forthcoming visit to England. But since the play must have been issued after 25 March, it is more likely that the last-minute changes and additions were made towards the end of that month, when rumours spread about the general's visit. This seems to have been

Massinger's usual practice, as we have evidence that for some of his plays he actually attended the printing house and made alterations while printing was in progress.[45] The possibility that the similarity of certain elements in the created world of the play to the political situation in England in February–April 1624 was coincidental must be taken into consideration although, on the other hand, this correspondence seems too detailed to be the result of mere chance. Moreover, an answer to the above problem would only tell us about the author's 'intentions', which are themselves beyond critical inquiry. We want to show how the text gained a political function, whether intended by the author or not, at the time when it was first circulated in print. In other words, our attempt will be to prove that The Bondman, when seen on stage or read in March–April 1624 was bound to evoke unambiguous associations in spectators or readers. Further, an attempt will be made to show that the major addressee of the play's 'political message' was not the 'man in the street', but Parliament. It may be recalled here that the play is dedicated to Philip Herbert, Earl of Montgomery, the brother of William, Earl of Pembroke and the Lord Chamberlain, who by this time had overcome his distrust of Buckingham and had taken his side in the House of Lords.[46] And Sir Henry Herbert, the Master of the Revels, was their close relative. The restitution of the Palatinate was the common aim of the Herberts and Buckingham, but this could be achieved only through the financial support of the House of Commons. There is no doubt that the propaganda campaign, advocating the cause, was carried out on an unprecedented scale before the commencement of Parliament and during its sessions, and it seems that The Bondman was one of many texts, the aim of which was to convince obstinate MPs (obstinate only when big words had to be converted into big money) about the necessary sacrifice of the nation, and of wealthy people in particular.

Let us, then, return to the play text for further evidence for what has been said above. It is still in scene iii that Timoleon appears in person. He is invited to the Senate, where he is offered a seat 'As to the Supreme Magistrate' (line 83). In a lengthy speech, Timoleon presents himself as a modest person: 'Such honours [are] / To one ambitious of rule and titles' (lines 84–5) – which he is not; and he does not consider himself good enough to rule others:

> He that would gouern others, first should be
> The Master of himself, richly indude
> With depth of vnderstanding, height of courage,
> And those remarkable graces which I dare not
> Ascribe vnto my selfe ...   (I.iii.100–4)

His modesty wins the praise of Archidamus:

> Sir, empty men
> Are Trumpets of their owne deserts: but you
> That are not in opinion, but in proofe

> Really good, and full of glorious parts,
> Leaue the report of what you are to fame,
> Which from the ready tongues of all good men
> Aloud proclaimes you. (104–10)

(Undoubtedly, Mansfeld was the most famous general in England at that time, fighting continuously, and sometimes successfully, against the Catholic League.) The reason for his arrival in Syracuse, Timoleon explains in the following terms:

> For you and for the liberty of Greece
> I am most ready to lay downe my life ... (115–6)

And as a 'stranger', he does not want to deprive local men of a chance to take command of the army:

> But yet consider men of Syracusa,
> Before that you deliuer vp the power
> Which yet is yours to me (117–9)

Before he accepts the command, Timoleon presents a condition:

> Stay yet, ere I take
> This seat of Iustice, or ingage my selfe
> To fight for you abroad, or to reforme
> Your State at home, sweare all vpon my sword,
> And call the gods of Sicily to witnesse
> The oath you take; that whatsoever I shall
> Propound for safety of your Common-wealth,
> Not circumscrib'd or bound in, shall by you
> Be willingly obey'd. (149–57)

The entire scene creates an image of an honest, just, and brave man, capable not only of undertaking military actions, but also of advising the Senate wisely in political matters:

> First then a word or two, but without bitternesse,
> (And yet mistake me not, I am no flatterer)
> Concerning your ill gouernment of the State,
> In which the greatest, noblest, and most rich,
> Stand the first file guilty. (166–70)

This is followed by a bitter attack against the selfishness of those with power and wealth in Sicily:

> Your haue not, as good Patriots should doe, studied
> The publike good, but your particular ends.
> Factious among your selues, preferring such
> To Offices, and honours, as ne're read
> The elements ...
> Your Senate house, which vs'd not to admit
> A man how euer popular to stand
> At the Helme of gouernment; whose youth was not
> Made glorious by action, whose experience

Crown'd with gray haires ...

is now fild
With greene heads that determine of the State
Ouer their Cups ...

or suppli'd by those
Who rising from bare arts, and sordit thrift
Are eminent for their wealth, not for their wisdome.

...

From whence it proceeds,
That the treasure of the City is ingros'd
By a few priuate men: the publique Coffers
Hollow with want; and they that will not spare
One talent for the common good, to feed
The pride and brauery of their Wiues, consume
In Plate, in Iewels, and superfluous slaues,
What would maintaine an Armie,   (171–201)

These, certainly, are strong words against the incompetence of the Senators, who gain their position not through their merits, but through their wealth. They could, of course, be applied to any government. However, there seems to be a topical allusion in the lines about such men preferred 'To Offices, and honours, as ne're read / The elements . . .' to the notorious case of an English envoy sent to the Emperor's court, who being one of the new men could scarcely read and write and was laughed at even by James himself. And the phrase 'Factious among your selues' echoes Issac Bargrave's sermon preached before the House of Commons on 28 February, in which he attacked 'factions' between various Protestant sects:

there is no way so ready to conuert a Lutheran [to Catholicism], as by the passion of a Caluinist; no names so promt to make a Protestant a Papist, as by the opposition of a Puritane. Thus they endeauour to destroy vs as wee destroyed their inuincible Nauy by sending fire, even the fire of dissension in the midst of vs. Oh let vs beate downe this pollicy of the world . . . Away with these distracting names of Lutheran, Calvinist, Puritan, &c. Wee are the children of the same father.[47]

More important, however, is the attack on the selfishness of the Senators who tend to mind their own interests rather than care for the future of the country. The reason why 'publique Coffers' are 'Hollow with want' is that few people have acquired the possession of the City's wealth and instead of contributing their riches – as good patriots should – to the public cause, they 'feed / The pride . . . of theire Wiues' and spend money on unnecessary luxuries, for they 'consume / In Plate, in Iewels, and superfluous slaues, / What would maintaine an Armie'. These lines (194–201) correspond in fact to a passage in *Robert Earl of Essex His Ghost* (1624), a pamphlet which Massinger seems to have read before the play had reached the press:

What though his majesties treasure be drawne deepe into, the poore countryman by these late hard yeares be impoverished, and merchandize and trading of your kingdom much decayed, &c. Yet, if your sumptuous buildings, your surfeiting diets, your prodigality in garments, your infinate plate, and costly furniture of your houses, and the pride of your wiues (specially) bee considered, England cannot be thought so poore ... And is England so base a state, as that people therein will not bestow some part of their superfluous expenses to keepe themselves from conquest and slavery?[48]

The consequences of this selfishness are detrimental to the country's safety, as we learn from Timoleon in the play:

> Yet in this plenty,
> And fat of peace, your young men ne're were train'd
> In Martiall discipline, and your ships vnreg'd,
> Rot in the harbour, no defence preparde,
> But thought vnusefull ...   (203–7)

This brings us to yet another contemporary source that Massinger seems to have used, namely to Thomas Scott's *Vox Coeli, or News from Heaven* (1624). A celestial conference of English royalty is taking place, with the participation of all the Tudor sovereigns and Prince Henry, to discuss contemporary politics of the 1620s and to vote on the Spanish match. During the discussion the following is said about the military status quo in England:

But then [i.e. in the past, when England was victorious over Spain] England was delighted in combats, warres, and victories, and now in stage-plays, maskes, revels, and carowsing, so as their courages are become rustie as their swords and muskets, which serve to grace the walls and not the fields, except in poore musters and sleight trainings, and that but once a yeare, which, upon the whole, is more for ostentation than service. Moreover, then Englands navy-royall could give a law to the ocean, and now time and negligence hath almost made all these ships vnserviceable, who lye rotting at Chatam and Rotcester.[49]

To which news Queen Elizabeth exclaims: 'What ... my royall-navy lye rotting, who are the bulwarkes and walles of England ...' And as this celestial dispute continues, we encounter another, similar passage:

if England would assume the anscient generosity of her ancestors, and forsake her new fangled pride and prodigality, wee know it is strong enough to beat Spaine ... for it were farre safer for England and Englishmen, if they wore worse cloathes, and had better hearts and swords, and if they were more martiall and less effeminate.[50]

In the play, this negligence of defence has caused the country's vulnerability to the enemy's attack:

> [TIMOLEON.] Now you finde
> That Carthage looking on your stupid sleepes,
> And dull securitie, was inuited to
> Inuade your Territories.   (I.iii.211–13)

The image of the country's 'stupid sleepes, / And dull securitie' once again may be found in *Vox Coeli*, this time in a fictitious letter written by Queen Mary (from Paradise) to Gondomar, undoubtedly the most hated person in England:

So whiles England lyes gasping on her bed of peace and securitie, let the king your master provide for warre.[51]

Similarly, in *Robert Earl of Essex His Ghost*, we find the following passage:

it is your parts, especially that are of his majesties councell and nobility, with faithful hearts to persuade and stirre him up, not to let the lyon in his princely breast any longer to sleepe and slumber, but to awake and rouse up himselfe, and to go forth against the Romish wolves, and Spanish foxes, who have devoured so many of Christs sheepe ...[52]

And the same Thomas Scott, in his *Certain Reasons and Argvments of Polecei* (1624) warns his countrymen that

if now, after they [i.e. the English] have raised so good opinion and hope of themselves in the world, they should grow faint, and fall backe into their former lethargie, they should lose all faith and reputation.[53]

And the accusation that Carthage was in fact 'inuited to / Inuade your Territories', due to Sicily's drowsiness, is also expressed in *Robert Earl of Essex His Ghost* as a warning to England that Spain may 'suddenly surprize you unawares by some new invasion'. In the play, Archidamus reacts humbly to Timoleon's harsh words:

> You haue made vs see, Sir,
> To our shame the Countries sickness: now from you
> As from a carefull, and a wise phisittian
> We doe expect the cure.   (I.iii.213–16)

Timoleon does not hesitate in announcing his 'cure':

> For the maintenance of the warre
> It is decreed all moneys in the hand
> Of priuate men, shall instantly be brought
> To the publike Treasurie   (219–21)

This decree instantaneously evokes opposition from among the Senators: 'This bits sore', 'The cure is worse than disease', 'This rough course / Will neuer be allowd of' etc. (lines 221–8). Similar indeed was the reaction of MPs in the English Parliament in March 1624 at the suggestion of raising sufficient funds for the war. Some suggested that since the war was caused by the Catholics on the Continent, their co-religionists in England should carry the economic burden of the war and should therefore be appropriately taxed, or their property be confiscated.[54] And Sir George Chaworth reached the conclusion in his parliamentary speech of 20 March 1624 that it would in fact be cheaper to give the King two subsidies and four fifteenths for himself and forget about the trouble in the Low Countries, for they could maintain themselves.[55]

When after the Easter break Parliament reassembled on 1 April, Buckingham gave a report to the Lords about his recent visit to the fleet, and he also informed them that 'the King of Spain had now in a readiness a far greater and stronger navy than that of '88'. The Lords had agreed to vote supply for setting out the fleet, but the parliamentary procedure did not allow for rapid actions. First, the subsidy bill had to be prepared, then discussed and passed. Even after a bill of this sort was passed, it took months before ready money could be gathered. This would postpone any military undertakings to a distant future. Exactly for this reason, Buckingham had reached the conclusion, astonishingly similar to that of Timoleon's in the play, that 'monied men may be dealt with to disburse such a sum of money as for the present is requisite, and they to be secured for the repayment thereof by Parliament, out of the subsidies now intended to be granted'.[56] On the same day, the Duke's suggestion was presented to the Commons, who – owing to low attendance during that session – decided to postpone the discussion of the matter until the following day. In a very characteristic way, on 2 April the Commons paid hardly any notice to Buckingham's proposal, and instead drew up a petition against recusants, after which the former issue was totally abandoned.

In the play, the unexpected opposition infuriates Timoleon who utters a lengthy set speech, a philippic rather, beginning with an exclamation: 'O blinde men!':

> But take your owne wayes, brood vpon your gold,
> Sacrifice to your Idoll, and preserue
> The prey intire, and merit the report
> Of carefull Stewards, yeeld a iust account
> To your proud Masters, who with whips of Iron
> Will force you to giue vp what you conceale,
> Or teare it from your throats ...
>
> (1.III.239–45)

As pointed out by B.T. Spencer, the metaphor of the 'whips of Iron' was unambiguously associated by the English with Spain.[57] The origin of this association is that after the defeat of the Armada in 1588, rumour spread throughout England that the Spanish, convinced of victory, had taken with them strange whips especially designed to inflict maximum pain on the English. Thomas Deloney, who was always up to date with the events of his day, immediately wrote a ballad, the very title of which is significant: 'A new Ballet of the straunge and cruell Whippes which the Spaniards had prepared to whippe and torment English men and women ...'. And in a pamphlet, contemporary with *The Bondman*, we find a warning that the Spanish 'will make no new scruple to whip you and your children with rods of iron'.[58]

> adorne your walls
> With Persian Hangings wrought of Gold and Pearle;
> Couer the floores on which they are to tread
> With costly Median silkes; perfume the roomes
> With Cassia, and Amber, where they are
> To feast and reuell, while like seruile Groomes
> You wayte vpon their trenches; feed their eyes
> With massie Plate vntill your Cupboards cracke
> With the weight that they sustaine; set forth your Wiues
> And Daughters in as many varyed shapes

81

> As there are Nations, to prouoke their lusts,
> And let them be imbrac'd before your eyes,
> The object may content you; and to perfit
> Their entertainment, offer vp your Sonnes,
> And able men for Slaues ...   (245–59)

The superfluous luxury of the Syracusans is the obvious target of Timoleon's attack. As mentioned above, this was the recurrent topic of political literature in the England of the 1620s. And the 'apocalyptic' vision of Syracuse being conquered by Carthage is analogous to the one we find in *Vox Coeli*, which refers, of course, to England and Spain. However, before we quote the appropriate passage from Thomas Scott's tract, it is worth pointing out that if we analyse Act I without paying any attention to the politics of the day, the play creates a moral contradiction. The anticipated cruelties inflicted upon the Syracusans by the enemy can only be avoided, Timoleon is saying, if the wealthy citizens sacrifice their riches for the maintenance of the army. In the play it so happens that in spite of the fact that the wealthy yield to Timoleon's appeal, and even join his army, risking both life and fortune, this does not prevent the calamities that fall upon the Syracusans when the army is away. Their sacrifice loses its meaning, and Timoleon's apocalyptic vision becomes, ironically and contradictorily, an anticipation of the consequences of this sacrifice.

As mentioned above, the threat of Spain is described in very similar terms in *Vox Coeli*:

E.6. So, if England match with Spaine, Spaine undoubtedly will in a short time over-match England.

. . .

Q.E. And then shall Englands men fall upon the edge of the sword; her virgins bee defloured and murthered, her wiues defiled and slaine in sight of their dying husbands, and their children and young babes shall have their braines dashed out against the walls, in sight of their dead parents.

P.H. Yea, then shall our nobilitie and gentrie dye upon the swords of those barbarous Castilians, and those who escape and survive their fury, shall be fettered and let captives and slaves to work in the mines of Peru and Mexico.[59]

This last image of the English turned into Spanish slaves is repeated in the letter, mentioned above, from Queen Mary to Gondomar:

Through your zeale and industry, I likewise doubt not but ... to see England made a province of Spaine, her nobility most murthered, and the rest carryed away slaves, to worke in the mines of Peru and Mexico.[60]

In the play, the reaction to this gruesome image is overwhelmingly physical: Leosthenes: 'The blood turns'; Timagoras: 'Obserue, how olde Cleon shakes'; Corisca: 'I am sicke, the man / Speakes poniards, and diseases'; Olimpia: 'O my Doctor, I neuer shall recouer.' One of the few who responds bravely and without the pricks of conscience to Timoleon's speech is Cleora, the heroine-to-be of the play. She uses the opportunity of this

physical paralysis of the Senate and makes a speech in which she expresses
her gratitude to Timoleon 'In the presence of so many Reuerend men, /
Strucke dumbe with terrour and astonishment' (272–3) for his revealing the
selfishness of the Sicilians. She then reinforces his arguments in the following
way:

> To all of you, I speake; and if a blush
> Steale on my cheekes, it is showne to reproue
> Your palenesse; willingly I would not say
> Your cowardise, or feare: thinke you all treasure
> Hid in the bowels of the Earth, or Shipwrack'd
> In Neptunes watry Kingdome, can hold the weight
> When libertie, and Honour, fill one scale,
> Triumphant Iustice sitting on the beame?
> Or dare you but imagine that your golde is
> Too deare a salary for such as hazard
> Their blood, and liues in your defence? For me
> An ignorant Girle, beare witnesse heauen, so farre
> I prize a Souldier, that to giue him pay,
> With such Deuotion as our Flamens Offer
> Their Sacrifices at the holy Altar,
> I doe lay downe these jewels, will make sale
> Of my superfluous Wardrobe to supply
> The meanest of their wants.   (I.iii.289–306)

The last three lines of Cleora's appeal to the Senators seem to be related to the
passage we find in *Robert Earl of Essex His Ghost*:

Was Rome so brave a State, as that the very ladies, to supply common treasure, and to
maintaine the warres, dispoyled themselves of their costly jewels and rich ornaments?[61]

and Thomas Scott urges the English to

turne your golden and silver coates, into coates of male, or iron jacks, and your silver
plate, into iron corslets of plate.[62]

And in *Vox Coeli*, this advice is exactly the same as that given by Queen Mary
to the Catholics in England: in case King James manages to gather more
money for the war than the King of Spain

you lords and knights morgage your manners and plate, and you ladies and gentle-women
pawne your ringes and jewels to make up the expected summe.[63]

The message in *Vox Coeli* is clear: if you, Protestants, do not do it, the
Catholics will.

Cleora's speech appeals to the Senators, who are deeply moved by her
words and by the fact that it is a woman who displays a 'braue masculine
spirit'. They agree to submit their wealth to the common need and to 'presse'
ten thousand 'Of Labourers in the Countrey men in-vr'd / To colde and
heate' (317–18), and the scene ends in a patriotic mood crowned with the
decision made by most of those present to take part in the war in person. And
having gone to pray in the temple (which, incidentally, shows Timoleon as a

religious man who worships the same gods as the Sicilians; ironically, Mansfeld was a Catholic – a fact never mentioned in English political literature of the period), they leave the stage to the slaves who begin their conspiracy; this forms the major plot of the play which is only loosely connected with the issues raised in Act I. These issues are neither developed nor discussed in what is to follow. They form an autonomous dramatic scene of a parliamentary debate, the understanding of which is not dependent on the rest of the play. However, an explanation for the lack of unity in the composition of *The Bondman* rests entirely on our reconstruction of the political milieu in March–April 1624, that is, during the period when the play was bound to evoke particular and predictable associations in spectators or readers and by doing so functioned as a political text.

In order to analyse this function with greater precision, let us recall some of the extra-textual pieces of evidence provided above. First of all, it has been shown that, apart from the historical sources Massinger used when writing *The Bondman*, the printed version exhibits a close relationship, hitherto unnoticed in criticism, with two contemporary tracts, both of which appeared in print in 1624. To be more precise, *Vox Coeli* and *Robert Earl of Essex his Ghost* were printed before or during the early days of the Parliament that assembled in February 1624. *Vox Coeli* is addressed to this Parliament, and Thomas Scott appeals to the 'illustrious and generous sirs' to undertake determined actions against the Spanish match and to declare war, at all costs, against Spain. Similar appeal is made in the second pamphlet, which indicates that they could not have been printed later than 20 March 1624, by which date an initial agreement between the King and the Houses of Parliament had been reached. In addition, internal evidence of *Vox Coeli* leaves no doubt that the text was written at least three years earlier, but was revised and updated for the *ad hoc* edition of 1624. For instance, Sir Francis Bacon is mentioned there as the 'now chancellor', whereas we know that Bacon was deprived of his office early in 1621; the Parliament referred to in the text proper is predominantly the Parliament of 1621, when Gondomar was still the Spanish ambassador (Gondomar left London in May 1622, replaced by Don Carlos Coloma), whereas the Parliament in the author's address is that of 1624. The factual discrepancies in *Vox Coeli* are too many to be listed here, but it seems certain that the text was rapidly revised to be printed before the new Parliament opened. Certain passages, complimentary to the Duke of Buckingham and elevating him almost to the position of England's saviour, lead us to suspect that the Duke furthered the publication of *Vox Coeli* as part of the propaganda campaign against the Spanish match and calling for the war against Spain.[64] It may, of course, be argued that both the pamphlets had been circulated in manuscript before they appeared in print and that Massinger may have read them before February 1624. Even if this were true, it would not change the fact that he used these sources consciously and selectively in order to create a dramatic version of a parliamentary dispute over issues that were actually debated in Parliament in March 1624. These issues could not have been predicted before that date. This implies that the November 1623 version of *The Bondman* must have been different from the one that was published a couple of months later. As was the case with *Vox Coeli*, *The Bondman* was updated, and was equipped with a new implied addressee, Parliament; or rather, and more precisely, only the first act was altered and updated and addressed to MPs. The basic change would be to create a dramatic situation, to introduce characters who would be able to evoke certain predictable associations in spectators or readers, and through these associations influence opinion on political issues of the day. Therefore, the implied function of the text is both political and normative. By introducing these changes and in effect creating an autonomous act, the author sacrificed the compositional unity of the text. As the result of this, Act I stands 'apart'.

If we take into account the fact that Timoleon's arrival in Syracuse to lead the Sicilian army against Carthage corresponds to the expected arrival of Mansfeld to England, the play becomes a political extrapolation at the time it was first circulated in print, or staged – in the new version – in a theatre. And the title page of the 1624 edition of *The Bondman* informs us that 'it hath been often Acted with good allowance, at the Cock-pit in Drury-lane: by her most Excellent Princesse, the Lady Elizabeth her Seruants'. It may be pointed out that the players were not the only people serving the Queen of Bohemia: Mansfeld served, so did Thomas Scott, the author of *Vox Coeli* and *Robert Earl of Essex His Ghost*, who in fact had been the chaplain to the English garrison in Holland since 1623.[65] The Duke of Buckingham had always been a faithful supporter of Frederick and Elizabeth and in the early spring of 1624 he had even more reason to be: about this time it was suggested that his daughter might marry Elizabeth's son. We learn this from, among others, a report to the King of Spain from Padre Maestro, a Spanish agent, in which Maestro mentions that Buckingham had received a letter from Elizabeth expressing hopes of a match between his daughter and her son, and adding that English Puritans did not want Prince Charles as successor, but Frederick, for whose sake Mansfeld came over to England.[66] This would support the repeated accusations against the Duke, as presented by the Spanish ambassador to James in April 1624, that Buckingham conspired with Parliament to dethrone the King if he refused to make war with Spain.[67] If this was true, and if Elizabeth and Frederick succeeded, Buckingham would have guaranteed succession rights to his daughter. Whatever his reasons, the Duke was certainly responsible for the shaping of England's policies during the period under discussion, and to achieve his goals he initiated a propaganda campaign in which drama was one of the instruments of agitation.

As a political extrapolation, *The Bondman* presents a dramatic context which reveals a striking similarity to the political context in the England of March 1624. The political and military alliance of two countries, indispensible for success, is sealed by the arrival of a famous and praiseworthy soldier–commander–politician. He is well received, although not without some embarrassment and pricked national pride, and taken to a meeting of parliament where decisions of great importance for the future of the country are to be made. This parliament, however, does not declare war – it seems to have been declared already – but assembles for two basic reasons: one, to assign to the arriving general the command of the army and two, to find financial means sufficient for its maintenance. The first issue involves little controversy, but the second does, owing to the opposition of some men in power who do not want to sacrifice their wealth to the common cause. In a series of speeches made by the general and some of the conscientious citizens, the selfishness and shortsightedness of that attitude is uncovered, and eventually patriotism wins over private concerns. The army leaves the city and returns victorious. Everything that happens between the departure and the return of the army is a local history, unconnected with known facts from English history, therefore this part of the play, constituting its plot, could not function as a political text, and was likely to have been considered by careful spectators or readers as something quite distinct from Act I. Once again, this may serve as proof that only part of a literary text may acquire a political function and neither this function nor its comprehension are invalidated by the remainder.

Because *The Bondman* was written and circulated before Mansfeld's arrival, its political extrapolation is clear: the general should be offered command of the English forces to fight the enemy abroad, and Parliament should overcome its reluctance to raise sufficient financial support for the war. Both Mansfeld's command and appropriate finances, in addition to the spontaneous enrolment under Mansfeld's ensigns, guarantee the final success. As such the appeal of *The Bondman* is in accordance with Buckingham's policies in March–April 1624. Its 'political message' is carefully balanced and free from any offensive or critical statements concerning James or his policy. Conversely, both the pamphlets that Massinger used when writing the new version of Act I are strongly biased against the King and are examples of what we would have labelled today as 'underground literature'. Massinger carefully selected the material for his play, concentrating on only a few current issues. This is why, for instance, there is little explanation given for the war with Carthage; we do not find the usual set speeches against the enemy describing treachery, cruelty and cunning Machiavellian policies; and there is no mention of religious controversy between the two sides, etc. All these issues would undoubtedly have been considered as 'dangerous matter' by the Master of the Revels, and in fact may have been detrimental to Buckingham's policies at this point.

Although it goes beyond the scope of critical analysis of a literary text, a reader may like to know whether the propaganda campaign, of which *The Bondman* was part, was effective. Its immediate result was satisfactory for Buckingham, but the consequences of its early success were disastrous. As expected, Mansfeld arrived in London on 14 April 1624, welcomed with great enthusiasm by the people. Whenever he appeared on the streets he was followed and applauded.[68] Men pressed forward to have the honour of touching the edge of his cloak; the Archbishop of Canterbury received him as he stepped out of his boat on the Surrey side of the Thames.[69] Numerous contemporary accounts tell us of his arrival and of the unusual welcome he enjoyed.[70] Soon after his arrival, he had a private audience with the Prince, and was also visited by Buckingham.[71] On 16 April he was taken in one of the Prince's coaches to Theobalds, where he was received 'extraordinarily well' by James.[72] The recovery of the Palatinate, according to Mansfeld, would be possible if he had 10 000 infantry and 3000 horse, 6 guns and £20 000 a month for the maintenance of the army. The demand must have been agreed beforehand with Charles and Buckingham. It is worth noting that 10 000 'pressed' men are mentioned in *The Bondman* (1.iii.16–18). James agreed to provide the above on condition that the King of France would do the same, that is, entrust Mansfeld with a similar force, and that the joint armies would be used only for the recovery of the Palatinate and the Valtelline.[73] After the audience, Mansfeld was offered a lodging in St James's Palace; ironically, in the very room prepared for the Spanish Infanta. He was also provided with a 'plentiful table', and 'every show of welcome', which was done, as one contemporary source informs us, 'not with any real intention to find him employment he desires, but to spite the Spaniards, who hate him, and to satisfy the Parliament of the King's resolution'.[74] The same source, dated 19 April 1624, informs us that at the time of Mansfeld's visit, Buckingham had urged the House of Commons to hasten the subsidies on account of the threat from Spain. This proves our point, raised above, that Buckingham used Mansfeld's arrival and his physical presence in London as an instrument in his dealings with the Commons. His earlier attempt to persuade MPs to advance part of the subsidy for the furnishing of the fleet with necessary supplies was a failure, as reported by various writers on 1 and 11 April.[75] A detailed account of Mansfeld's visit is also included in a report, dated 3 May (24 April in English terms), from the Venetian ambassador in England to the Doge and Senate:

God has sent Mansfelt here, his repulse [*sic*] from France was lucky. His coming ... has brought honour to himself and greater advantages to others [*sic*] than could have been expected. Buckingham visited him at his own quarters, showed him every courtesy and expressed excellent sentiments. Last Sunday, he went to Theobalds to the king who welcomed him gladly, although some doubt whether he was really glad to see an instrument of opposition to his ideas [*sic*]. At his return the prince took him in his own carriage, and then lodged him in his own palace in the very apartment prepared for the Infanta, with forty dishes a meal ... Many are amazed ... The people say he has come to be naturalised and to invest his money in England. After seeing the king and prince he presented his proposals in writing as they desired. He askes for 10,000 foot, 3,000 horse and six guns ... I spoke to the French ambassador in Mansfeld's favour as soon as he arrived, especially begging him to assure every one that Mansfelt had not been repulsed from France [sic].[76]

The immediate results of Mansfeld's visit were as follows: on 15 April, commissioners had been appointed to treat with the Dutch about sending troops to their assistance. On 18 April orders had been given to fit out twelve ships of the royal navy, and on 21 April the Council of War had been appointed.[77] Mansfeld left England on 25 April, taking with him a jewel worth £4000 that he had received as a present in addition to a diamond ring worth £2500 and a 'coach with six horses', and the news that England was preparing for war.

The later results were as follows: on 4 October a warrant was issued by the Council of War to empower the Treasury to advance £15 000 for the levy of troops for Mansfeld, in addition to £40 000 to pay his men for two months. On 29 October it was ordered to levy 12 000 pressed men for Mansfeld's service. On 7 November he received a commission to take command of the troops. In December the troops were gathering at Dover, where neither food nor money was waiting for them. Mansfeld asked for another £20 000 due for December, but there was no money in the Treasury; it took some time before Prince Charles could borrow the needed sum on his personal security. In the meantime, the starved soldiers looted nearby villages, stealing cattle and breaking into houses. Many deserted, and those who stayed in Dover threatened to hang the mayor and burn the town; in consequence, martial law was imposed there. At last, on 31 January 1625, this expeditionary force was able to leave Dover, and on the following day the ships cast anchor off Flushing. After some days, the troops were transferred in boats to Gertruidenberg, a town near Breda, but due to frost only some of them reached their destination. The others were almost starved to death. The fate of those at Gertruidenberg was no better. With little or no money sent from England, the army was decimated by weather, diseases and lack of food. At the end of March and before they managed to come near a battlefield, out of 12 000 men barely 3000 were capable of carrying arms. Such was the fate of an army which had been considered in England as capable of changing the situation on the Continent, capable of recovering the Palatinate and hammering the last nail into Antichrist's coffin.[78]

About the same time as Massinger's *The Bondman* reached the press, Thomas Dekker and John Ford's (?) *The Sun's Darling* was licensed for the public stage by Sir Henry Herbert on 3 March 1624:

For the Cockpit Company, The Sun's Darling; in the nature of a masque by Deker, and Forde.[79]

The curious composition and the lack of consistency in the plot of this play have puzzled its critics. We may actually distinguish three major trends in the meagre pile of criticism of *The Sun's Darling*. One interprets the play as an unusual mixture of morality and masque forms:

The authors have combined in this production the two dramatic forms in which natural and moral philosophy has hitherto been presented. The form of the morality has been used to stage the conflict in man's soul as he wanders from the paths of righteousness. The form of the masque has been used to present the properties of the four elements and affections. *The Sun's Darling* is a combination of the two . . . Raybright . . . is the counterpart of Man, Humanum Genus . . . The masque is built around the familiar doctrine of the incompatibility of the elements and humours, which must be harmonized . . .[80]

The second trend is characterized by the acknowledgement of the fact that as a 'morality' the play lacks consistency and is simply 'odd', and by attempts of the critics to account for this attenuation of composition by later additions:

But though there is no evidence the *The Sun's Darling* was composed before 1623, there is evidence that additions to it were made long after 1623. The last three lines of Act IV and the first part of Act V break sharply from the character of the rest of the play and refer almost unmistakably to the Scottish troubles and the preparations for the Bishops' Wars in 1638 or perhaps in 1639 . . . the masque as a whole is an odd piece for a London theatre . . . To the modern reader it seems confused and somewhat pointless.[81]

And Fredson Bowers, accepting Bentley's suggestion of additions being made in 1638/39, cautiously remarked that

It is tempting to speculate that *The Sun's Darling* was written for performance at Whitehall in 1623 sometime after Prince Charles's return from Spain on 5 October, that it was intended basically as a compliment to James I and his son Prince Charles, and that it was subsequently produced at the Cockpit, probably in March 1624, as indicated by Sir Henry Herbert's Office Book.[82]

The above suggestion was refuted by C. Hoy:

I doubt that any dramatist (or pair of dramatists) would be either naive enough or daring enough to greet Prince Charles on his return from his flighty jaunt to Spain in the dubious company of Buckingham with a morality play about a prodigal son who, squandering the gifts of a bounteous father, rambles capriciously and self-indulgently through three-quarters of his earthly sojourn in the company of Folly, a dissolute clown, and Humour, a whore whose whim decrees his every move. As a welcome home to Prince Charles, *The Sun's Darling* could only be a devastatingly satiric greeting, and it is not to be imagined that anything of the sort was ever intended by the authors.[83]

The third trend in the criticism of this 'odd' play is almost total neglect, as if nothing could be added to the opinions quoted above. In our view, the extant text[84] is an altered version of the authors' original, but – with the possible exception of some few lines – there is no need to look for the origin of these alterations in the late 1630s, but rather at about the time the play was licensed. This theory does not invalidate the possibility of later minor additions, which may have been made when the text was updated to be staged under new political circumstances. As was the case with *The Bondman*, an attempt will be made to show that the extant text fails as an artistic unity, and through this failure a second layer of meaning is created, the significance of which may be elucidated only by relating the text to contemporary political events, especially those described on the preceding pages of this chapter. A close analysis of this relationship will lead us to the conclusion that the additions to *The Sun's Darling* must have been made during the first weeks of the Parliament of 1624, that is, in February/early March, and that the *ad hoc* function of the altered text was similar to that of *The Bondman* – to promote the necessity of England's involvement with the war on behalf of Frederick and Elizabeth of Bohemia.

In the address to the reader, the text briefly defines itself: 'it is not here intended to present . . . the perfect Analogy betwixt the World and man . . . nor their Co-existence . . . But drawing the Curtain of this Morall, you shall finde him [i.e. Man] in his progression as followeth . . .'[85] and what follows is an introductory poem, in which the four seasons of the year are described as being parallel to the changing age and experience of man. As the play opens, Raybright, the Sun's Darling, and the protagonist of this 'morall', is awoken by the heavenly spheres, so that he would be able to face and experience reality, instead of being duped by illusory dreams. From the dialogue that follows between Raybright and the Priest of the Sun, we learn that the former descends directly from the Sun, defined either as his ancestor, or as his father,[86] and that Raybright's present melancholy and misery are caused by his disillusion with life. The latter, in turn, has been caused by what seem to have been recent events:

> PRIEST. You have had choice
> Of beauties to enrich your marriage-bed.
> RAYBRIGHT. Monkyes and Parokeetoes are as prettie
> To play withall . . .
> troath sir
> I care for no long travels with lost labor   (50–6)

The Priest's diagnosis is:

> 'Tis melancholy, and too fond indulgence
> To your own dull'd affections . . .   (62–3)

And then he reminds Raybright of 'the care your ancestor the Sun takes of yee' (65). To which Raybright answers:

> The care, the scorn hee throws on mee.
> PRIEST. Fie, fie;
> Have you been sent out into strange lands,
> Seen Courts of forreign Kings, by them been grac'd,
> To bring home such neglect?
> RAYBRIGHT. I have reason for't.
> PRIEST. Pray shew it.
> RAYBRIGHT. Since my coming home I have found
> More sweets in one unprofitable dream,
> Then in my lives whole pilgrimage.   (66–72)

The dialogue, which could evoke certain associations with Prince Charles's recent return from Madrid, is concluded with the appearance of the Sun who agrees to fulfil Raybright's desire to enjoy for one year

> the several pleasures here,
> Which every season in his kinde,
> Can bless a mortal with.   (189–91)

And thus, Raybright, or – perhaps – 'Mankind', goes on his earthly journey, accompanied, unfortunately, by another morality character, Folly, who, in turn, is presented as Humour's servant. And it is the sweet whispers of Humour that make Raybright reject Spring's love, which causes her death. In what follows Raybright also rejects Youth and Health, both offered to him by Spring, and all the temptations of Summer and Autumn. Every season is given a full act, the exposition occupying the first one. So in Act V Raybright comes to the court of Winter, who is the only man among the seasons. As might be expected from a play belonging to the morality tradition, it is only then that Raybright realizes the true nature of his companions, Folly and Humour. The play may indeed be, and has been, interpreted as only a curiously late example of a morality play. However, in Act V this one-sided interpretation cannot satisfactorily explain the text.

It may be observed that the seasons in the play are not presented as transitory, following one another in one place, but rather they are presented as rulers in their own right, living in courts of their own, governing different countries; to experience them, Raybright has to travel from one country to another. In this way, the passing of time is not stressed, and in consequence Raybright's journey loses its metaphorical character as a man's journey through life. Raybright is not much older at the end of the play than at its beginning. His experience is acquired chiefly through his travels from one court to another.

The country of Winter is described to us in terms very similar to any description of a contemporary duchy or kingdom. It has its own society, and Act V opens with ordinary people's dispute:

1. CLOWN. Hear you the news neighbor?
2. CLOWN. Yes, to my grief neighbor; they say our Prince Raybright is coming hither, with whole troops and trains of Courtiers; wee'r like to have a fine time on't neighbors.
3. CLOWN. Our Wives and Daughters are ...   (V.i.1–5)

They are immediately reprimanded by Winter:

> Bold sawcie mortals, dare you then aspire
> With snow and ice to quench the sphere of fire:
> Are your hearts frozen like your clime, from thence
> All temperate heat's fled of obedience:
> How durst you else with force think to withstand
> Your Princes entrie into this his land;
> A Prince who is so excellently good,
> His virtue is his honor, more then blood.   (V.i.17–24)

It is interesting to note that Winter does not identify himself with the climate: he accuses his subjects of having hearts as cold as their 'clime' – something that logically he should praise in them. Also, in Act v Raybright is constantly referred to as a 'Prince' (our 'Prince', or your 'Prince') – something not to be found in the previous acts. It is this opening of Act v that Bentley declared to be an allusion to the Bishop's War in the late 1630s. It may be so, but later changes and additions do not necessarily argue against others made in February/March 1624, the existence of which we shall now attempt to prove.

In the same scene, Winter goes on, in a lengthy speech, to praise Raybright for his wisdom and mercy (1.26), for his laws that are impartial and therefore 'truly just' and 'heavenly' (27–8), for his 'moderation' which gives his subjects 'an example how to live'. The last feature of course contradicts everything that the text has hitherto told us about Raybright: he is supposed to be after all a prodigal son, on his way to learn his lesson; therefore, to speak about his moderation and wisdom is to reject the whole idea of a morality. We learn also that Raybright is a ruler in his own right, for he has his court and his army, as indicated in the dialogue opening Act v, and it is this army that Winter's subjects fear. Winter patiently explains to them that the Prince's every thought is 'an act of pitie' (61), that he is 'all religious, furnish'd with all good / That ever was compris'd in flesh and blood', and therefore he can only 'direct you in the fittest way / To serv those powers, to which himself does pay / True zealous worship.' (62–6) The implication of course is that Winter's subjects should not worry, because the Prince is just and of the same religion as they are. In addition, he is related to heavenly powers, and should in fact be himself 'deified' (66–7). This, however, does not appeal to the people, who – prompted by Folly – decide to mutiny, without listening to Winter's prophecy:

> This Prince shall com, and by his glorious side
> Lawrel-crown'd conquest shall in triumph ride,
> Arm'd with the justice that attend's his cause,
> You shall with penitence embrace his laws:
> Hee to the frozen northern clime shall bring
> A warmth so temperate, as shall force the Spring
> Usurp my privilege, and by his Ray
> Night shall be chang'd into perpetual day.
> Plentie and happinesse shall still increase,
> As does his light; and Turtle-footed Peace
> Dance like a Fairie through his realms, while all
> That envie him, shall like swift Comets fall,
> By their own fire consum'd.   (90–102)

Thus, the Prince's arrival is described in predominantly military terms: his 'Lawrel-crown'd conquest shall in triumph ride'; this conquest is the result of the Prince's 'cause', not identified here, but it is 'arm'd with the justice that attend's' it; the conquest shall bring 'warmth' that will change the climate of the 'frozen' north, changing the night into perpetual day with the consequent increase in 'Plentie and happinesse' and the irretrievable fall of his enemies. This is evidently a military expedition of the Prince, the aim of which is to conquer Winter's country, which is frozen and suffers from the lack of light, wealth and peace. The power behind the Prince's actions is, of course, the Sun. This is confirmed by Winter's welcoming speech:

> to that glorious light
> Of heaven, the Sunne which chases hence the night,
> I am so much a vassaile, that I'le strive,
> By honoring you, to keep my faith alive
> To him, brave Prince, thro you, who did inherit
> Your fathers cheerefull heat, and quickning spirit;
> Therefore as I am Winter, worne and spent
> So farre with age, I am Tymes monument,
> Antiquities example . . . (129–37)

If we look at these lines closely, we shall notice that Winter's speech is not without grievance: because only the light of the Sun chases the night away, Winter feels neglected, but – as a 'vassaile' – he will 'strive' to keep his 'faith alive', which indicates that the faith had almost gone. Furthermore, Winter underlines the fact that he had been 'Winter' for far too long and that he is 'worne and spent / So farre with age'. He does not seem to like being winter at all! – a curious feature that makes him exceptional among the seasons presented in the play. This is why he welcomes the Prince's army in spite of the fact that its military goal is the destruction of Winter's dominion. Within the created world of the play this does not make any sense at all, and becomes meaningful only when related to an extra-textual reality known to the audience. In order to define the reality alluded to, several additional quotations are needed.

To Winter's welcoming speech Raybright replies:

> Never till now
> Did admiration beget in me truly
> The rare match'd twins at once, pittie and pleasure;
> So royall, so abundant in earth's blessings,
> Should not partake the comfort of those beames,
> With which the Sun beyond extent doth cheere
> The other seasons, yet my pleasures with you,
> From their false charmes, doth get the start as farr
> As heaven's great lamp from every minor starr. (141–9)

Thus, Raybright's arrival evokes in him two emotions: pity and pleasure. But why pity? The answer is provided above: Winter is 'so royall', so 'abundant in earth's blessings', that it is a shame and a pity that – equipped with his superior qualities – he should not enjoy the beams of the Sun, which, on the other hand, are rather inappropriately ('beyond extent') distributed among other seasons; this injustice being largely due to the latter's 'false charmes'.

This again contradicts the previous four acts, and destroys the morality. For these reasons, Raybright feels pleasure in bringing relief to the night-trodden north. At this point, Bounty speaks for the first time, stating cautiously that if Raybright's words are of his heart, without any mischief behind them, then they can hope to enjoy the 'lasting riches' of Raybright's presence there (150–4).

Bounty is addressed by Raybright in the following significant way which, at the same time, gives us the 'clue' to the 'mystery' of the play:

> RAYBRIGHT. Winters sweet bride,
> All Conquering Bounty, queen of harts, life's glory,
> Natures perfection; whom all love, all serve;
> To whom Fortune, even in extreame's a slave,
> When I fall from my dutie to thy goodness,
> Then let me be ranck'd as nothing.
> BOUNTY. Come, you flatter mee.
> RAYBRIGHT. I flatter you! Why Madam? you are Bounty;
> Sole daughter to the royall throne of peace.
>   . . .
> For you he is no souldier dares not fight,
> No Scholar he, that dares not plead your merites,
> Or study your best Sweetness, should the Sun,
> Eclips'd for many yeares, forbeare to shine
> Upon the bosome of our naked pastures.
> Yet where you are, the glories of your smiles
> Would warm the barren grounds, arm hartless misery,
> And cherish desolation. Deed I honor you,
> And as all others ought to, I serve you.   (154–73)

Thus, Bounty turns out to be Winter's 'sweet bride', and she is also labelled the 'queen of harts', 'life's glory' and 'nature's perfection'. We also learn that she is the 'sole daughter to the royall throne of peace', and that for her and her country the Sun had been 'eclips'd for many yeares'. Her miserable situation changes with Raybright's arrival, the aim of which is to serve Bounty and Winter.

Having reached this point in our account of the play's development, we may observe that when interpreted in isolation, all of this makes little sense. The traditional morality play motif of Mankind reaching wisdom in old age is totally destroyed in Act v. Raybright's arrival with his troops in Winter's country turns out to be a military victory rather than one of mind and character. By chasing away the evil forces of the night, he brings peace and comfort there. The other seasons turn out not to be tests and proofs of Raybright's prodigality, but just the opposite: the seasons are false and untrustworthy, and it is therefore Raybright's victory that he rejected them to 'take pleasure' to Winter and his bride, Bounty. Raybright – if treated as a stock morality character – does not experience anything in Winter's country; he arrives there with a 'just cause' and conquers the land with the power that he represents: with the Sun's beams. For some reason Bounty turns out to be Winter's bride, although they are not usually associated with one another at all. The couple have been neglected by the Sun for years, something that Raybright hopes to change by his service. Thus, the ultimate result of Raybright's journey through life turns out to be the liberation of Winter and Bounty from the evil forces of the night. This marks a sudden and inconsistent shift from the major plot of the play, and so creating a number of insoluble contradictions if we are to treat the text as a morality play, or even a variation on the theme of a morality play. This indicates that either the authors wrote a bad, inconsistent play, or – which seems more likely – that the original text was altered, or rewritten, either by the authors, or by (an)other poet(s), and this altered version reached the press and is the only one extant. The chief reason for this alteration would be to create a text capable of evoking in spectators or readers predictable and desired associations with the political issues of the day.

As indicated above, some critics have already hinted at this possibility, although others rejected it as impossible on the grounds that if Raybright 'represented' Prince Charles and the Sun, King James, the play would then constitute a severe criticism of Charles in particular by presenting him as a prodigal son. This, of course, would be true if the play revealed consistency as a 'pseudo-morality', which is not the case. In our opinion, Raybright of Act v has little in common with Raybright of Acts I–IV, even though the authors were at pains to fit him to the original story. But he does not fit at all, something that could not have escaped contemporaries' attention. The entire 'morality episode' of Act v does not follow or expound the 'moral' of the 'fourth season' we find in the address to the reader:

> And now the Winter, or his nonage takes him,
> The sad remembrance of his errours wakes him;
> Folly and Humour, Faine hee'd cast away,
> But they will never leave him, till hee's Clay.
> Thus Man as Clay Descends, Ascends in spirit;
> Dust, goes to dust, The soule unto It's Merit.   (21–6)

However, on the basis of the quotations provided above, we may ascertain that it was not difficult for a contemporary audience to associate 'Winter' with the Winter King, that is, with Frederick the Elector Palatine. He is mentioned in the play as being 'royall' and he is praised in a way reminiscent of *The Life of the Duchess of Suffolk*.[87] His 'sweet bride', Bounty, is labelled the 'queen of harts', by which name Elizabeth of Bohemia was well known in the period under discussion. She is also called the 'sole daughter to the royall throne of peace', which unmistakably refers to James I – the peacemaker. Similarly, it would be possible to associate Raybright with Prince Charles, and the Sun with the 'heavenly powers' of the House of Stuart, if not with James in person. Thus, in Act v the text alludes directly to contemporary

politics, and creates the following 'meaning': the Winter King and Queen
have for many years been deprived of the Sun's, that is, James's, favour and
patronage. The Sun/James – instead of bringing relief to the royal couple
who had fallen into distress – has paid more attention to other
'seasons'/countries (like Spain). This caused Winter's/Frederick's loss of
faith in the Sun/James. But the King, being the wise peacemaker, sent
his Raybright/Charles and troops on a rescue mission, by which
Winter/Frederick regained his faith in him, and the night of the winter would
soon be turned into perpetual day of joy. The 'seasons' referred to in Act v are
not the same seasons of the preceding acts. They are blamed for distracting
the Sun's attention with their 'false charms'. They do not seem to create
unequivocal parallels with any definite monarchs or countries, but they were
certainly responsible for the 'eternal night' of Frederick and Elizabeth. It is
only Raybright's military expedition that turns Winter's and Bounty's land
to a 'new Elisium' (l.271).

What follows is 'Winter's festivall', which turns out to be a masque
introduced by Conceit and Detraction, and with the participation of the four
elements and four temperaments. These are joined together by the 'nymph of
harmony'. Raybright is given instruction by Winter how to find the way to
Paradise, and although tempted again by Humour, chooses the right way.
The Sun appears in person and gives Raybright the 'moral' of the play:

> Thy sands are numbered, and thy glasse of frailtie
> Here runs out to the last: here is this mirror
> Let man behold the circuit of his fortunes;
> The season of the Spring dawns like the Morning,
> Bedewing Childhood with unrelish'd beauties
> Of gawdie sights; the Summer, as the Noon,
> Shines in delight of Youth, and ripens strength
> To Autumns Manhood, here the Evening graws,
> And knits up all felicitie in follie;
> Winter at last draws on the Night of Age ...   (304–13)

However, this description applies to a morality and not to *The Sun's Darling*.
The extant text does not create a 'mirror' which would let a man 'behold the
circuit of his fortunes'; Spring is not Childhood for Raybright, who – even
before his visit there – had been to many foreign courts and had intended to
marry. There is no conspicuous change in his personality in the Summer,
supposedly 'representing' his 'Youth', nor in the Autumn/Manhood. And the
last act, to the last line preceding the masque, is not a continuation of the
morality pattern at all. Therefore it appears that the masque refers to a
from different text than the one extant. It refers to the original 'moral play' written
for a court performance, which – owing to the political circumstances – was
re-written and adapted for a public stage, with the intention of evoking in
spectators particular associations with the political situation of the day, and
through these associations to draw their attention to England's obligation to

enter the war for the recovery of the Palatinate and Bohemia. When staged in March 1624, the play served a propaganda function similar to that of Massinger's *Bondman*. To acquire this function both the plays had to be substantially altered, which had a damaging effect on their compositional and artistic unity.

4 The matter of Spain

A marginal note in one of the several extant copies of Thomas Middleton's *A Game at Chesse* informs us that the play was licensed by Sir Henry Herbert on 12 June 1624. However, there is no mention of it in Sir Henry's Office Book, and we learn only from other sources that the play was staged early in August and was presented with enormous success for nine consecutive days. In the Privy Council Records (August 1624), we read a note informing us that the play had actually been 'seene and allowed by Sr Henry Herbert k^t M^r of the Reuells, vnder his owne hand, and subscribed in the last page of the said Booke' (*CSP, Domestic*, 1623–25, p. 329). A number of other allusions and references to the play have been preserved, along with descriptions of its actual staging, and the diplomatic and official correspondence; all of these documents have been reproduced by other authors, so there is no need to deal with them here in detail.

The fact that this strongly anti-Spanish satirical piece was licensed in the first place has puzzled the critics. No other play in the entire Jacobean period has provoked so much comment from contemporaries, no other play caused a comparable scandal, involving the offended Spanish ambassadors, the Privy Council and the King himself, by whose order the play was suppressed, the actors were questioned, a warrant was issued for Middleton's arrest, and Sir Henry was summoned to explain himself. It seems logical to assume that Herbert, usually very cautious, and others involved in the 'scandal', took the risk of staging the play only because they felt themselves secure and were convinced that if trouble arose they would be protected by some influential personages. Because the play reveals striking congruity with the new ideology of the 'war party' headed by the Duke of Buckingham and Prince Charles, it is therefore equally plausible that these two sponsored the production.

We should, perhaps, begin our discussion of Middleton's *A Game at Chesse* with a rudimentary reconstruction of the laws that govern the created world of the play. Because certain rules of chess are employed here, the laws are naturally different from those known to us from everyday experience, and – generally speaking – from those that govern the human world.[1] The created universe is basically divided into three interrelated spheres: the world of chess – as presented on stage, the implied human world – off-stage, and the metaphysical world that controls the first two, and which is defined in

Christian terms. The interrelationship between these worlds has drawn little attention from the critics, who have instead elaborated on 'who is who' in the allegory.[2] We shall therefore make an attempt to elucidate the links between the particular worlds of A Game at Chesse, and on this basis try to show that to a certain extent the play 'explains itself';[3] this will bring us to the problem, neglected in criticism, of who are the players of this 'game': at first sight there seems to be none, but perhaps a closer analysis of all chess references in the text will at least imply their existence; further, we shall point to those elements in the text that allude to current political events and to the ideology that backed the English Protestants' cause during the early phase of the Thirty Years War.

The implication of the title is confirmed early in the Induction: we are about to witness

> The noblest Game of all, a Game at Chesse
> Betwixt our side and the Whitchouse, the men sett
> In theire iust order readie to goe to it;   (43–5)[4]

And the stage direction informs us that 'Enter severally in order of Game, the White and Blacke-Houses' (on the margin of lines 53–7). We also learn that the game is played according to certain rules (74–5), which are not yet defined, but the implication is that these are chess rules which should not be violated.[5] The appearance of chessmen on stage is – as Error tells us – a materialization of his dream, and the game – due to the intervention of some 'power' – is going to go on before Ignatius Loyola as a 'projection' of Error's dream.[6] Of course, the irony of this artistic device, reminiscent of medieval dream-visions, is that the game has its origin in Error's mind, which in itself impairs the verisimilitude of the ultimate result.

In what follows we have a series of encounters of chessmen from both the houses, two, three or four pieces at a time, with the exception of three instances, when we are presented with a 'panoramic' view of the 'chessboard'. The first instance is to be found in the stage direction quoted above, when the two full houses appear on stage, and make their exit towards the end of the Induction.[7] This simple device informs the reader or spectator that in spite of the fact that the play presents a sequence of episodes, this is a 'true' game of chess. Simply, the stage becomes 'too small' to accommodate both the houses. The implication is that the two houses are off-stage, which is also confirmed by the successive appearances of various chessmen and by references they make to the houses that are not visible. We are thus witnessing episodes of a larger game strategy, and the text constantly reminds us of it. This, however, is not a simple game, but a dramatic text which attempts to imitate certain laws that govern the chess world, and by equipping the chessmen involved in the action with certain human qualities, it creates a peculiar relationship between the human and the chess worlds.

There are scores of references to the game of chess throughout the play.

The text constantly reminds us that we are witnessing nothing but a chess game, as if this were in doubt. However, the rules of the game – as we know them – are constantly violated in the created world, which may lead us to at least two possible explanations of that fact: (1) the rules of chess in the created world are simply different from those observed in the extra-textual reality; we are after all observing a 'materialized' dream, and because of the nature of dreams, lack of consistency is possible, and anything can happen; but, on the other hand, if we stress the dream nature of the created world, we are bound to face serious problems when making the final evaluation of the play's 'message', for this is Error's dream. The other possibility is: (2) since it was impossible to combine the rules of the game with the rules of the genre, some of the rules had to be violated or neglected[8]. As critics have observed, 'the discrepant natures of theatre and of chess ensure that Middleton must depart from the practice of a real chess game'[9] and 'chess cannot be used both accurately and effectively as the structure for a play ... on their own, the chess pieces provide too narrow a range of human motivation';[10] as P. Yachnin put it:

It will not be difficult to prove that Middleton's grasp of the technical aspects of chess was not particularly firm, and that what he meant to do ... was not to fit the dramatic action to the chess, but rather to exploit the allegorical significance of chess in order to give point to a dramatic situation.[11]

Consequently, the constant chess references serve the important function of allegorizing human actions on stage as a 'game-of-the-chess-type', which in fact does not pretend to be a literal, or mimetic, representation of a chess game, but rather – by violating the rules of the game known to spectators or readers – creates a significant metaphor.[12] Had the rules of the game been observed completely, or indeed more carefully, it would have been impossible to create a metaphor of a similar kind, not to mention some dramatic action, which would have been confined to strict, basically non-theatrical rules.[13] Thus, in order to create a vivid and intelligible metaphor, and a dramatic action of some sort (weak though it be), chess rules had to be violated or neglected. Any consistent implementation of these rules brings confinement to the dramatic action, and only occasionally is the effect successful, as in the 'temptation' scene in Act II scene i, when the Black Bishop's Pawn commands the White Queen's Pawn to come 'nearer', so that he can embrace her; the black Pawn cannot do it himself, because it is not 'his' move: his helplessness is determined by chess rules, and in this particular example the effect must have been comical indeed, if we imagine the lascivious Pawn begging the other one to come nearer so that he could fulfil his sexual wishes.

All the references to chess made in the play are basically of two types: the general one, examples of which refer to the game of chess as such, and the self-referential type, examples of which describe the particularities of the situation on the chess-board, or of the game strategies that we are witnessing or are about to witness. There is no need to list all of these here, and only characteristic examples will be provided.

TYPE I – 'The noblest Game of all, a Game of Chesse' (Induction, 42), 'the best Game that e're Christian lost' (I.i.14), 'right Christian Conflict' (I.i.29), 'Pawns that are lost, are euer out of playe' (III.i.355), etc.

It seems that the references belonging to this type serve the important function of communicating the following message: the game we are witnessing is not the first of its kind; the 'Christian Conflict' has been going on for some time, with both the Houses taking active part in the game (as implied by comments like: 'I knowe youre play of ould' (II.i.311)), apparently without a decisive victory for either side. This presupposition finds confirmation elsewhere in the text. We are told, for instance, that 'The Deuill has beene at worke since 88 on' (IV.iv.6), and that '7 yeares since' the 'White Kingdome' was promised to the Black House (I.i.270–1), and that the Black Knight had 'labour'd' seven years to accomplish the conquest (II.i.189). The game we are witnessing lies within a long 'game tradition' and its greatest importance is that this is the last game, in which the final blow is given to the Black House and the power that stands behind it.

TYPE II – The abundance of self-references recurring in the chess world may be illustrated by the following selected examples: 'Take heede S^r, weere entrapt' (I.i.341); 'Who comes to take mee' (II.i.163); 'There's check agen' (II.i.215); 'Would I stood farder off' (II.ii.172); 'I playe thus them' (II.i.31); 'Hee maye skip over mee' (III.i.31); 'If shee were tooke, the Game would bee ours quickly' (III.i.278); 'Hee's taken by default / By willfull Negligence, guard the sacred persons' (III.i.288–9); I am snapt too, a Black Pawne in the Breech of mee' (III.ii.35–6); 'I haue my Game to followe' (IV.i.21); 'I'me now about a Mr: peice of playe / To entrap the white Knight' (IV.ii.79–80); 'Stand you now idle in the heate of Game?' (IV.ii.143); 'Neuer was Game more hopefull of our Side' (IV.ii.151); 'And the Games ours – wee giue thee Checkmate by / Discouerye, King, the Noblest Mate of all' (V.iii.177–8); 'See, all's confounded, the Game's lost, Kings taken' (V.iii.203); etc.

The function of most of the above examples is to define dramatic action (and stage business) in terms of chess. The 'chess nature' of what the text presents to readers (in particular), or to spectators, is too weak to explain itself: it has to be supported verbally and all the references to chess fill the gap resulting from the incompatibility of drama and chess rules. In other words, the text constantly defines itself as a game of chess,[14] something that otherwise would not have been so obvious. But a game it is not: it is a dramatic piece that adapts certain selected rules of chess in an attempt to create the desired metaphor. In the play, the world of chess is not autonomous and self-explanatory, as it incorporates a number of features, attributes and laws that are external to chess, and there is constant allusion to the world(s) outside the chess-board.

To begin with, the text locates the game within a certain phase of history–

human history to be more precise. At least three historical characters known to us are mentioned by name: Ignatius Loyola in the Induction, Doctor Lopez in Act IV.ii.121 and the Pope in III.i.26. In connection with Lopez, the 'maiden Queen' of the White House is also mentioned (IV.ii.122) (the text leaves no doubt that the White House is a 'hereditary kingdom'), who may with ease be identified as Queen Elizabeth I. There are numerous references made to historical events: the defeat of the Spanish Armada in 1588, the expulsion of the Jesuits from Venice in 1606, the canonization of Loyola, the expedition of the English navy to help the Spaniards fight pirates in the Mediterranean in 1620. Almost the whole of Europe is referred to: countries and cities are recurrently mentioned, so are streets and boroughs of London. In addition, the abundance of topical reference to contemporary events, to people, and even to political pamphlets, allow us to date the game as 'taking place' in the year of Prince Charles's visit to Spain, that is, in 1623. In this way the world of chess becomes inseparable from the world external to it, and this relationship is created with considerable precision. The basic method employed here is the violation of chess rules, by which the chess world is expanded beyond the chess-board and beyond the temporal confinement of the game proper. Consequently, the understanding of the text depends largely on our knowledge of chess rules and of the extra-textual reality(ies) alluded to, and without this knowledge the play makes little sense. As R. Sargent put it, 'a work of art so geared to a contemporary situation is likely to be too much of its own time to be for all time'.[15] The created dramatic conflict is not only similar to some human conflicts, but it is, the text tells us, a part of these conflicts. In other words, the chess world is incorporated into the human world.

Let us now provide several examples of the numerous violations of chess rules in the game. Already in the illustrated poem prefixed to one of the early editions of the play, *The Picture Plainly Explained After the Manner of the Chess-Play*, we read that

> A Game at Chesse is here displayed,
> Betweene the *Black* and *White House* made,
> Wherein Crowne-thirsting Policy,
> For the *Blacke-House* (by falacy)
> To the White-Knight, checke, often giues,
> And to some straites, him thereby driues;
> The *Fat-Blacke-Bishop* helps also
> With faithlesse heart to giue the blow:
> Yet (maugre all their craft) at length
> The *White-Knight*, with wit-wondrous strength,
> And circumspectiue Prudency,
> Giues Check-mate by Discouery
> To the *Blacke Knight* ...   (1–13)

This has appalled a critic:

Whoever wrote the poem knew nothing of chess; he made three unpardonable blunders, twice saying that a Knight checks another Knight, and once saying that the White Knight checkmates the Black Knight by 'discovery'. Then as now, no Knight could be checked or checkmated, and of the attacking forces the Knight was the only piece which could not give check by discovery. It is incredible that the author of this poem knew the rudiments of chess. He was equally ignorant of the crisis of the play. From the simplified scene and abbreviated speech, 'Check by discovery', on the title-page . . . he assumed that the White Knight checkmates the Black Knight.[16]

In our view, the author's 'message' is totally different: the quoted lines inform a conscientious reader that a very peculiar game of chess is going to be presented, a game in which different rules are valid, and that the chess formula is employed only as a pretext to present in a concealed manner the 'games' that politicians play.

As mentioned above, some of the violations of chess rules lead to the temporal 'expansion' of the chess world, as the following examples will illustrate:

> BLACK KNIGHT. . . . is this fellowe
> Our prime Incendiarie, one of those
> That promist the White Kingdome 7 yeares since
> To our black house?   ·   (I.i.268–71)

> WHITE QUEEN'S PAWN. Yesterdayes cursed evening, –   (II.ii.206)

> BLACK KNIGHT. That holie Man
> So wrongfullie accusde by this lost pawne,
> Has not beene seene these 10 dayes in these parts,   (II.ii.224–6)

> WHITE KING. . . . showe him the testimonie
> Confirmed by goodmen, how that fowle Attempter
> Got but this morning to the place, from whence
> Hee dated his forgd lines for ten dayes past: (III.i.214–17)

> BLACK KNIGHT'S PAWN. Tis hee, my Confessor! hee
> might ha' past mee 7 yeare together . . .   (IV.i.1–2)

Similarly, the locational references 'expand' the chess world territorially: most of these allude to European geography in connection with historical or contemporary political events. However, there are several of a different type, originating from the dramatic action:

> BLACK BISHOP. Awaye, upon the wings of Speede take posthorse
> Cast thirtie leagues of Earth behind thee suddainlie
> Leaue letters Antedated wth our house
> Ten days at least from this,   (II.i.206–9)

> BLACK BISHOP. [he is] at this instand 30 leagues from hence,   (II.ii.228)

> (s.d. opening v.i) Musique, Enter the Black Knight
> in his Litter!

Other violations of basic chess rules which do not stem from the pre-dominantly 'human' nature of all the chessmen can be provided:

1. The movements of chessmen and pawns in particular do not follow chess rules consistently (e.g. pawns can move only forward, which is not the case in the play).

2. Three of the chessmen change sides during the game (the King's Pawn, the Fat Bishop and his Pawn). The black pieces constantly try to convert the opposite ones to their 'House'.

3. Pieces of the same House make their entrances together.

4. There is one black bishop missing. As a matter of fact, he has to be missing unless Middleton were to allow the black side to play with three bishops, after the Fat Bishop's betrayal. Interestingly, this omission is explained by the Black Knight:

> Our Second Bishop absent,
> Wch hash yet no Employment in the game,
> Perhaps nor euer shall, it maye bee wun
> Without his motion, it rests most in ours   (II.ii.82–5)

To the above list we may add P. Yachnin's comment that

any interpretation which sees the play as representing a chess game breaks down in I.i.243 s.d., when the Black Knight enters out of turn ... In his allegorical adaptation of chess, Middleton is demonstrably indifferent towards technical precision. In A Game at Chess, we hear nothing of castling or pawn promotion, the Queen is accorded less influence in determining the outcome of the game than her Pawn, and on the whole, the knowledge of chess which Middleton reveals is of the most elementary kind.[17]

In our view, Middleton is not at all 'demonstrably indifferent towards technical precision', and the play does not reveal his knowledge of chess as being 'of the most elementary kind', because chess is not played seriously here: chess rules are violated on purpose to create a second layer of meaning.

As we have said above, the chess world extends far beyond the temporal and locational boundaries of a chess-board, and is incorporated into the off-stage world of contemporary politics; particular chessmen, with few exceptions, have been identified with various personages involved in the 'Spanish match'.[18] On this level, the 'main intention of the play is', as M. Heinemann put it, 'overwhelmingly simple. The seduction attempts represent Catholic and Jesuit attempts to capture the individual soul, while the great Spanish design of a "universal monarchy" is the stake the arch-schemer Gondomar plays for till he is defeated by the skill of Charles and Buckingham.'[19] It may therefore be worthwhile to discover how this 'simple intention' is created in a literary text, and how the politics of the play may be related to a given extra-textual reality.

Let us first describe the nature of the conflict in which both the sides are involved. Certainly, this is not a simple game of chess. As far as game strategy is concerned, the major difference between the houses is that the Black House is active and undertakes a number of actions in order to win. The other side is chiefly passive, only occasionally undertaking defensive action, as in the forged letter plot, or in the Fat Bishop's attack on the White Queen. From the start of the game, it is obviously this passivity that leaves the White House vulnerable to danger from the aggresive black pieces.[20] This vulnerability is deepened as the danger comes both from without and within the White House, a fact that the innocent white pieces do not at first acknowledge.[21] It is through the seemingly trivial sub-plots that the twofold source of danger is revealed, and this enables the White House to take effective action. The black pieces, too, have their Achilles heel: it is the danger of their true nature being 'discovered'; precisely for this reason they are at pains to conceal their real intentions and, whatever they do, they do it in great secrecy, as the Black Knight declares openly: 'When went a man of his Societie [i.e. a Jesuit] / To mischeife with a wtnesse' (II.i.204–4). As pointed out by R. Sargent, in the play

the word discovery is used constantly and . . . a number of 'discoveries' are made during the course of action . . . The first discovery occurs in Act II when the White Queen's Pawn discovers that the Jesuit Pawn is a dissembler (II.i.149; II.ii.258) . . . Act III has several discoveries. The White Knight discovers that the white pawn had been telling the truth . . . The clearing of the White Queen's Pawn leads on immediately to the discovery of the duplicity of another white pawn . . . The sight of the parti-coloured pawn leads the Fat Bishop to announce that he will 'instantly discover / One that's all black' (III.i.284). The White King responds, 'I long for that discovery' (287) . . . Act V contains only one 'checkmate by discovery' but in the resolution of the sub-plot . . . the black pawn . . . concludes, 'I'm quit with you now for my discovery' (v.ii.57) . . . From Middleton's point of view the whole play must have been intended as a discovery.[22]

In order to protect themselves from being 'discovered', the black pieces put on a mask of dissimulation. As the Black Knight puts it himself

> . . . what wee haue donne
> Hath beene dissemblance euer.   (v.iii.157–8)

And this confession does not refer only to the dissembling we have been witnessing ever since the play began, but – indirectly – to the entire period since 'the devil hath been at work'. The abundance of words and phrases denoting dissimulation, elusiveness of appearence, falsehood, cunning conceit and treachery used in the text is significant in itself, but to make his point clear even to children Middleton constantly employs the simplest device used in drama – his characters revealing their true nature to readers or spectators. There is never any doubt about the 'character' of particular chess pieces, there is nothing to surprise. And when some of the white chessmen turn out to be traitors of their 'house', their treason is revealed by others before they can act. Thus, when the White King's Pawn appears at the end of Act I and scares the Black Bishop's Pawn, the latter (and the implied reader or spectator) is informed by the Black Knight that

> Hee's made our owne (man) halfe in Voto youres,
> His hearts in the black house ...   (I.i.342–3)

Almost as soon as the Fat Bishop appears on stage, we learn from the Black Bishop that 'twere a Mr: peice of Serpent Subteltie / To fetch him a this side agen' (II.ii.61–2). And the Fat Bishop 'discovers' himself

> Black Knight! expect a wonder er't bee long;
> You shall see mee one of the Black House shortlie   (III.i.58–9)

The same device is applied to the black pieces, who constantly uncover their true natures either in asides, or when planning new deceits. The reader or spectator therefore becomes much better informed than the white chessmen on stage, which directs attention and expectation not to the question 'who is right and who is wrong' (this is made explicit by the text), but to 'when and how' the white pieces are going to discover the dissemblers. This is why the final 'discovery' becomes checkmate in the allegorical world of chess: as soon as their technique of playing is revealed, the black pieces lose their ability to continue the game and are checkmated with ease.[23]

As presented in the play, the expansion of the Black House in the 'world' is not realized through military action (with perhaps one exception there are no belligerent cries in the play), but through cunning diplomacy, the main instrument of which is secret service or 'intelligence', bribery and intrigue ('plots'). This applies both to the chess world on stage and to the activity of the black pieces in the 'human world' off-stage. As early as in the first scene of Act I, the Black Queen's Pawn informs the White Queen's Pawn that the Jesuits are 'true Labourers in the Worke / Of the Vniuersall Monarchie' (56–7) and that they are

> ... mayntaynde in manie Courts and palaces,
> And are inducst by noble personages
> Into great princes Seruices, and prooue
> Some Councellors of State, some Secretaries
> All seruing in Notes of Intelligence,
> (As parish clearkes theire morturarie Bills)
> To the Father General; so are designes
> Oft times præuented, and Important Secrets
> Of State discouerd, yet no Author found
> But those suspected oft that are most sound[24]   (59–68)

It may be added that the Black House is constantly associated with Jesuits, and the latter with Spain (as in I.i.334–7); the aims of the Society of Jesus are identical with those of the Black House – to form a 'Vniuersall Monarchie' (as in I.i.264). Still in the first scene of Act I, the Black Knight expresses his satisfaction with the work of his agents:

> The Busines of the Vniuersall Monarchie
> Goes forward well now! the great Colledge pott
> That should bee always boyling, with the fuell

> Of all Intelligences possible
> Thorough the Christian kingdomes ...   (264–8)

The secret diplomacy of the Black House is also revealed through dramatic action: the Black Bishop's Pawn brings 'A packet [of 'intelligence'] from the Assistant Fathers' from 'all parts' (i.i.324–6), and soon after the White King's Pawn – the traitor – brings intelligence from his own House (cf. line 71 quoted above) and announces that nothing shall happen to 'extenuate' the Black House's 'cause', and that

> ... I will striue
> To crosse it wth my Councell, purse and power,
> Keep all Supplies back, both in meanes and men
> That maye rayse agaynst you ...   (350–3)

The secrecy of their actions is also implied in the scene when the White Queen's Pawn has managed to escape the lust of the Black Bishop's Pawn, and the black pieces deliberate on what counter-actions to undertake, with the solution that the Black Pawn should presently travel 'thirty leagues' and ante-date letters providing himself with a sufficient alibi. The problem, however, is how to get 'forth unspied', which is solved by the Black Queen's Pawn, who discloses 'a secret vault' (ii.i.218). In the scene that follows, a 'cabinet of intelligences' is brought forth, and the Black Knight elaborates on its content (ii.i.225–62). He also boasts about his past successes,

> Was it not I procurde a pretious safeguard
> From the White Kingdome to secure our coasts
>   . . .
> Who made the Jayles flie open (wthout miracle)
>   . . .
> Whose policie was't to put a silencst Muzzle,
> On all the Barking Tonguemen of the Time
>   . . .
> In the most fortunate Angle of the World,
> The Court has held the Cittie by the Hornes
> Whilst I haue milkt her ...[25]   (iii.i.88–112)

And he boasts again in Act iv:

> ... I haue sold the Groome a'th Stoole 6 times,
> And receiude monye of 6 seuerall Ladies
>   . . .
> I haue taught o' frends too
> To conuey white house Gold to our black Kingdome
> In cold bakte pasties and so coozen Searchers,
>   . . .
> Letters conuayed in Roules, Tobacco-Balls
> When a Restraynt comes by my politique Councell
> Some of our Jesuites turne Gentlemen Vshers,
> Some Faulkers, some park keepers, & some Huntsmen,
>   . . .

praye what use
Put I my Summer Recreation to?
But more to informe my knowledge in the State
And strength of the White Kingdome! no fortificatiō
Hauen, Creeke, Landing place 'bout the white Coast
But I got draught and platforme, learnd the depth
Of all theire channells, knowledge of all Sands
Shelues, rocks, and riuers for inuasion proper'st[26]
A Catalogue of all the Nauie Royall
The Burden of the Ships, the Brassie Murderers,
The number of the men, to what Cape bound:
Agen, for the discouerie of the Inlands,
Neuer a Sheire but the State better knowen
To mee then to the Brest Inhabitants
What power of men and horse, Gentries Reuennues,
Who well affected to our Side, who ill
Who neyther well nor ill, all the Neutrallitie,
Thirtie eight thousand Soules haue been seducd, P.
Since the Jayles Vomited wth the pill I gaue 'em.   (IV.ii.43–77)

The same Black Knight reveals that he has the ability to change 'to anye shape' he likes (IV.iv.45). Therefore, it is not surprising that in the play he is made the arch-Machiavellian politician, the 'brain' of the Black House's expansionism.[27] And, literally, the Black Knight's brain becomes a symbol of his House's desire to form a 'universal monarchy':

BLACK KNIGHT. ... thou hast seene
    A Globe stands on the Table in my Closett?
BLACK KNIGHT'S PAWN. A thing Sir full of Cuntryes, and hard words,
                    . . .
BLACK KNIGHT. Just such a thing (if ere my Skull bee opend)
    Will my Braynes looke like,
BLACK KNIGHT'S PAWN. Like a Globe of Countries
BLACK KNIGHT. I, and some Mr-Polititian
    That has sharpe State Eyes will goe neere to pick out
    The plotts, and euerie Clymate where they fastend
    Twill puzzle 'em too;[28]   (III.i.137–48)

The ability to deceive the opponent by false appearance, the ability to pretend to be something different from one's own true nature, while employing 'decent' and 'Christian' language, seem to be the instruments of the black chessmen's quest for power. These are in fact the *sine qua non* of their ability to play the game: as soon as their dissimulation is 'discovered', the game is over. These abilities also enable the black pieces to pretend that they are Christians, something that the text constantly negates, and something that the white pieces constantly fail to acknowledge. The latter brings us to yet another sphere in the created universe, the metaphysical one.

The major issues in the dramatic conflict throughout the play are basically of a religious and moral character. Most of the chessmen involved in the game keep talking about Christianity, faith, sin, salvation, damnation and so on. The cause of the conflict is that all these notions mean something totally different to the representatives of both the houses. They become in fact antonyms, out of which we could form a list of dichotomous pairs. 'Christianity' as used by the White Queen's Pawn in her first dialogue with the Black Queen's Pawn, means 'heresy' to the latter (and vice versa). Because the text tells us precisely who is 'right' and who is 'wrong', the colour symbolism of black and white is deepened by further opposites: faith–heresy, Christianity–Antichristianity, chastity–lechery, religion–irreligion, God–Devil etc.

Immediately the play begins we are told the nature of the game we are to witness. The Black Queen's Pawn trying to convert the White Queen's Pawn, tells her that her faith

> Disarmes youre Soule e'en in the heate of battayle,
> Your Firmnes that waye makes you more infirme
> For the right Christian Conflict ...   (1.i.27–9)

Initially, therefore, the game of chess is defined as a 'Christian conflict', the aim of which is the conquest of the soul. This is congruous with the tradition, in which 'the metaphor [of chess] had a continuing facility for the fight of Good and Evil, with Hell the fate of the captured piece, and checkmate had become an easy figure for both moral and temporal ruin'.[29] Consequently, we may deduce the supernatural powers that are involved – indirectly(?) – in the conflict: beyond doubt these are the Christian God and the Devil, who are in fact, as we shall attempt to prove, the implied players of this game. As noted by critics:

A common statement in the chess treatises of the time is that chess is like a battle between the two opposing forces. In many of the chess moralities the battle is presented as a spiritual one between the individual soul and the Devil, or between God and the Devil for possession of man's soul.[30]

It is easy to see that in Middleton's play, it is only the white pieces that express their faith in God and they firmly believe that God is not only on their side, but is responsible also for their fortunes on the chess-board. The White Queen's Pawn, for instance, in the opening scene admits that she finds 'Th'assistance of a sacred strength' to 'ayde' her (1.i.98–9). She also admires the 'Makers Glorie' in the 'dignitie of the Creature [= man]' (1.i.199–200). She strongly believes in salvation ('spatious Vertue', 11.i.39), and calls 'heauen' to help her when in danger of being raped (11.i.134 and 159). To preserve her virginity, she prefers death to shame:

> Then take my life sir,
> And leaue my honor for my guide to heauen,   (11.i.151–2)

Having escaped the danger, she praises God for her safety:

> The cheife of his ill Ayme being at my honor,
> Till heauen was pleasde by some unlookte for accident
> To giue mee courage to redeeme my selfe   (II.ii.134–6)

And when through a cunning trick of the Black House, she is to be punished severely for libel, she calls 'uertue' [= heavenly powers] for help (II.ii.238–9), and then rationalizes the absence of heaven's immediate intervention:

> Vertue! to showe her Influence more strong,
> Fitts me wth patience mightier then my wrong.   (II.ii.292–3)

When the Black Queen's Pawn makes yet another attempt to deceive the White Queen's Pawn, and acts 'trecherie wth an Angells Tong', she describes that part of the game as the 'most noblest Combate' of 'glorious and most Valiant Vertue' with the 'Deuill' (III.1.225, 246–7). The White King's wisdom is acclaimed by the White Bishop as 'heauens Substitute' (III.i.315). The White Knight, in turn, in his prophecy declares that the 'truths Triumph' [i.e. the White House's victory] over the 'Serpent' fashioned by 'falshood' [i.e. the Black House] will be possible through the intervention of 'just Heauen' that will 'finde a Bolt to bruize his head' (IV.iv.8–12). The latter conviction is corroborated by the White King, when the White Queen is saved from the danger through 'heauens blessings' (IV.iv.83), and, again, after the black pieces have been checkmated and put into the 'bag':

>   whilst wee winner-like,
> Destroying (through heauen's power) what would destroy
> Welcome our White Knight wth Lowde peales of Joye.   (v.iii.239–41)

And the White Queen's Pawn expresses her gratitude to 'That power' that has 'preserved' her from the 'Deuill' (v.ii.74).

Thus, the actions of the white pieces are guarded by a supernatural power, identified in the text as the Christian God. Consequently, the victory of the White House becomes the victory of God, whose 'game strategies' are realized by His chessmen and eventually bring destruction to the forces of the other side; strictly speaking, of the other player: the Devil. In this sense, a game of chess becomes an allegorical presentation of the struggle between metaphysical forces, and since the White House is identified at one point with Lutheranism (II.i.185–6), the opposition becomes more precise: Lutheran God (= Christian God) vs. Catholic God (= the Devil). We cannot therefore agree with the opinion that

The White side pretend they are at chess play with the Devil. They become self-appointed guardians of virtue in the face of the Devil's advance ... the more we know of the White House the more devilish their characters appear and the more affinities there are between them and the Black House.[31]

Let us now find more support in the text for the opinion that the black pieces are in fact identified with 'hellish forces'. To begin with, it may be pointed out that throughout the game the black chessmen do not make a single reference to God, or 'heaven', with the exception of situations in which they 'dissemble' and pretend to take the side of their adversaries and 'talk their language'. The latter implies also that even the black pieces consider their opponents as guarded by the deity, a feature that clearly makes the White House distinctive. Moreover, the text makes constant allusions to the metaphysical power that 'stands behind' the black pieces, and there is no doubt as to the identity of that power, as the following examples will illustrate.

In the Induction, when Ignatius Loyola learns about Error's dream, he appeals to some 'power' (49) to 'show' him the game of chess. A question may also be raised as to where exactly Loyola comes from, when he appears on stage in a London theatre. He is dead after all, and this leaves no doubt that it is his ghost that appears. Although he mentions his canonization (which, naturally, implies that the Church of Rome treats him as a saint), according to the Protestant dogma he cannot be a saint and, besides, blessed souls cannot return to earth as ghosts: this is the ability of damned souls only. As the founder of the hated Jesuits, the only association he could evoke in contemporary Protestant audiences was with the Devil, and the only place he could be coming from was hell.[32] And although in the text there is no direct reference to Loyola's 'summoning' on to the stage from hell, a contemporary source informs us that in the first staging of the play

there were remarkable acts of sacrilege and, among other abominations, a minister summoned St Ignatius from hell.[33]

The same source tells us that hell 'consisted of a great hole [i.e. the 'bag'] and hideous figures [i.e. devils]',[34] and one is tempted to imagine that the play opened with Ignatius being cast out of the 'bag' by devils, which would actually explain his initial exclamation of surprise: 'Hah! where!.'[35]

The White King's Pawn turns out to be a traitor to his own House, for he had been 'foolde / Out of [his] Faith', and from his 'Alleagance drawen' (I.i.358–9), and is therefore – as the Black Knight states it – a 'lost Pawne' (360). He is lost in both senses of the word – as a chessman and as a Christian who had rejected his faith. Thus, turning to the Black House is identified with the Christian concept of damnation. Another traitor, the Fat Bishop, finds the same destiny:

> BLACK BISHOP. Oh twere a Mr: peice of Serpent Subteltie
>   To fetch him a this side agen,
> BLACK KNIGHT. And then dam him
>   Into the Bagg for euer ...   (II.ii.61–4)

Incidentally, the white pieces are never even threatened with the 'Bagg'. The word 'Serpent' used in the quoted passage has undoubtedly 'devilish' connotations here ('that old serpent, called the Devil, and Satan'–Rev. 12.9), which is complemented by the concept of eternal damnation. The word is repeated with the same meaning later in the play, when the White Knight talks about 'The glitteringst Serpent that ere falshood fashiond' (IV.iv.10). The cunning falsehood of the black chessmen is identified with 'sin' by the White King and is defined as the 'Mr: peice of darkness, shelterd / Under a Robe of Sanctitie' (II.ii.142–3). The White King elaborates on the subject in the following way:

> The pride of him that tooke first fall for pride [i.e. Satan]
> Is to bee Angell shapte, and imitate
> The forme from whence hee fell, but this offender
> Far baser then Sins Master, first by Vowe
> To holie Order, wch is Angells method
> Takes pride to use that Shape to bee a Deuill; (II.ii.146–51)

That the Devil stands behind the black pieces' machinations is confirmed by the White Queen's Pawn, when she is surprised by false evidence against her: 'What new Engine / Has the Deuill raysde in him now?' (II.ii.217–8). The Black Knight, in turn, is described as being able to 'teach the deuill how to lye' (III.i.222), and the Black Jesting Pawn as being similar to 'the Deuill striding o're a Night-Mare / Made of a Millers daughter' (III.ii.8–9). The Black Knight's Pawn's change of attire in Act IV.i had been interpreted as a symbolic one:

On the human plane, the Jesuit's change betokens the abandonment of the last of his vows of chastity, obedience, and poverty. It had, however, been the devil's custom to appear on the stage dressed as a gallant, and the Black Bishop's Pawn is the devil of the pawns' plot, an identity the White Queen's Pawn belatedly recognizes.[36]

As the White Duke observes, with an obvious reference to the Black House, 'The Deuill has beene at worke since 88 on' (IV.iv.6). In a comment reminiscent of Hamlet's, 'That one may smile, and smile, and be a villain', the White Knight exposes the Black Knight's dissembling nature:

> In yonder smile sitts bloud and Trecherie basking
> In that perfidious Modell of Face-Falshood
> Hell is drawn grinning, (IV.iv.14–6)

Similarly, the White Queen's Pawn discovers the true nature of the Black Bishop's Pawn:

> The World's a Stage on wch all parts are playde
> You'de thinke it most absurd to haue a deuill
> Presented there not in a Deuills shape,
> Or wanting one to send him out in yours, (V.ii.19–22)

and

> The Sillables of Sin flie from his lips,
> As if the letter came new cast from hell (V.ii.44–5)

When the Fat Bishop makes an unsuccessful attempt to surprise the White Queen, and overlooks the White Bishop guarding her, he blames the Devil for his misfortune (IV.iv.74). Devil = the player, one may observe, who made an obvious mistake in this particular move.

The culminating point of the main plot is the White Knight's and the White Duke's visit to the Black House. As part of the welcoming celebrations an 'Altar' is discovered, along with 'Statues' (s.d. v.i.40/1). In the song that follows, we find an address to the metaphysical power that governs the 'Black World':

> Maye from the Altar flames aspire
> Those Tapers set themselues afire
>
> . . .
>
> And those Brazen Statues moue
> Quickened by some power aboue   (v.i.45–9)

And a stage direction informs us that 'some power abouc' has reacted to the wish: 'The Images moue in a dance' (v.i.48–50). The text does not tell us what sort of images these were,[37] but through the recurrent associations of the Black House with Catholicism and with 'Hell', we may suspect they were intended to represent certain attributes of both. All these are rejected by the White Knight in an aside as 'a taste / Of the ould Vessell still, the erroneous rellish' of Popery (v.i.39–40).[38]

After the checkmate, the black pieces are thrown into the 'hell-bag', and the White King comments:

> Tis theire best course that so haue lost theire fame
> To putt theire heads into the Bagg for Shame,
> And there behold the Baggs Mouth, like Hell[39] opens
> To take her due, and the lost Sonnes appeare
> Greedilie gaping for Encrease of Fellowship
> In Infamie, the last desire of Wretches,
> Aduancing theire perdition-branded foreheads
> Like Enuies Issue, or a Bed of Snakes: (v.iii.195–202)

The black chessmen quarrel in the bag, which amuses the White Knight: 'Contention in the pitt is Hell diuided' (v.iii.218), and as the Black Knight passes by to join the others, he is given a sarcastic farewell:

> Roome for the mightiest Machiauill polititian,
> That ere the Deuill hatcht of a Nuns Egg: (v.iii.225–6)

And the play ends with the White King's words:

> So, now lett the Bagg close, the fittest Wombe
> For trecherie pride and malice . . .   (v.iii.238–9)

All the examples quoted above provide sufficient grounds, it seems, for a more general statement concerning the nature of the 'Black World': it is a world deprived of the Christian God; instead, it is governed by God's powerful and cunning adversary – the Devil, who very appropriately becomes the second player in this 'game'.[40] The black pieces only pretend to be Christians, and – as indicated above – this ability to deceive by false appearance is presented throughout the play as the most powerful instrument of their 'chess' strategy. In this sense, the game of chess becomes a metaphor for the struggle of two metaphysical powers: the Christian world of the White House vs. the non-Christian world of the Black House.[41] The same struggle, the text suggests, is reflected in the politics of the human world off-stage ('the world's a stage', v.ii.19). Thus, knowing the true nature of the Black House, we may pass to the question: how is its devilish desire to enslave Christian souls realized in theatrical and dramatic terms?

As observed by D.M. Holmes, 'Middleton's imputation of sexual depravity within the Jesuit organization, through the persons of the Black Bishop's Pawn and the Black Queen's Pawn, begins in the opening scene and continues throughout the play'.[42] In fact, most of the actions of the Black House are defined in sexual terms. The entire black world is filled with lust, lasciviousness, desire to rape and deflower, 'hot inflammation', by adultery and all sorts of depravation. Sexual desire is the dominating driving force of all the black pieces active on stage. Even when discussing their political aims, the black pieces always contaminate their language with sexual innuendo, if not with sexual frankness, by which an equation is made between political and sexual desires.[43]

Once again, the initial 'signal' of this 'sexual pattern' in the play is made by Ignatius Loyola in the Induction. Having introduced himself to the audience as the 'father' of Jesuits, he wonders 'what angle of the world' this is, because

> Here's too much light appeares shot from the Eyes
> Of truth and goodnes neuer yet deflowrde,
> Sure they [Loyola's disciples] were neuer here ... (9–11)

'Here', of course, refers to the theatre stage, *ergo* London, *ergo* England – a traditional temporal and locational unity of an induction with the theatrical performance. So, from the opening of the play, the activities of the Jesuits are expressed in sexual terms: they are to deflower truth and goodness in order to replace light with darkness (with an obvious symbolism of the latter two).[44] When Error tells Ignatius about the 'Chesse' dream (43), he wants to know whether any of his 'Sonnes' were 'placst for the Game'(46); to which Error replies:

> Yes, and a daughter too, a secular daughter
> That playes the Black Queenes pawne, hee the Bl. Bishops. (47–8)

Apart from the characteristically Elizabethan and Jacobean ambiguity of the meaning of the word 'game', 'a daughter of the game' was a contemporary synonym for a harlot, as used in Shakespeare's *Troilus and Cressida* (iv.v.63), which is confirmed by the Black Queen's Pawn's function later in the play. At the same time, Error identifies himself and Ignatius with the Black House,[45] 'our side' (44), which makes the initial equation: Error + Loyola = the Black House. However, Ignatius is not satisfied with the activity of his 'children', finds them 'Not worthie of the name of my disciples' (68), because if he were in their place (i.e. alive) he 'would haue cut / That Bishops Throate . . . And told the Queene a loue-tale in her Eare / [That] Would make her best pulse dance' (69–72). Again, the 'loue-tale' that makes the 'best pulse [read: desire] dance' has obvious sexual connotations.

What is traditionally considered in the criticism of the play as a 'sub-plot' or 'pawns' allegory', consists in fact of a series of attempted sexual assaults by black pieces on the white ones. Under the disguise of virtue and religion, primitive sexual lust is concealed, something the white pieces will eventually learn to discover. Language is the effective instrument wielded by the black side, the language of religion, ethics and 'honest politics', and very often it is overwhelming lust and the desire for immediate sexual fulfilment, leading to hasty and premature action, that reveals the falsehood of their use of language. The best example of this is to be found in Act II, scene i, when the Black Bishop's Pawn almost succeeds in converting the White Queen's Pawn to 'Catholicism', that is, in raping her.[46]

When the White Queen's Pawn asks him to 'command' her 'something', so that he could check her faith and obedience, the Black Queen's Pawn cannot restrain his desire any longer:

> I do command you first then –
> . . .
> To meete mee
> And seale a kisse of loue uppon my Lip,   (II.i.53–7)

and further

> If I can at that distance send you a blessing,
> Is it not neerer to you in mine Armes?   (73–4)

and

> Come, come, bee neerer,
> . . .
> bee neerer, why so fearefull?
> Neerer the Altar the more safe and sacred,   (110, 122–3)

Because the White Queen's Pawn resists, the aggressor threatens to rape and kill her:

> thy nice Virginitie
> Is recompence too litle for my Loue   (136–7)

and therefore

> Take heede I take not both [i.e. virginity and life], wch I haue uowde
> Since if longer thous resist mee,   (153–4)

After the White Queen's Pawn's brave escape, her oppressor is reprimanded by the Black Queen's Pawn (Loyola's 'daughter of the game'):

> Are you mad?
> Can lust infatuate a man so hopefull,
> No patience in youre bloud, the Dogstar reignes sure
> Time and fayre Temper would haue wrought her plyant,   (II.i.172–5)

The same pair of black pawns make yet another attempt to ravish the chastity of the White Queen's Pawn in Act IV, this time through the deception of a 'magical mirror'. The innocent pawn is lured with a promise of marriage, but the black side wants to have consummation first:

> BLACK QUEEN'S PAWN. [to the WQ's Pawn] ... you must be coupled:
> BLACK BISHOP'S PAWN. Shee speakes but Truth in this, I see no reason then,
>   That wee should misse the rellish of this night   (IV.i.136–8)

Ironically, the Black Bishop's Pawn – who is a Jesuit – seems to have some moral scruples and he admits to the pander, 'You knowe I cannot marrie by my Order' (154), but these are not the scruples of a holy man, but, rather, of a devil who cannot receive a sacrament 'by his Order', as is the case with the devil in Marlowe's *Doctor Faustus*. He is instructed to 'Venture / Uppon a Contract' (155–6), and the scene ends with the Black Queen's Pawn revealing her true intentions:

> Now Ile enioye the Sport and coozen you both,
> My blouds game is the Wages I haue workte for   (171–2)

But it is not only the two black pawns who are presented in the play as bawds in disguise. When, in Act II, scene i, the Black Knight receives 'intelligence' from various countries, he comments on the news concerning the English papists:

> Oh this is the English house, what newes there tro?
> Hah! by this hand, most of these are bawdie Epistles   (230–1)

and, further

>   hee writes here
> Some wiues in England will committ Adulterie,
> And then send to Rome for a Bull for theire housbands,   (246–8)

Thus, lechery and carnal sin are inseparable from Catholicism on- and off-stage. Both recur in the imagery used by the black pieces throughout the play.

Having escaped the danger of the Black Bishop's Pawn, the White Queen's Pawn makes an official complaint against him

> Who making meeke Deuotion keepe the doore [i.e. act as pander]
> His lips being full of holie Zeale at first,
> Would haue committed a fowle Rape uppon mee,   (II.ii.124–6)

Owing to the surreptitious evidence supplied by the Black House, the accusation is rejected and the innocent victim of the intrigue is handed over to her oppressors to receive punishment. As one may expect after what has been said to this point, the punishment is planned by the black pieces in a characteristic way. First, the Black Knight exclaims in fury:

> Vessell of foolish Scandall! Take thy freight
> Had there beene in that Cabinet of Nicenes
> Halfe the Virginities of the earth lockt up
> And all swept at one cast by the Dexteritie
> Of a Jesuiticall Gamster, 'tad not Valued
> The least part of that generall worth thou hast taynted, (II.ii.275–80)

And the instrument of torture will be

> ... a Roome fild all wth Aretines pictures[47]
> More then the twice 12 labours of Luxurie [=lust],
> Thou shalt not see so much as the chast Pummell
> Of Lucrece Dagger peeping, naye, Ile punnish thee
> For a Discouerie, Ile torment thy modestie, (II.ii.284–8)

When asked by the White Knight about his opinion on carnal sin, the Black Knight says that this is

> The Trifle of all Vices, the mere Innocent,
> The uerie Nouice of this house of Claye: Veneric! (v.iii.137–8)

And, besides, one can always obtain absolution by paying for sins a sum prescribed in *Taxa Paenitentiaria*:

BLACK KNIGHT. [reads] For Adulterie a Couple of Shillings, and for fornication five pence

> ...
>
> for Licing wth
> mother, Sister, and daughter – I marrie Sir, thirtie
> three pound 3 shilling, 3 pence, –
>
> ...
>
> Simonie, nine pound
>
> ...
>
> Sodomie sixpence, (IV.ii.99–112)

The 'story' the Black Knight tells the White Knight may serve as another example of the black chessmen's 'sport' activities:

> Ile tell you what I told a Sauoye Dame once,
> New wed, high, plumpe and lusting for an Issue,
> Wthin the yeare I promised her a childe
> If shee could stride ouer St Rumbants breeches
> A Rellique kept at Mechlin, the next morning
> One of my followers ould hose was conuayde
> Into her chamber where shee tryde the Feate,
> By that and a Court Frend after grewe great, (IV.iv.35–42)

The Black King is no exception here, and his lascivious nature is fully exposed in the letter he sends to the Black Bishop's Pawn:

> ... wee had late intelligence ... that you haue at this instant
> in chace, the white Queenes pawne, and uerie liklie
> by the carriage of youre Game to entrap and take
> her, these are therefore to require you by the burning

> affection I beare to the Rape of Deuotion, that
> speedilie uppon the surprizall of her, … you make some
> attempt uppon the white Queenes person whose fall or
> prostitution our Lust most uiolentlie rages for,　　　　　　(II.i.16–26)

It is interesting to note that here also, the King's words give us the ambiguous meaning of the sense of the 'game': words like 'chace', 'carriage of youre Game', 'entrap and take her' may refer both to a game of chess and to attempted rape. The same ambiguities may be found elsewhere in the play, as when the Black King says, 'That Queene would I fayne finger' (III.i.276). The quoted passage leaves no doubt that the black side understand the game as a game of lechery. This is additionally confirmed by the treacherous Fat Bishop's words:

> The Black Kings bloud burnes for thy Prostitution
> And nothing but the Spring of thy chast vertu
> Can coole his Inflammation, instantly
> He dyes uppon a plurisie of Luxurie
> If hee deflowre thee not,　　　　　　(IV.iv.67–71)

Even the 'innocent' technical comments the black pieces make on the game are not free from sexual innuendo, as in the following examples:

> BLACK KNIGHT. Wee shall match you
> Playe how you can, perhaps and mate you too;　　　　　　(III.i.319–20)

> FAT BISHOP. I take you now, this is the time wee euer hopde for,
> Queene you must downe;　　　　　　(IV.iv.64–5)

To sum up what has been said to this point, we may observe that the created world of the play is divided into three interrelated spheres: the chess world, the political world 'off-stage', and the implied metaphysical world. This triad has a hierarchical, vertical order: the implied struggle of the metaphysical powers (God vs the Devil) is realized through human political conflict (Protestantism vs Antichrist, or England vs Spain), and the latter is metaphorically realized in a game of chess (the Black House vs the White House). Consequently, the attributes of the powers in the highest sphere are bestowed upon those below: for example, the Devil's attributes are 'inherited' by the Spaniards (Catholics, or Antichrist) in the political world, and, further, by the black pieces in the game of chess. In this sense, the game becomes a model of the universe torn in two conflicting sides and creates implications of both a theological and a political character, which are in fact inseparable. Critics of the play have primarily concentrated on the relationship between the chess world and the world of politics, strictly speaking on the relationship between the play and an episode in Anglo-Spanish relations in 1623–24. This led to numerous articles identifying, more or less convincingly, particular chessmen with their contemporary 'equivalents', and to various, often conflicting, interpretations of particular episodes in their relation to historical events. So much has been written on the subject that there seems no point in repeating the critical discussion here. Moreover, it seems that the ideological implications of the play have been almost totally neglected in scholarship. It is not our intention here to refute the validity of the 'political' interpretations of the play. In most cases they remain valid, but are perhaps incomplete, because the play is not only 'about' particular episodes in Anglo-Spanish relations (such as the Spanish match),[48] but it creates a consistent and significant model of the universe with implications reaching far beyond a conflict between two countries. In point of fact, as T.H. Howard-Hill's meticulous study has revealed, most of the conspicuously political allusions in *A Game at Chesse* are later additions, for – generally speaking – the play exists in two versions, with the second an enlargement of the first. For instance, in the Archdall-Folger manuscript, which is the early version, the Fat Bishop's part did not exist at all; when it was added it enabled the Black Knight to become more prominent in the play and to carry out his plot to capture the Fat Bishop. Similarly, the enlargement of the White King's Pawn's part made it possible for the critics to identify him as Lionel Cranfield, Earl of Middlesex. As Howard-Hill put it in an unpublished paper, it is not unlikely that the additions

were the result of rehearsals, during which the play's theatrical deficiencies became noticeable. Middleton had written a *serious religious allegory* [my italics]; what the players apparently wanted and finally got was humorous topical satire.

In what follows, we shall make an attempt to show that the model of the universe created in the play is based on a clearly defined ideology, which may, in turn, be related not only to the contemporary political tracts that scholars have uncovered while searching for Middleton's sources, but also to the theological component of what seems to have become the war ideology of the party led by the Duke of Buckingham and Prince Charles.

As mentioned on several occasions in the preceding chapters, in the 1620s – and in accordance with a long tradition – Spain was considered by many Englishmen as the greatest political and military threat to England, and to Protestantism in general. This persistent belief that Spain was the cause of all the calamities that had befallen the Protestants both at home and abroad, and that military action against this single enemy would radically change the situation on the Continent, led to a naive line of foreign policy, headed by the Duke of Buckingham and Prince Charles, the consequences of which were both embarrassing and disastrous. But in March/April 1624, when the initial agreement between reluctant and pacifist James and his belligerent Parliament had been reached, it seemed that at last the English were taking up the initiative, and new hopes appeared for the recovery of the Palatinate and, possibly, for the restitution of Frederick and Elizabeth as the King and Queen of Bohemia. The latter two issues were of course acknowledged as the direct political causes of England's obligation to enter the war. But it seems they were not sufficient, for the war party found it necessary to advocate their cause by nationalistic and religious propaganda, thereby creating strong ideological support for their actions. In spring 1624 this ideology was readily provided by sundry theological treatises, evoking once again the myth of the elect nation (England), elected by God to give the final blow to Antichrist (Pope, Spain, and their Jesuitical fifth column). Thus, all the signs on heaven and earth showed that the time had come for God's people to take arms for their divine cause. In other words, a political cause gained a religious dimension. Even if this newly created ideology had no direct effect on England's military strength, it certainly appealed, or was hoped to appeal, to the Puritan MPs who were to decide on the subsidies needed for the war. It is not a coincidence that a number of works calling for decisive action against the forces of Antichrist are dedicated to the Parliament of 1624.

For instance, Thomas Taylor's *Two Sermons: The One a Heavenly Voice, Calling All God's People Out of Romish Babylon. The Other An Everlasting Record of the Utter Ruine of Romish Amalek* (1624),[49] is dedicated to 'The Right Honovrable ... Knights and Burgesses of the Lower-House of Parliament' (sig.A2). And in the 'Epistle Dedicatory' we find the following significant passages:

all the eyes of the land are held upon you, to helpe us against these Babylonians, who have been and are so bussie to bring us backe into our former Babylonish Captivitie (A2ᵛ)

and

Looke backe, worthy Gentlemen, upon the zeal and former love of your famous predecessors, who pulled downe the nests of these Antichristian birds: and hating neutrality ... awaken your zeale, to make the hopes of Babylonians utterly to perish ... In this great work against Antichrist, shew your love to Iesus Christ. If ever you will doe him an honourable service, this is the time. (A3ᵛ)

Also, Edmund Gurnay's furious attack against the Pope, entitled *The Romish Chaine* (1624)[50] is dedicated to Parliament, and a considerable number of other works are dedicated to the Earl of Pembroke,[51] who had by this time joined the war party and may have provided financial support for the writers.

Both sides involved in the conflict, Catholics and Protestants, claimed that only they constituted the 'true' Church of God, and that they were direct descendants of the early Fathers of the Church and, consequently, continued the pure Christian religion, unstained with the sin of heresy. In Protestant literature of the period, we find numerous historical accounts proving ancient roots of the reformed church, in reply to what seems to have been a frequent question of the other side: 'Where was your church before Luther?' As was mentioned earlier, the most influential of these works was Foxe's *Acts and Monuments*, commonly known as *The Book of Martyrs*, which gave rise to Englishmen's belief that they were God's people, the 'new Israel', the elect nation. Focusing on particular stories depicting the martyrdom of Protestant saints, Foxe framed these stories in an account of ecclesiastical history which purported to show that this faith was the same for which the martyrs of the primitive Church had died, the same which had been brought uncorrupted to Britain in the beginning directly from the apostles. This account of Church history the book also linked to a history of the long succession of native rulers down to Elizabeth, shown as owing their authority directly to divine appointment and . . . the book made plain that all the signs to be found in scripture and history showed the will of God was about to be fulfilled in England . . . That is to say, Foxe set the apocalyptical conception of England in a valid historical perspective.[52]

Furthermore:

Foxe's account of the Reformation included the struggle of the elect everywhere, but it was chiefly occupied with the struggle of one English ruler after another to keep the faith pure and defend the people of the faith. This was the central engagement in the whole age-long struggle of Christ and Antichrist.[53]

It is not coincidental, then, that a number of works reviving the subject appeared in print in the first half of 1624, in what seems to have been an ideological campaign of the war party. In order to prove our point, let us first quote in chronological order appropriate entries to be found in the Stationers' Register:

17 December 1623	*A Treatise of the Perpetuall Visibilitie and Succession of the True Church Especially in the Ages Before Luther*
20 January 1624	Daniel Featley, *The Fisher Held in His Nett. The Protestant Confermed with the Popish Difference. A Iustification of the One and a Refutation of the Other in Matter of Faith and Fact*
23 January 1624	H.G., *A Gagg for the Pope and the Jesuites or the Arraignement and Execucon of Antechrist*
8 February 1624	Thomas Bedford, *Luthers Predecessors*
11 February 1624	Thomas Sutton, *The Good Fight of Faith*
7 April 1624	James Wadsworth, *The Copies of Certaine Letters Which Haue Passed Between Spaine and England in Matter of Religion*
14 April 1624	Francis White, *A Reply to Jesuit Fishers 'answere' to 'certaine questions' propounded by his Maiestie*
	A.B. *The Principle of All Principles Concerning Religion*
27 April 1624	Henry Burton, *A Censure of Symony*
	Robert Johnson, *The Necessities of Faith*
3 May 1624	The *Sermons* of Samuel Hieron
24 May 1624	Thomas Taylor, *The Vtter Ruine of Romish Amalecke*
2 June 1624	Anthony Wotton, *Run From Rome*
11 June 1624	Thomas Beard, *Antechrist the Pope of Rome or the Pope of Rome Antechrist*
28 June 1624	George Webbe, *The Protestants Calendar*
2 July 1624	Edmund Gurnay, *The Romish Chain*

The Stationers' Register of course provides in most cases only abbreviated and corrupt forms of particular titles; for example, the content of George Webbe's work is fully revealed by its printed title: *Catalogus Protestantium: Or, The Protestants Kalendar Containing A Surview of the Protestants*

Religion long before Luthers daies, euen to the time of the Apostles, and in the primitive Church. We may therefore observe that the political propaganda campaign initiated shortly after Prince Charles and the Duke of Buckingham returned from Madrid was accompanied by sundry theological treatises, printed in an unusual number in the first half of 1624, and that the fusion of immediate political aims with 'eternal truths' gave rise to a new ideology. The first target of this ideology was to establish the divine provenance of the Protestant cause, to confirm the special role to be played by the English, God's elect people, and to prove the Antichristian character of the enemy by creating an image of the Catholics composed of devilish attributes.

The strong belief that God elected the English people to give the final blow to Antichrist is to be found in many publications that came out when Parliament was in session. For instance, Samuel Hieron's *The Papist Rime, answered* (1624) tells us that the English are God's elect people, of whom 'one part in heauen liues, / The other here with Satan striues'.[54] The enemy that the English have to destroy is defined more precisely by Thomas Scott in *The Belgick Sovldier* (1624):

I go about to prove, that Warre hath beene better then peace, and that the Commonwealth and *Religion* of *England* haue had their glory and propagation by opposing *Antichrist*, and in plaine termes reputing *Spaine* our *Antagonist*.[55]

In other tracts by the same author, which critics have in fact considered to have been Middleton's sources, we find numerous claims made for the belief that God protects England against Spain. Thus, in *Vox Coeli* (1624), when Queen Elizabeth talks about the attempt to poison her undertaken by the treacherous Spaniard, Lopez, she declares that 'God, in his infinite mercy and providence, still protected and defended me, to their owne confusion'.[56] Referring to the defeat of the Spanish Armada, Prince Henry says that 'God looked on England with his indulgent eye of pitty and compassion, and on that great and mightie navall army with contempt and detestation',[57] which is further confirmed by Queen Elizabeth: 'Yea, God was so gracious to England.'[58] God is also made responsible for bringing an end to the first Anglo-Spanish match, that of Queen Mary and King Philip: '[Henry VIII:] so God gave limits to Philips ambition, and your [i.e. Queen Mary's] owne desires, by making you forsake earth, and he England'.[59] God also prevented Philip and Mary from having children:

[Q.M.] If we had had any males, England had beene long since a province to Spaine.
[Q.E.] God knew so much, and therefor prevented it; wherein I blesse his mercy and providence, as also your sterilitie.[60]

Queen Elizabeth also believes that 'God of his mercy will confound all those who wish or desire it (i.e. the Spanish match), whether it be Gondomar, the Jesuits, Englands recusants, Spaine, the Pope, or the divell'.[61] And in *Robert Earl of Essex His Ghost* (1624) Scott described Spain as the 'profest' enemy of God.[62]

The same is repeated by Thomas Taylor in *The Epistle Dedicatory* to MPs, quoted above. In Samuel Hieron's sermon, *Penance for Sinne* (1624) we find further confirmation of God's particular care for England, and the author tells us that numerous 'bloudy designes' against England were never accomplished, because of God's 'mercy and goodnesse', and he reminds his countrymen of 'what God hath done for vs in defeating Popish plots, and in turning their bloudy deuices vpon their owne pates'.[63] And the English Protestants saw Spain and the Roman Catholics as one inseparable danger, both being associated with Antichrist. As early as in 1584 Richard Hakluyt had written of the Spaniards as supporters of the great Antichrist of Rome,[64] and this concept was given an additional impetus by the ominous defeat of the 'invincible' Armada, 'the antichristian fleet'. Ever since that time, Catholics in general, and Spaniards, the Pope and Jesuits in particular, were constantly referred to as Antichrist, or Antichristians. When Simond Harward spoke of 'antichristian Catholics', he meant Spaniards, and Henry Smith spoke of the papists as 'Antichrist and all his wicked confederates'.[65] Christopher Hill's *Antichrist in Seventeenth-Century England* provides dozens of further examples of the these attitudes. And, as pointed out by Hill, the belief that the Pope was in fact Antichrist 'was not the monopoly view of any theological party'.[66] Thus, Buckingham and the war party made use of an ideology which actually united different Protestant sects, otherwise hostile to one another, by providing them with a common enemy. War against Spain was, as seen from this particular point of view, 'not only a divine command but a covenant on the part of God to fight for England against the enemy of God's church'.[67] One of the consequences of this was that the English Catholics were treated as traitors, both in a religious and a political sense. An English Catholic was, as Scott put it, 'Spaynes subject and a Romish slaue'.[68] And the Jesuits, trained in Spain, formed a fifth column in England and other Protestant countries, as evidenced by many contemporary tracts.[69]

For instance, in Thomas Scott's *Vox Coeli* we find a letter from Queen Mary to Gondomar, which includes the following instructions:

Forget not to continue and fortifie your intelligence with the seminaries and Jesuites in England, as also with the Catholique ladies of that kingdome . . . Be sure to be intimately acquainted with all factions and discontented Catholikes, for they will prove fine agents and instruments to execute your masters commands.[70]

In *A Game at Chesse* it may be observed that the Black House is not composed of 'Spaniards' only: we have Jesuits there, who do not necessarily have to be Spanish, and the Pope, who is the supreme ecclesiastical authority of the house. Thus, we are fully justified in treating the composite nature of this house on at least two interrelated levels: political, in which the black pieces attempt to undermine the safety of the White Kingdom and hence may be related to a certain episode in Anglo-Spanish relations; and religious, in which the Black House may have with ease been identified by Protestants with Catholicism in general, and the forces of Antichrist in particular. The very fact that the Pope is mentioned as being on the black side is significant in itself, for the Pope in contemporary Protestant literature was simply Antichrist, as the following examples will illustrate. George Downame, for instance, declared in 1603 that 'the head of this Antichristian body & catholic apostatsie, we hold to be the Pope of Rome; and consequently that the Pope is that graund Antichrist'.[71] He is 'an enimie of religion because he sets himself aginst (1) God's glory (2) Mans salvation', added John Rainolds,[72] and George Goodwin stated that 'What Christ *prescribes*, That Anti-Christ *proscribes*'.[73] In his hideous wickedness, Antichrist requires that 'all men should acknowledge and adore him for God', claimed Anthony Wotton,[74] and Thomas Taylor made an equation between Antichrist and 'the Catholique Heretike'.[75] George Webbe held 'the Pope to be Antichrist',[76] so did Edmund Gurnay,[77] and Daniel Featly in *An Appendix to the Fisher's Net* (1624) included a long 'Catalogue of Authors, who from age to age testifie that the Pope is Antichrist, or Rome Babylon, or both'.[78]

As in the play, Antichrist's major desire is to form a universal monarchy. To achieve this, he has to defeat England first and enslave God's elect people. This is where theology and politics unite, as is evident from a passage from Thomas Scott's *A Speech Made in the Lower House of Parliament, By Sir Edward Cicell, Colonel* (1624):

First, who is the greatest Enemy we haue in request of our Religion. The Catholike King is euident, by the protection he giueth our Papists and traytors, and by his nourishing the Seminaries and Iesuites of our Nation. 2. Who is the greatest enimy we haue, in respect of the State. It followeth the Catholike King, whose ambition ... is reflecting more vpon vniversall Monarchy, then greatnesse of religion. That it hath been his Ambition to create himself Monarch of the world, his consultations, & designes haue giuen cleare testimonie, and under pretence of Religion, he colours his quarrell for it. So that England is ... the cheife marke of his offence, because both in respect of Religion and State, England is the greates impediment in his way.[79]

To achieve his goal, Antichrist has formed a Jesuitical fifth column in England, who are busy preparing the ground for an invasion. As Thomas Taylor observed in 1624:

And wheras the Babylonians have mightily increase of late their hopes, numbers, and strength, not only those forraigne frogs and Locusts, the Priests and Iesuites, have in great armies invaded our Countrey, but our home-adversaries have greatly multiplied.[80]

Thus, as in Middleton's play, the danger comes from without and within. Because the Jesuits are Antichrist's faithful followers, and because their aim is to 'gouerne the world', their treacherous activities have to be exposed to the general public, as done by John Gee in *The Foot Out of the Snare: With a Detection of Sundry Late Practices and impostures of the Priests and Iesuites in England* (1624).[81] The variety and abundance of epithets with which Jesuits are labelled is indeed amazing. Even the 'Egyptian grasshopers' mentioned in Middleton's play are taken out from theologians' imagery. Thomas Taylor, for instance, claimed that 'the kingdom of Antichrist is called spiritually by the name of Aegypt, Rev.11.8., for it resembles that Kingdome, especially in three things, 1. In Idolatry 2. In cruelty and oppression of the Israel of God 3. Most of all in blindnesse and darkness.'[82] And in Two Sermons (1624) he compared papacy with 'Egypt covered with darknesse'.[83] J. Paul Parrin referred to the 'ministers' of Antichrist as 'Balaamites and Egyptians'.[84] Their physical appearance is revolting, for they are, indeed, the Devil's offspring.[85] As hinted in the play, the black pieces are what 'the devil hatch'd of a nun's egg' (v.iii.226); interestingly the same roots of papacy may be found in George Goodwin's Babels Balm: Or the Honey-Combe of Romes Religion, which appeared in print shortly before Middleton wrote his play:

> Once, Satan hatch't an Egge, full of foul Hope,
> Whose Birth, by Fraud and Pride became a Pope[86]

This brings us to the dominating attribute of the Black House, as presented to us in the play, in which it is constantly associated with the Devil. This, again, is congruous with political and religious literature of the period, in which Antichrist, the Pope and Catholicism were constantly described in satanic terms. From Thomas Scott's Inglands Ioy (1624) we learn that the papists both in Spain and in England

and all that deal with them, care not by what meanes or treachery they compasse their owne ends, deny Christs presence in Heauen . . . extenuate the power of the God-head, by allowing a dyety to Creatures, and an inuocation to Diuells.[87]

He also labels the Catholic religion 'the doctrines of the Diuell'. And Thomas Beard in Antichrist the Pope of Rome (1624) attempted to prove that Catholics believe in fact in the Devil only:

they that shall view the liues of the Popes, shall not find this strange, that Antichrist shall worship the deuill.[88]

The same opinion was shared by Thomas Taylor, who claims that Rome is like Babylon, which was full of 'false gods' and where 'Dragon was worshipped also among them as God',[89] and by Samuel Hieron, in a 'reply' to a Catholic:

> If thou knewest Romes Impurity,
> Thou wouldst not brag of Sanctity:
> A Sinke of Sinne, a sea of Euill,
> A place professed of the Diuell.[90]

And in Robert Abbott's The Danger of Popery (1625) the Devil fights for Antichrist, against God, by 'seducing' people who – if they follow him – are damned for ever[91] (like the White King's Pawn in the play). Antichrist is to come, declared John Rainolds, with 'the full power of Satan'.[92] Richard Bernard prophesied that 'Papistry' 'with the old Serpent, called the diuel, or

Sathans, thy father, with thy lewd mother, that great whore . . . shall bee cast aliue where the Dragon is, into the *Lake of fire*, burning with brimstone'.[93]

Similarly, like the black pieces in the play, Spaniards and Jesuits are constantly accused of falsehood and mastery in the art of dissembling. In Samson Lennard's translation of Parrin's *Luthers Fore-Runners* (1624), we read that

The first worke of Antichrist, is to take away the truth, and to change it into falsehood and errour and heresie. The second, to couer falsehood with the truth, and to confirme an vntruth, by seeming faith, and by virtue, and to mingle falsehood with things spiritual.[94]

And he speaks in the same work of 'errours and impurities of Antichrist', which are 'framed by some art, and vnder the name of Christ'.[95] According to Richard Bernard, the 'bloudy Antichristian Aduersary' has the ability of:

Counterfeiting the habit of an hones man: so Sinne craftily putteth vpon himselfe the shew of Vertue . . . For as Satan can transforme himselfe into an Angell of light, and his Apostles into the Apostles of Christ: so can Sinne, the seed of Satan, put vpon it selfe the counterfeit of vertue.[96]

And Robert Abbott in his *Danger of Popery* (1625) reminded his countrymen that Antichrist 'deceiues by the signes and great wonders of the beast' and that 'they that come in *sheepes cloathing*, may be inwardly rauening Wolues'.[97] Thomas Taylor maintained that the 'secrecy of working' is one of the features of 'Antichristianisme', because Antichrist does not 'destroy by fire and sword' in 'open defiance of Christ', but 'pretending to worship him intendeth to kill him'.[98] 'Papisme is Paganisme', declared George Goodwin in *Babels Balm* (1624), and Rome is the 'deceiuable Synagoge of Satan'.[99] The very title of Henry Mason's work is significant: *The New Art of Lying, Covered by Iesuites under the Vaile of Equivocation* (1624), and in it we find the following passage:

in the kingdome of Antichrist *iniquity* should reigne vnder the couert of holiness . . . for now wee see those who exercise *a mastery of iniquity*, and speake lies, pretending thereby to maintaine and preserve trueth as . . . may euidently be seene in a new-found Art of *Equiuocation*. For the Masters and maintainers thereof doe tell vs, *That by speaking according to this Arte of dissembling, sinnes are auoided.*[100]

It may be recalled here that in the play, the White Queen's Pawn calls the Black House, the 'house of Impudence / Craft and Aequiuocation' (II.ii.193–4). And we have shown above that all the actions of the black pieces, as presented in the play, are in fact characterized by dissimulation, which is attributed to the Black House in general. But this is not the only similarity between the black world created in the play and Antichrist in sundry Protestant treatises.

As has been shown above, the driving force behind the actions of the black pieces is insatiable sexual desire. As a matter of fact, to Protestant theologians, lechery was intrinsically connected with Antichrist, Catholicism, the Pope, Catholic priests and Jesuits. Already in 1603, George Downame declared that

a smal part of their vncleannes (which they sought by al meanes to cōceal) is knowē to the world: yet notwithstāding very many of them haue bene detected and knowne to be most filthy fornicatours and adulterers, besides Iohn the 8. or rather Ioane who was a harlot in mans apparell.[101]

And God, Downame continues, has justly 'rewarded' their 'lustes' 'insomuch that they commit abominations against nature', a list of which he provides.[102] Papists in England and Spain, claimed Thomas Scott after the expulsion of the Jesuits had been announced in April 1624, 'are poluted with incests and fornication'.[103] The play makes it clear that Catholic nuns are not free from blame. The Black Knight's Pawn admits that 'the savin tree' is 'Too frequent in nuns' orchards' (1.i.235–6), and we know that the leaves of this particular tree were used to cause abortions; furthermore, the Black Knight mentions '6 thousand Infants heads' found in the ruines of a 'Nunnerie' (V.iii.141–2) as reported by 'Huldrick Bishop of Augsburge in his Epistle / To Nicholas the first' (145–6). In Samuel Hieron's Sermons (1624) we encounter a rhymed poem, The Papists Rime, answered, in which we find the following stanza:

> The forced-vowes of singlenesse
> Haue brought forth beastly filthinesse:
> Thou maiest behold in History
> The fruits of Monkish Lechery.[104]

And note 't' to the above, on the margin, explains that 'There were 6000 infants heads found in Pope Gregory his mote, as appears by the letter of Volutianus, Bishop of Carthage, or as some thinke, of Huldericus (Bishop of Augusta) to Pope Nicholas: against the forbidding of Priests marriage.'[105] It is not unlikely that Middleton used Hieron's marginal note as a source for the pieces of information included in the lines quoted above. Whatever the case, priests and nuns were also ridiculed in George Goodwin's satirical poem in Babels Balm:

> Pure Priests, from their pure Nunnes pure Broods may see,
> Many a nimble Night-mare Sp'rit is knowne,
> To make such pure Sp'rt-haunted Virgins groane.
> Wiues of their owne theil none, Neighbours haue these:
> In such Flesh (may be) they can God well please.
> Religion, thus, hath foam'd vp Luxurie:
> A Lazie Life bred many Prodigie.[106]

Speaking in the name of the Protestants, Robert Abbott declared in A Hand of Fellowship, To Help Keepe ovt Sinne and Antichrist (1623) that

We presse vpon the seat of Lust, and teach our appetites, that as we must liue, so we must liue honestly ... We cannot abide the slighting of Fornication, the blanching of Priests Minions and Concubines, the stink of Stews.[107]

James Wadsworth, in turn, provides the reader of his The English Spanish

Pilgrime (1629) with ten 'Commandements' of the Jesuits, of which the tenth is 'to gouern their neighbours wife'.[108]

The Catholics, however, do not worry particularly about their sins, because – as in the play – they can always 'buy themselves out'. As George Downame put it, Antichrist's

most odious merchandise is his setting to sale all maner of sinne, which is called *Taxa paenitentiaria apostolica* [also mentioned in the play], whereby is promised impunity to euery one hauing cōmitted any sin, be it neuer so grieuous, paieth according to the rate for his absolution: as namely for adultery, incest, Sodomy, the abominatiō not to be spoken of cōmitted with beasts, wilful murder, paricide, periurie, and such like.[109]

This is reiterated by Robert Abbott in *The Danger of Popery* (1625), where we learn that the Church of Rome 'giues libertie to many sinnes, as ... incest, fornication, periury, rebellion and what not'.[110] And Henry Burton wrote a whole book on the subject, *Censure of Simonie* (1624), in which, among other things, he disclosed how easy life is for a Catholic 'adulterer', as his sin is 'but simple fornication at the worst, and (according to Roman-Catholike Doctrine) *a Veniall sin*, which his nature is now and then necessitated vnto, for his healths sake'.[111] A similar sentiment is expressed in the Black Knight's speech, quoted above, in which he trivializes 'venery'.

Sexual depravity, however, is to be expected from the followers of Antichrist and their Church, which is a notorious 'whore'. To be more precise, this Church is the Whore of Babylon. In his *Two Sermons* (1624), Thomas Taylor, having proved that Rome is Antichrist, compares Rome with ancient Babylon:

They are alike in perfidiousnesse and treachery. Babylon was a Cittie estranged from the Covenant of God: so is Rome, once in covenent, and married to Christ, but after breaking her faith by *her horrible whoredom and Idolatries*, shee can call Christ no more *Ishi* ... and though shee can shew Baptisme, and rehearse the Creed and Ten Commandements, (as an Harlot can shew the Marriage Ring) yet is shee a wife no longer ... Hence is this Papall Babylon called the *great* whore, the whore of Babel.[112]

Similarly, J. Paul Parrin in *Luthers Fore-Runners* (1624) calls the Church of Rome 'the Apocallipticall whore' and 'the mother of fornication' and simply 'the whore'.[113] George Goodwin in *Babels Balm* calls Catholicism 'Common *Whore*, or Couchant Wolfe most vile'.[114] As Robert Abbott put it:

Some also there are that are carnally minded, who liue in pleasure with the whoore of Babel; such are said to commit fornication with her, and to be drunk with the wine of her fornications.[115]

To conclude, the evidence provided above supports our initial assertion that the features of the created world of the play, and the laws that govern them, form in fact a model of a universe congruous in its implications with the contemporary ideology of the war party headed by the Duke of Buckingham and Prince Charles. The propaganda campaign, initiated on a political and anti-Spanish basis only, evolved into an ideology which fused the latter components with nationalistic and theological ones. The conflict between the Black House and the White House in Middleton's play becomes an allegory for what was seen as the conflict between Protestantism in general and God's people (i.e. the English) in particular, and the forces of Antichrist, represented by Catholics in general and the Pope, the Jesuits and Spaniards in particular. In short, the Black House is deprived of true religion: instead of God, the Devil is worshipped there; the goal of all the actions undertaken by the black pieces is to prepare the ground for universal monarchy: for this reason, the white world is infiltrated by Jesuits, and cunning 'diplomats' like the Black Knight; in order to achieve their wicked aims, the black chessmen dissemble: they pretend to be Christians, but there is only sin in their intent (which is metaphorically represented in the play by their insatiable lust). The obvious implication of the play is that the first counter-action that the White House (England) should undertake is to discover the adversary's machinations and hypocrisy. In the play, this is achieved by the White Knight and the White Duke, as in 'real life' by the Duke of Buckingham and Prince Charles. Moreover, the play, as seen from this point of view, is a political extrapolation: it foresees the inevitable fall of England's enemies. As the play suggests, the Madrid visit has opened England's eyes, and marks the beginning of the end of the forces of Antichrist. It is further indicated that the struggle has a metaphysical dimension as the final battle between the people of God and the ministers of the Devil, and the special role to be played in this 'game' is bestowed upon the English, God's chessmen.

Conclusion

ENGLAND's preparations for the 'holy war' against Antichrist led to a rather surprising conclusion. With no regard as to whether the propaganda campaign against the Spanish match and advocation of the war was effective, it may be pointed out that the immediate and subsequent results of Buckingham's adventurist policies were disastrous, to say the least. At first, the Duke – or the matchmaker – managed to enforce his second plan: in September 1624, James conceded to his son's marriage to the French Princess, Henrietta Maria, and promised to fulfil numerous conditions made by the French. The immediate result of the latter was a suspension of the laws against the recusants and a breaking of the promise to summon Parliament in November, for in that month the marriage treaty was signed and the risk of a parliamentary dispute on the matter had to be avoided. On 24 December the courts were forbidden to admit any further prosecution of the recusants, and two days later the Lord Keeper was ordered to set at liberty all Roman Catholics in prison for offences connected with their religion, and the Lord Treasurer was commanded to repay all fines. But without Parliament no money could be raised. Thus, England was entering the war on the Continent as a close ally of a Catholic country, and with insufficient subsidies. Consequently, Mansfeld's expedition, discussed in chapter 3, had been sacrificed to Buckingham's new political stratagem. To the amazement and fury of the English people, the next strategic step of the new monarch (James died in March 1625) and his friend was not the recovery of the Palatinate by French aid, but the loan of English ships to help the King of France slaughter the French Protestants, the Huguenots of Rochelle. As G.M. Trevelyan put it

in four years of war with Catholic powers [i.e. 1625–8] nothing was achieved abroad, while at home the quarrel between Crown and Parliament broke out more fiercely than in the days when Gondomar was dictating the policy of James. The causes of our failure abroad were the military inefficiency usual with England after a long peace, the ignorance of the Parliament men about foreign affairs, but above all else the incompetence displayed by Buckingham. Six times in these four years English fleets or armies were sent out on expeditions, diplomatically ill-conceived and militarily unsound, and six times they returned home with shame.

[*England Under the Stuarts* (London and New York, 1965), p. 124]

The crisis in which England found herself led to the assassination of Buckingham in 1628 and to the temporary abolition of Parliament by Charles

I, and – in the longer term – the foundations were laid for civil war. In this respect, the propaganda campaign of 1623/24, in which drama played a significant role, may serve as an example of politicians' attempts to create an ideological cover for their discrepant political goals in order to manipulate public opinion and win popular support. Ever since then, literature has always been used as an effective means of political propaganda.

The theatrical season of 1623/24 is interesting not only for its political implications. The plays discussed in the preceding chapters of this book share one predominant feature: their persuasive function, the aim of which was to support an ideology backing a political cause. In order to explain this function, historical and political background has been reconstructed and related to particular texts. It has been our aim to show that the plays in question are linked with one another not only by the fact that they were written, or revised, printed or staged within one theatrical season in London, but also by the political situation of the period, which in fact determined their appearance. Consequently, we may treat them as a group of related texts. The relationship is not generic, as the plays belong to different genres: there is a masque among them (*Neptune's Triumph*), quasi-morality (*The Sun's Darling*), biographical drama (*The Life of the Duchess of Suffolk*), historical drama (*The Bondman*) and an allegory (*A Game at Chesse*); rather, the relationship is functional. When circulated in print, or performed on stage, these texts acquired an important political function as part of the propaganda campaign initiated by the Court faction of the Duke of Buckingham and Prince Charles. The ramifications of this campaign were a result of employing all the means available at the time to disseminate an ideology that would not only stir national and religious feelings in wide circles of English society, but would also – above all, perhaps – influence the proceedings of a Parliament that was to decide on the immediate future of the country.

There is little doubt that this group of plays was larger than has been preserved to the present, as a number of texts, for example, Maynards's masque, or plays like *The Hungarian Lion* and *Match or No Match*, although lost, may be included in this group by virtue of external evidence or significant titles. It is also worth pointing out that this 'theatrical propaganda campaign' was not confined to London; we know, for instance, that Lady Elizabeth's Men toured the country in April 1624 presenting a play entitled *The Spanish Contract* (now lost). This supports our initial assertion that the appearance of these politically 'engaged' plays in one theatrical season cannot result from either mere chance or from playwrights' spontaneous response. Although in most cases it appeared impossible to prove direct sponsorship by the Duke and the Prince (or their supporters), it seems very likely that they may have been responsible for the political orientation of this particular season.

Naturally, by supporting what was basically an anti-royalist policy, the texts under discussion had to overcome a serious obstacle before reaching the press or the stage: they had to pass through the hands of Sir Henry Herbert, the censor, who was a careful guardian of his monarch's interests. Owing to his position at court, Sir Henry was undoubtedly well aware of political scheming and this knowledge would make him particularly sensitive to the subtleties of dramatic literature. Any conspicuously political text was certainly 'dangerous matter' to him, and when necessary he did not hesitate to use his pen to 'reform' a play, as was the case with *The Life of the Duchess of Suffolk*. To obtain a licence without Sir Henry's intervention, political allusion had to be disguised, which is why the plays are equipped with a 'mask' of non-referentiality: they refute their link with the present by setting their plots in the indefinite mythological past (*Neptune's Triumph*, and, partly, *The Sun's Darling*), or in the historical past (*The Bondman, The Life of the Duchess of Suffolk*), or in the timeless allegory (*A Game at Chesse*). On the surface, none of the texts deals openly with contemporary English matters. They can only be related to contemporary events and persons through similarity of plot, episode, or character. Therefore, on an ideological or political level, communication is possible only with an aware audience.

To facilitate this level of communication, texts had to be equipped with a number of signals which would draw the attention of the audience to the similarity of event and character appearing in the created world to their extra-textual and contemporary equivalents. To establish this link and understanding, playwrights subordinated their texts to the persuasive function they wanted to achieve, with little or no regard to the plays' artistic integrity. The text of *The Bondman*, for instance, has been altered by the author in order to create a conspicuous parallel between a parliamentary debate in the created world and a debate in the English Parliament of 1624. Focusing on achieving the persuasive function, Massinger neglected the artistic unity of his text, and as a result most of Act I bears little relation to what follows. Similar kinds of change were made in *The Sun's Darling*, in which Act V violates the unity of the original version to the extent that it might belong to a different play; and the original version of *A Game at Chesse* was altered as a response to demand for political satire. In all these cases the persuasive function is achieved at high cost. A comparison can be found in modern theatre, when in production of an old play a director attempts to adjust the available text to contemporary political or social issues and, consequently, makes cuts in the original, or even supports his idea with additions from other texts. This leads us to a more general conclusion. The more a literary work is 'engaged' in contemporary politics and the more the persuasive function becomes a goal in itself, the more confined its meaning becomes to one particular time and society (or section of society). This determines a temporary and relative insignificance outside the milieu in which this type of literature is created. The most popular and 'politically' scandalous play of the 1623/24 season, *A Game at Chesse*, is trivial, if not meaningless, to today's audiences, even in Britain. And nobody could suspect it of being 'political' today. The same applies to *The Sun's Darling* and to *Neptune's Triumph*. It is interesting to note that literature which is created in countries with totalitarian regimes, and under severe censorship, often reveals the same 'flaw' as the texts discussed in this book: whenever these works are engaged with contemporary, local political issues, their ability to communicate meaning depends largely on their audience's knowledge of issues; the literature is therefore short-lived and often confusing or incomprehensible to outsiders, as is the case, for instance, with political cabaret.

Although this book deals with a very brief period in the history of drama, it seems that certain established relationships between literature, censorship and politics may be applied to any other period (and not necessarily in Britain). The fact that institutional censorship does not exist in several countries today does not mean that there are no 'invisible' forms of censorship. Apart from political, military, or moral censorship, we may distinguish an economic form, enforced – for instance – by publishers. In most countries of the world, however, there is still political censorship, either institutional or clandestine, in operation. One is tempted to generalize and observe that it exists only in those countries where governments believe in the existence of a social force capable of overthrowing, or severely undermining, the stability of the current political system. In those countries, writers face the same or similar problems to those faced by playwrights of Elizabethan and Jacobean England. To avoid the censor's interventions, the same means and 'tricks' are employed, by which a conscientious spectator or reader is instructed to 'read between the lines' of a text which seemingly bears no relation to contemporary politics, or is instructed to draw a parallel between the created world (or its part) and the world he/she inhabits. All the censors of the world know that theatre above all other arts has enormous potential for signalling and communicating 'dangerous matter', not through words alone, but through acting, characterization, costumes, stage design and music.

Chronological table

Numbers in brackets are dates of the particular month

1623

	Plays licensed by Sir Henry Herbert	Other dramatic and theatrical events	Non-dramatic literature entered in the Stationers' Register	Political events
October	(2) *A Fault in Friendship* (a lost play by 'Young Johnson and Broome' for the Prince's company) (17) *More Dissemblers Besides Women* (an 'Old Play' for the King's Company) (29) *Hardshifts for Husbands, or Bilboes the Best Blade* (a lost play by Samuel Rowley for the Palsgrave's Company)	(13) Lady Elizabeth's Company recorded at Leicester (27) The Prince's Company recorded at Leicester	(10) *The Catholique Judge: Or a Moderator of the Catholique Moderator* (13) *The Joyfull Returne of Prince Charles from Spain* (17) Thomas Adam's *The Barren Tree*	(5) Prince Charles and the Duke of Buckingham returned from Madrid without the Infanta. In spite of rejoicing in London, the Spanish marriage still seemed possible until the end of October. (31) Buckingham was reported to have spoken openly against the Spaniards.

November		
(19) *Two Kings in a Cottage* (a lost play by Bonen for the Palsgrave's Company)	(1) *The Maid in the Mill* acted at court 'with reformations'	(1) Arrival of the letter from the Earl of Bristol, announcing that the Pope's dispensation was expected hourly in Madrid
	(5) *The Spanish Gipsy* acted at court	(11–13) Two Privy Council meetings were held and it was decided not to have a match with Spain without the Palatinate. Summoning of Parliament proposed for the first time.
(28) *The Faiyre Fowle One, or The Bayting of the Jealous Knight* (a lost play by Smith for a 'Strange Company at the Red Bull')	(20) A lost masque by John Maynard staged at Yorkhouse (end of November?) Massinger completes his first version of *The Bondman*	A new proxy dispatched for the English ambassador in Madrid, valid until March
		(15) Prince Charles sent letters to the Earl of Bristol depriving him of any power in the delivery of the procuration.
		In an audience with the Spanish ambassadors James admitted in public that the restitution of the Palatinate had never been considered a condition of the Spanish match.
		(29) This was the fixed date for the marriage in Madrid. Bristol received his dispatches from Prince Charles on the 26th.

Chronological table (*cont.*)

1623

Plays licensed by Sir Henry Herbert	Other dramatic and theatrical events	Non-dramatic literature entered in the Stationers' Register	Political events
December			
(3) *The Noble Bondman* (by Massinger for the Queen of Bohemia's Company)	(12) First report of preparations for the staging of *Neptune's Triumph*	(7) Samuel Ward's *A Peace Offering to God, for the Prince's Safe Return*	(c.15) News arrived from Spain: the marriage had been prevented virtually on the eve of its celebration
(4) *The Hungarian Lion* (a lost play by Richard Gunnel for the Palsgrave's Company)	(26) *The Maid in the Mill* acted at court	(17) *A Treatise of the Perpetuall Visibilitie and Succession of the True Church Especially in the Ages Before Luther*	(20) The Privy Council decided on Parliament by a majority of seven to five.
	(27) *The Bondman* acted at court		(30) Bristol recalled from Madrid.
(6) *The Wandering Lovers* [= *Lover's Progress?*] (by Fletcher for the King's Company)	(28) *The Buck is a Thief* (a lost play) acted at court	(17) *Mephibosheth's Hearts Joy upon . . . . the Happie returne of our Prince Charles*	(?) Anti-Spanish publications began to issue from the presses abroad. These were smuggled and circulated in England.

January			
(2) *The History of the Duchess of Suffolk* (by Thomas Drue for the Palsgrave's Company)	(1) *The Wandering Lovers* acted at court	(12) John Meredeth's *The Judge of Heresies*	(14) New proposals presented by the Spanish ambassadors, which pleased James to the extent that he seriously thought about reviving negotiations.
(6) *The Four Sons of Amon* (a lost play for the Prince's Company)	(4) *The Changeling* acted at court	(18) Henry Mason's *The New Art of Lyeing Covered by Jesuites Vnder the Vaile of Equivocacon*	(20) Council met to consider the Spanish proposals; the councillors divided into three factions: five for the Spanish match, three opposed and four remained neutral. Prince Charles declared that the marriage with the Infanta was out of the question.
(26) *The Whore in Grain* (a lost play for the Palsgrave's Company)	(6) *Neptune's Triumph* 'put off; *More Dissemblers Besides Women* acted at court	(20) Daniel Featley's *The Fisher Held in His Nett*	
	(18) *The Winter's Tale* acted at court	(23) H.G.'s *A Gagg for the Pope and the Jesuites or the Arraignment and Execucon of Antechrist*	
	(27) The Queen's Company paid for performances at Leicester		

Chronological table (*cont.*)

Plays licensed by Sir Henry Herbert	Other dramatic and theatrical events	Non-dramatic literature entered in the Stationers' Register	Political events
		1624	
February	(8–10) The 'usual' Shrovetide masque cancelled ('in order not to offend any [ambassadors]')	(8) Thomas Bedford's *Luther's Predecessors*	(11) The massacre of English merchants at Amboyna.
	(17) Lady Elizabeth's Players paid £100 for presenting 'tenne severall plaies before his Ma.ty'	(8) Giffin William's *Seven Golden Candlesticks*	(15) Viscount Kensington arrived in Paris with a secret mission connected with the possibility of starting marriage negotiations with France.
		(11) Thomas Sutton's *The Good Fight of Faith*	(19) On this day the new Parliament commenced.
			(24) In the Commons, Buckingham gave an account of his and Prince Charles's stay in Madrid, and blamed the Spaniards for various 'offences' suffered there.
			(26) The MPs calles for a bill against the recusants.
			(27) General Mansfeld's envoy arrived in London.

March				
	(3) *The Sun's Darling* (by Dekker and Ford for the 'Cockpit Company') (12) *The Bondman* licensed for print	(20) Lady Elizabeth's Company recorded at Dover (?) *The Bondman* acted at the Cock-pit in Drury-lane by Lady Elizabeth's Company	(3) Issac Bargrave's *Sermon Preached Before the Honourable Assembly of the Commons House of Parlement*	(1) Sir Benjamin Rudyard gave a speech in the Commons urging war against Spain: much applause. The Commons drew up a petition to the King. (3) The Commons' petition adopted by the Upper House, but rejected by the King. (5) Mansfeld's envoy received by the Venetian ambassador; James refused to see him. (8) Proclamation forbidding 'all misbehaviours insolences, c., against foreign ministers and their servants' issued. (11) The King's demand for payment of his debts and for money for the war in Germany rejected by the Commons. (14) James presented new proposals, asking for five subsidies and ten fifteenths. (20) The Commons granted three subsidies and three fifteenths after the King's declaration of the utter breach with Spain.

1624

	Plays licensed by Sir Henry Herbert	Other dramatic and theatrical events	Non-dramatic literature entered in the Stationers' Register	Political events
April	(6) *A Match or Not Match* (a lost play by Rowley for the Palsgrave's Company)	(9) Lady Elizabeth's Players paid £30 for presenting three plays before the King in December and January	(7) James Wadsworth's *The Copies of Certaine Letters Which Haue Passed Between Spaine and England in Matter of Religion*	(2) Buckingham appealed to MPs to raise money for the war before the subsidies were granted, a suggestion neglected by the Commons.
	(10) *The History of Henry the First* (a lost play by Davenport for the King's Company)	(24) Lady Elizabeth's Players attempted to stage *The Spanish Contract*, a lost play, in Norwich; they were prevented.	(8) Ferdinando Texeda's *The Exhortacon of a Spanish Converted Monk*	(3) The Commons sent a petition to James demanding the full execution of penal laws against the recusants, which offended the King.
	(17) *The Way to Content All Women or How a Man May Please His Wife* (a lost play by Gunnel for the Palsgrave's Company)		(14) Francis White's *Reply to Jesuit Fishers 'answere' to 'certaine questions' propounded by his Maiestie*	(6) Breach of the negotiations with Spain announced by James.
				(14) Mansfeld arrived in London, welcomed by cheering crowds.
	(17) *The Renegado, or the Gentleman of Venice* (by Massinger for the 'Cockpit Company')		(27) Henry Burton's *Censure of Symony*	(15) Commissioners appointed to treat with the Dutch about sending troops to their assistance. Charges against Middlesex laid before the Privy Council.

(16) Having seen Prince Charles and Buckingham, Mansfeld received by James. Initial agreement reached as to the force of the expeditionary army to be led by Mansfeld on the Continent.

(18) Orders given to fit out twelve ships of the royal navy.

(19) It is reported that during Mansfeld's visit Buckingham had urged the Commons to hasten the subsidies.

(21) The Council of War appointed.

(22) First reading of the subsidy bill in the Commons.

(24) Spanish ambassadors demand an explanation for military preparations in England.

(25) Mansfeld leaves England.

(28) Thomas Gataker's *Discussion of the Popish Doctrine of Transubstantiacon*

Chronological table (*cont.*)

1624

	Plays licensed by Sir Henry Herbert	Other dramatic and theatrical events	Non-dramatic literature entered in the Stationers' Register	Political events
May	(3) *The Madcap* (a lost play by Barnes for the Prince's Company)		(1) John Gee's *The Foote out of the Snare*	(13) Impeachment of Middlesex.
	(3) *Jugurth, King of Numidia* (a lost play for an unidentified company)		(3) Hieron's *Sermons*	(17) Carlisle sent to France to negotiate the marriage.
	(15) *The Tragedy of Nero* (licensed for print)		(24) Thomas Taylor's *The Vtter Ruine of Romish Amalecke*	(19) Order to equip thirty merchant vessels for war. Jesuits expelled from England.
	(21) *Honour in the End* (a lost play for the Palsgrave's Company)		(24) John Gee's *New Shreds of the Old Snare*	(31) Treaty signed between France and the United Provinces.
	(27) *A Wife for a Month* (by Fletcher for the King's Company)			

	(27) *The Parricide* (a lost play for the Prince's Company)		
June	(11) *The Fairy Knight* (by Dekker and Ford for an unspecified company) (12) *A Game at Chesse* (by Thomas Middleton)	(2) Anthony Wotton's *Run From Rome* (11) Thomas Beard's *Antechrist the Pope of Rome or the Pope of Rome Antechrist* (28) George Webbe's *The Protestants Calendar*	(5) A treaty signed with the United Provinces and under its provisions regiments of English soldiers sailed to serve under Dutch command. (19) Three French armies ordered to prepare for active service. (26) Spanish ambassadors leave England.
July	(7) Herbert licensed a scene that was added to *The Virgin Martyr* (9) The King's, Lady Elizabeth's, Prince's Companies and the Children of the Revels received payment at Leicester	(2) Edmund Gurnay's *The Romish Chain*	Negotiations with the French continued
August	(6–7) Nine consecutive performances of *A Game at Chesse* (18) A warrant issued to have Thomas Middleton brought before the Privy Council		Difficult marriage negotiations continued throughout August.

Chronological table *(cont.)*

1624

	Plays licensed by Sir Henry Herbert	Other dramatic and theatrical events	Non-dramatic literature entered in the Stationers' Register	Political events
September	(3) *The Captives, or the Lost Recovered* (by Heywood for the Cockpit Company)			(26) Suspension of laws against recusants, being the immediate result of the continuing marriage negotiations.
	(?) *A Late Murther of the Son Upon the Mother* (a lost play) by Webster and Ford for an unspecified company			
October	(14) *The City Night Cap* (by Davenport for the Cockpit Company)			(1) Parliament prorogued
	(15) *The Angell King* (a lost play for the Palsgrave's Company)			(4) A warrant issued by the Council of War to advance money for the levy of troops for Mansfeld.
	(19) *Rule a Wife and Have a Wife* (by Fletcher for an unspecified company)			(29) It was ordered to levy 12 000 pressed men for Mansfeld's service.

November	(22) *The Bristowe Merchant* (a lost play by Ford for the Palsgrave's Company)		(7) Mansfeld received commission to command the troops.
	(3) *The Parliament of Love* (by Massinger for the Cockpit Company)		(10) Marriage treaty signed with the French.
	(3) *The Masque* (a lost play) licensed for the press		(17) Siege of Breda began.
			(21) Rejoicing in London at the news of the completion of negotiations.
December	(?) *The Spanish Viceroy* (a lost play) acted without a licence	(14) A ballad entitled *Duchesse of Suffolk*	(12) Marriage treaty ratified.
			(24) Courts forbidden to admit any further prosecution of the Recusants under the penal laws.
			(26) Order issued releasing all Roman Catholics in prison for offences connected with their religion.
			Mansfeld gathers troops in Dover.

Notes

Introduction

1 *Tudor Drama and Politics. A Critical Approach to Topical Meaning* (Cambridge, Mass., 1968).

2 See the discussion of the political implications of these proclamations in Godfrey Davies's 'English Political Sermons, 1603–1640', *The Huntington Library Quarterly*, vol. III, No. 1 (October 1939), pp. 1–2.

3 For examples of the Master of the Revels' censorship see J.Q. Adams (ed.), *The Dramatic Records of Sir Henry Herbert, Master of the Revels, 1623–1673* (New Haven and London, 1917), pp. 18–23.

4 F. Dahl, *A Bibliography of English Corantos and Periodical Newsbooks 1620–1642* (London, 1952), p. 18.

5 Ibid.

6 Ibid., pp. 18–19.

7 Ibid., p. 22.

8 *Pepysian Ballads*, I, p. 94.

9 See the *Transcript of the Registers of the Company of Stationers of London; 1554–1640 A.D.*, ed. E. Arber (London, 1877), vol. IV, p. 87.

10 *Calendar of State Papers* (hereafter CSP), Domestic (1623–25), p. 481.

11 Ibid., p. 485.

12 *CSP, Domestic*, vol. CX, p. 18.

13 See the discussion of the play and the circumstances surrounding its staging in W.P. Frijlinck's edition of *The Tragedy of Sir John Olden Barnavelt* (Amsterdam, 1922), pp. XI–CLVIII.

14 Adams, *Dramatic Records of Sir Henry Herbert*, p. 18.

15 Ibid., p. 6.

16 Ibid., p. 21.

17 This was *The Late Murder in the White Chapel, or Keepe the Widow Waking*, a play by Dekker, Rowley, Ford and Webster.

18 Quoted from C.J. Sisson, *Lost Plays of Shakespeare's Age* (Cambridge, 1936), p. 101.

19 Ibid., p. 115.

20 See M. Butler, *Theatre and Crisis 1632–1642* (Cambridge, 1984), pp. 105–6.

21 W.W. Greg, *A Companion to Arber* (Oxford, 1967), pp. 222–3.

22 Ibid., p. 225.

23 See Walter Scott (ed.), *The Somers Collection of Tracts* (London, 1809), p. 520, n.1.

24 *CSP, Venetian* (1619–21), p. 491.

25 *The Autobiography and Correspondence of Sir Simond D'Ewes, Bart., During the Reigns of James I and Charles I*, ed. James O.Halliwell, (London, 1845), vol. I, pp. 158–9.

26 See Louis B. Wright, 'Propaganda against James I's "Appeasement" of Spain', *The Huntington Library Quarterly*, vol. VI, No. 2 (1942–3), pp. 149–72.

27 Ibid., pp. 154–5.
28 Davies, 'English Political Sermons', p. 5.
29 *Somers Collection of Tracts*, vol. I, pp. 556–7.
30 This was also labelled the 'Howard party'. However, as a modern historian put it: 'The distinction between the aims of the Spanish and those of the Howard faction is considerably obscured by the practice of referring to the latter as the "Spanish party". These people were pro-Spanish in the sense that they favored an alliance with Spain over the one with France, which their Scottish rivals for political influence favored and over the open war which the more zealous English Puritans wanted to wage against Spain in the Indies and elsewhere.' C.H. Carter, *The Secret Diplomacy of the Habsburgs, 1598–1625* (New York and London, 1964), p. 128.
31 *Harleian Miscellany* (London, 1809), vol. III, p. 338.
32 S.R. Gardiner, *Prince Charles and The Spanish Marriage: 1617–1623. A Chapter in English History* (London, 1869), vol. II, p. 26.
33 Ibid., p. 163.
34 *CSP, Venetian* (1619–21), p. 111.
35 *CSP, Venetian* (1623–25), p. 196.
36 Quoted from M. Heinemann, *Puritanism and Theatre* (Cambridge, 1980), p. 157.
37 See my article 'An Allusion to the Alleged Catholicism of Some Jacobean Players in John Gee's *New Shreds of the Old Snare* (1624)', *Notes and Queries* (forthcoming).
38 See the chapter on Warsaw in my *Gentlemen of a Company* (Cambridge, 1985).
39 J.T. Murray, *English Dramatic Companies, 1558–1642* (London, 1910), vol. II, p. 314.
40 See the chapter on Pomerania in my *Gentlemen of a Company*.
41 (London and New York, 1983); see in particular pp. 18–36.

1. The matter of Prince Charles's return

1 John Taylor, *Prince Charles his welcome from Spaine; who landed at Portsmouth on Sunday the 5ᵗʰ of October, and came safely to London on Monday the 6ᵗʰ of the same, 1623. With the Triumphes of London for the same his happie arrival* (London, 1623); quoted from *The Somers Collection of Tracts*, vol. I, p. 552.
2 Ibid., p. 553.
3 Apart from printed works, there are in the collection of the Society of Antiquaries a couple of verse broadsides describing the journey of Prince Charles to Spain and his happy return. There are also some ballads in manuscript in the Bodleian. See C.H. Firth, *The Ballad History of the Reign of James I, Transactions of the Royal Historical Society*, 3rd series (London, 1911), vol. V, pp. 50–1.
4 *CSP, Venetian* (1623–25), pp. 140–1.
5 Ibid., pp. 145–6.
6 *Letters*, vol. II, p. 527.
7 *CSP, Venetian* (1623–25), pp. 157–8.
8 John Orrell, 'Buckingham's Patronage of the Dramatic Arts: The Crowe Accounts', *Records of Early English Drama* (1980:2), p. 12.
9 *CSP, Venetian* (1623–25), p. 136.
10 *Neptune's Triumph for the Return of Albion* was published in London later that year. All the quotations are from vol. VII of *Ben Jonson*, ed. by C.H. Herford and Percy and Evelyn Simpson, (Oxford, 1941), pp. 681–700.
11 *CSP, Venetian* XVIII (1623–25), ed. by Allen B. Hinds (London, 1912), p. 175.

12 Quoted from *Ben Jonson*, vol. x [Play Commentary. Masque Commentary] (Oxford, 1950), p. 658.

13 *CSP, Venetian* XVIII, p. 192.

14 *The Letters of John Chamberlain*, ed. by N.E. McClure (Philadelphia, 1939), vol. II, p. 538.

15 *CSP, Venetian* XVIII, pp. 196–7.

16 Chamberlain to Sir Dudley Carleton, 17 January, 1624; *Letters*, vol. II, pp. 538–9. The fact that the performance was cancelled was also recorded by Sir Henry Herbert in his Office-Book:

> Jan.6 – Upon Twelfe Night, the maske beinge put off, More Dissemblers besides Women, by the king's company, the prince only being there, Att Whitehall

Quoted from J.Q. Adams (ed.), *The Dramatic Records of Sir Henry Herbert, Master of the Revels, 1623–1673*, (New Haven and London, 1917), p. 51.

17 See Finett's lengthy and detailed account of the entire 'incident' in his *Finetti Philoxenis* (London, 1656), pp. 133–5; and for various payments made in connection with the preparations for the masque see *Ben Jonson*, vol. x, pp. 660–3.

18 See above pp. 21–2.

19 Reproduced in his 'The London Stage in the Florentine Correspondence, 1604–1618', *Theatre Research International*, vol. III, No. 3 (1978), pp. 157–76.

20 Ibid., p. 164.

21 Ibid., p. 173.

22 See R.E. Ruigh's discussion in his *The Parliament of 1624. Politics and Foreign Policy* (Cambridge, Mass., 1971), pp. 16–42.

23 Ibid., p. 26; see also S.R. Gardiner, *Prince Charles and the Spanish Marriage: 1617–1623. A Chapter in English History* (London, 1869), vol. II, pp. 438–9.

24 *CSP, Venetian* XVIII, p. 156, and also Ruigh, *Parliament of 1624*, pp. 27–8.

25 Ruigh, ibid., p. 28.

26 Ibid., p. 31.

27 *Letters*, vol. II, p. 534.

28 Gardiner, *Prince Charles*, p. 446.

29 In point of fact, the King is the only spectator that the masque requires. From this point of view, this is a unique example of a dramatic text which is in a way 'self-sufficient' – in its implied staging it does not need an audience, and the only indispensible spectator for the act of communication to take place is James I. The masque is not only addressed to him, but also incorporates the King into the world it creates. Without the King, no act of communication can take place.

30 J. Goldberg, *James I and the Politics of Literature* (Baltimore and London, 1983), pp. 58–9.

31 Ibid.

32 Stephen Orgel, *The Jonsonian Masque* (Cambridge, Mass., 1965), pp. 97–8.

33 As mentioned in n.29, the text in fact requires only one spectator in its implied staging, but of course in the case of a printed text there is an implication of a reading audience.

34 Orgel, *Jonsonian Masque*, p. 101. Another example is *The Masque of Beauty* (1608), in which Boreas opens the masque by asking 'Which among these is Albion, Neptune's son?' and January points to the King.

35 Gardiner, *Prince Charles*, pp. 302ff.

36 In fact, this was entirely an idea of Charles and Buckingham, who begged a reluctant James to give them permission to go; see Gardiner, ibid., pp. 297–302.

37 Ibid., pp. 304–5. A contemporary source tells us that 'the Marquis of Hamilton (upon the sudden news of the prince's departure) had nobly reprehended the king, for sending the prince with such a young man without experience [i.e. Buckingham]'; see George Englisham, *The Forerunners of Revenge* (London, 1642), in *Harleian Miscellany* (London, 1809), vol. II, pp. 79–80.

38 Written by A.W. (London, 1650), pp. 148–9.

39 *CSP, Venetian* XVIII, p. 135.

40 *Letters*, vol. II, p. 515.

41 For example: John Taylor, *Prince Charles his welcome from Spaine* (London, 1623); William Hockham, *Prince Charles his Welcome to the Court, or a true subjects love for his happy returne frome Spaine* (London, 1623); Samuel Ward, *A Peace offering to God, for the Princes safe return* (London, 1623); Thomas Reeve, *Mephibosheth's Hearts Joy upon his Souereignes safety to be imitated by the Subiects of this Land upon the Happie returne of our Prince Charles* (entered the Stationers' Register on 17 December 1623).

42 Quoted from M. Hume, *The Court of Philip IV. Spain in Decadence* (London, 1907), p. 100.

43 Ibid., p. 120.

44 *Letters*, vol. II, p. 517.

45 See *Ben Jonson*, vol. X, p. 666, note to lines 195–203.

46 *Letters*, vol. II, p. 507.

47 N.W. Bawcutt, 'New Revels Documents of Sir George Buck and Sir Henry Herbert, 1619–1622', *Review of English Studies*, XXXV (1984), p. 326.

48 The Child adds: 'and either has her frisking Husband: / That reades her the Corrantos, euery weeke' (293–4). Corantos were the forerunners of English newspapers, and they were published more or less regularly once a week. The context in which the allusion is made implies that corrantos are criticized as one of the sources of gossip. This also explains why 'Mr Ambler, Newes-master of Poules' is included in the gossips' dish. I have been unable to identify the remaining characters in this group.

49 *Letters*, vol. II, p. 522.

50 That is, Buckingham as Lord High Admiral.

51 L.S. Marcus, 'The Occasion of Ben Jonson's *Pleasure Reconciled to Virtue*', *Studies in English Literature*, 19 (1979), p. 272.

2. The matter of the King and Queen of Bohemia

1 That the play was actually printed in London we learn from the title page: 'Imprinted by A.M. for Jasper Emery, at the Fowerdeluce in Paules Church-yard, 1631.'

2 J.Q. Adams (ed.), *The Dramatic Records of Sir Henry Herbert, Master of the Revels, 1623–1673* (New Haven and London, 1917), p. 27.

3 This play was published in 1961 (1962) by the Malone Society. The playwright in question may also have been a player himself, for one Thomas Drew is mentioned as an actor in Queen Anne's company in 1612, and again in 1617 and 1619; see J.T. Murray, *English Dramatic Companies, 1558–1642* (London, 1910), vol. I, pp. 193–7.

4 For other examples of Herbert's censorship see Adams, *Dramatic Records*, pp. 18–23.

5 See I. Ribner, *The English History Play in the Age of Shakespeare* (Princeton, N.J., 1957), p. 295; see also *Henslowe's Diary*, ed. by R.A. Foakes and R.T. Rickert (Cambridge, 1961), p. 133.

6 See *Chronicles of England, Scotland, and Ireland* (London, 1587), vol. III, pp. 1142–5.

7 F.C. Mann (ed.), *The Works of Thomas Deloney* (Oxford, 1912), pp. 389–93. This was reprinted in December 1624.

8 Several examples of publications of this sort may readily be provided: John Burgess, *Certaine letters declaring in part the passage of affairs in the Palatinate* (Amsterdam, 1620); John Harrison, *A Short Relation of the departure of the high and mightie Prince Frederick King Elect of Bohemia; with his royal vertuos Ladie Elizabeth* (Dort, 1619); [anon.] *The Present State of affaires betwixt the Emperor and the King of Bohemia* (London [?], 1620); [anon.] *The reasons wh. compelled the states of Bohemia to reject the archduke Ferdinand* (Dort, 1619); [anon.] *Troubles in Bohemia and other Kingdomes procured by Jesuits* (n.p., 1619). See also bibliography.

9 J.D. Spikes, 'The Jacobean History Play and the Myth of the Elect Nation', *Renaissance Drama*, N.S.,VIII (1977), p. 127.

10 This play in fact would have been very appropriate for revival in 1623/24 for it deals directly with another Spanish match in English history, that of Mary Tudor.

11 It may be added that both Charles Brandon and Katherine seem to have been great admirers and patrons of theatre. A company of players existed under the Duke's patronage as early as 1525, and the troupe was frequently recorded in the provinces until their patron's death in 1545 when, in turn, the players passed under the patronage of Katherine. After the Dowager Duchess's return from exile, she had a new company in her service until 1563; see Murray, *English Dramatic Companies*, pp. 71–2.

12 J. Pratt's edition of *Acts and Monuments* has been used here (Oxford, 1877), pp. 569–76.

13 This was Sir John Mason; see Georgina Bertie, *Five Generations of a Loyal House* (London, 1845), vol. I, p. 29.

14 This piece of information, provided by Foxe, is confirmed by Polish sources. We learn from the latter that the estate of Kroże was actually bestowed upon the Duchess by the King of Poland, Sigismund Augustus, for the sum of 3676 thalers. On her return to England, Katherine sold the lease to Prince Nicholas Radziwiłł for the same amount of money. See F. Sulimierski, Br. Chlebowski, W. Walewski (eds.), *Słownik geograficzny Królestwa Polskiego i innych krajów słowiańskich* (Warsaw, 1883), vol. IV, p. 719. See also M. Baliński, T. Lipiński, *Starożytna Polska pod względem Historycznym, jeograficznym i statystycznym opisana* (Warsaw, 1846), vol. III, p. 535.

15 *Foxe's Book of Martyrs and the Elect Nation* (London, 1963), p. 13.

16 Ibid., pp. 13–15.

17 See note 7.

18 *Honovr in His Perfection* (London, 1624), pp. 34–5.

19 See L.M. Oliver, 'Thomas Drue's Duchess of Suffolk: A Protestant Drama', *Studies in Bibliography*, vol. III (1950–1), pp. 241–6. It was, however, noted by J.D. Spikes ('Jacobean History Play', p. 143, n.38) that 'A strong argument ... can be made for the topical reference in the play to one of the latest issues of 1623. Frederick had assumed the crown of Bohemia and had almost as quickly been expelled not only from Bohemia but also from his own Rhenish palatinate by the Hapsburg Emperor Ferdinand.' And Margot Heinemann in her *Puritanism and Theatre ...*(Cambridge, 1980), noted in passing that the Duchess's 'sufferings as a refugee in Europe could be seen as a moving stage parallel with those of Queen Elizabeth of Bohemia, a Protestant heroine to the popular audience' (p. 202).

20 It may be noted that a couple of months before the play was staged, in September 1623, *The Familiar Discources of Erasmus* were entered in *The Transcript of the Registers of the Company of Stationers ...*, vol. IV, p. 66.

21 An illustration with an inscription in the church at Wesel, commemorating the birth of Peregrini, was reproduced by D.M. in *The Gentleman's Magazine*, vol. 77 (March 1807), pp. 209–10. M. Green's account of Katherine's fortunes is to be found in an earlier issue of *The Gentleman's Magazine*: vol. 76 (August 1806), pp. 691–2.

22 See G. Bertie, *Five Generations*, pp. 136–7.

23 Since no modern edition of the play is available, I have introduced my own line references.

24 The first character in the play to bring the news of Count Palatine's election to the Polish throne is one Cranwell, who announces the King's arrival at Katherine's court: 'The County Pallatine, new king of Poland' (1.i.132).

25 I was unable to find any confirmation of this part of Foxe's account in the Polish sources. There is, however, little doubt that the Duchess of Suffolk met Alasco in England, where he spent many years of his life as an active reformer. Following the accession of Mary Tudor, Alasco was forced to leave England and after a long period of exile in Denmark and in Germany, he eventually obtained the King of Poland's permission – thanks to the intervention of Prince Nicholas Radziwiłł – to return to Poland. We may, therefore, ascertain that Alasco actually met the Duchess during her exile in Germany, or that he heard about her vicissitudes and, after his return to Poland in 1556, he exerted himself to help Katherine and achieved his aim once again through the intervention of Radziwiłł, who was also a Protestant and one of the most powerful and influential nobles in Poland.

26 Queen Mary died on 17 November 1558. The news of her death reached Katherine surprisingly quickly, for the Duchess still managed to send a New Year's gift for Elizabeth; see Lady Cecilie Goff, *A Woman of the Tudor Age* (London, 1930), pp. 225–6. A letter has also been preserved, dated 25 January 1559, written by Katherine to the new Queen (ibid.). It seems, however, that the Duchess returned to England in the summer of that year (ibid., p. 251). Another source informs us that she travelled to England via Königsberg in the Duchy of Prussia, which – although Poland's fief – was a Protestant country. This is a letter, dated London 6 March 1567, written by Katherine to Duke Albert Hochenzollern to thank him for his kindness to her husband and herself when they were in Prussia; see *Calendar of the Clarendon State Papers Preserved in the Bodleian Library*, ed. by the Rev O. Ogle and W.H. Bliss (Oxford, 1872), vol. I, p. 497, entry 284.

27 See Goff, *Woman of the Tudor Age*, p. 167. That the King of Poland, Sigismund Augustus, was actually a suitor for Katherine's hand we learn from a modern guide to Grimsthorpe Castle, where the Duchess lived after her return to England. Today this is the property of the family of the late Gilbert James, the third Earl of Ancaster. Unfortunately, the guide is a popular publication and does not provide the name of the author, nor the source of the information it includes. From private correspondence with the late Lord Ancaster it appears that in the family collection there are no documents, letters, or souvenirs connected with Poland.

28 See H. Zins, *Polska w oczach Anglików XIV–XVI w.*, (Warsaw n.d.), pp. 71–2.

29 Quoted from Goff, *Woman of the Tudor Age*, pp. 166–7.

30 Ibid.

31 *Great Brittaines Generall Ioyes* (London, 1613), p. A₄ᵛ.

32 *A Marriage Triumph Solemnized* (London, 1613), p. C₄ᵛ. For the description of the betrothal and wedding celebrations see C. Oman, *Elizabeth of Bohemia* (London, 1964), pp. 59–100. This includes many other examples of poems written on that occasion.

33 L.W. Payne, Introduction to his edition of *The Hector of Germanie*, Publications of the University of Pennsylvania, Series in Philology and Literature, vol. xi (Philadelphia, 1906), pp. 30, 36.

34 See R.A. Foakes's Introduction to *King Henry VIII*, The Arden Edition (London, 1968), pp. xxxi–xxxii.

35 In point of fact, Elizabeth and her children were the immediate line of succession until 1630.

36 See C.V. Wedgwood, *The Thirty Years War* (New York, 1961).

37 Harrison, *A Short Relation*, pp. 4–5.

38 Wedgwood, *Thirty Years War*, p. 106.

39 *The Letters of John Chamberlain*, ed. by N.E. McClure (Philadelphia, 1939), vol. ii, p. 300.

40 In his *English-Mans Love to Bohemia* (Dort, 1620), which was actually dedicated to Sir Andrew Gray, 'Colonell of the forces of Greate Britaine, in this noble Bohemian Preparation'.

41 This was published in London in 1620.

42 The English preparations for sending aid to Bohemia were in fact both clumsy and slow. For instance, on 28 June 1620 Chamberlain wrote to Sir Dudley Carleton: 'Our 4000 men are fallen to 2000 the rest beeing to come after by way of supplie, and yet for this poore number here is such sharking and sharing, and such a deale of discontent, that I can scant promise myself any hope of successe' – *Letters*, vol. ii, p. 307. By April 1620 only £13 000 had been collected in England, compared with 50 000 florins regularly remitted to Bohemia by the Dutch; see S.R. Gardiner, *Prince Charles and the Spanish Marriage: 1617–1623. A Chapter in English History*, (London, 1869), vol. i, p. 323.

43 Gardiner, ibid., pp. 292–3.

44 Ibid., p. 309.

45 See R.E. Ruigh, *The Parliament of 1624. Politics and Foreign Policy* (Cambridge, Mass., 1971), pp. 1–15; M.A. Breslow, *A Mirror of England. English Puritan Views of Foreign Nations, 1618–1640* (Cambridge, Mass., 1970), pp. 10–27.

46 Wedgwood, *Thirty Years War*, p. 178; Ruigh, *Parliament of 1624*, pp. 27–8.

47 Wedgwood, ibid.

48 Ibid., pp. 179–81.

49 Ruigh, *Parliament of 1624*, pp. 16–42.

50 For a detailed account of Elizabeth's flight from Prague see Oman, *Elizabeth of Bohemia*, pp. 232–43.

51 Ibid., pp. 230–1.

52 Ibid., p. 232.

53 Ibid., p. 242.

54 Ibid., pp. 242–3.

55 Ibid.

56 This is what happened in Prague: 'Much frenzied packing was done on that dark November afternoon, but Frederick's chamberlain, on a last progress through the deserted royal apartments, discovered something important which he had left behind. He picked it up and, hurrying down the courtyard, was just in time to catch the 1st coach drawing away from the palace doors. Not until the bundle "thrown in" by Christopher Dohna rolled from the "boot" on the floor of the carriage and burst into a roar, did his astonished fellow-travellers discover that the infant Prince Rupert was amongst them'; quoted from ibid., pp. 224–5.

57 In September and October 1610; ibid., p. 46.

58 Early in 1623, Elizabeth wrote to James I, complaining that: 'Your Majesty will understand by the king's [i.e. Frederick's] letters how the Palatinate is in danger of being utterly lost if your majesty gives us not some aid' – quoted from A. Fraser, *King James* (London, 1974), p. 202. In a speech given in Parliament on 30 May 1621, Sir Robert Phelips reminded MPs that 'The Children of the King are in a miserable estate, releived by other charyty ... can it be for the honour of England to receive such a wound ... and shall we suffer the Kings Children to be kept upon charyty and not releive them' – quoted from Breslow, *Mirror of England*, p. 25.

59 The memory of England's great Elizabeth was becoming a source of near idolatry. Her triumphs over Catholicism and Spain were seen in sharp contrast with the 'peace-making' of James I.

60 *Tom Tell-Troath: Or, A free Discourse touching the Manners of the Time. Directed to his Majestie by Waye of humble Advertisement*, (n.p., n.d: c. 1623), in *Harleian Miscellany* (London, 1809), vol. II, pp. 419–38; quoted from p. 420.

61 *CSP, Venetian* (1619–1621), p. 436.

62 R.E. Schreiber, *The Political Career of Sir Robert Naunton 1589–1635* (London, 1981), p. 70.

63 Wedgwood, *Thirty Years War*, pp. 105–6.

64 For instance, in 1620 a treatise was printed under the title *An Answer to the Question: Whether the Emperour that now is, can bee the Judge on the Bohemian Controuersie or no?* Another 'theoretical' treatise on the subject was *A Briefe Information of the Affaires of the Palatinate* (n.p., 1624), the author of which provides historical justification of Frederick's cause.

65 Wedgwood, *Thirty Years War*, pp. 105–6.

66 Ibid.

67 G.E. Bentley, *The Jacobean and Caroline Stage* (Oxford, 1941), vol. I, p. 136.

68 Ibid., p. 150. It may be mentioned here that one of the lost plays, *The Hungarian Lion* by Richard Gunnell (who was also a member of the company) was staged in December 1623, and may have been connected – as the title suggests – with the political events on the Continent. The only Hungarian connection of the early 1620s with significance for the interests of the English was Prince Bethlehen Gabor of Hungary, who was one of Frederick's faithful allies in the period under discussion. Therefore, it seems quite plausible that the name of 'Hungarian Lion' referred to him. Gabor was very well known in England, and as a supporter of Frederick he was also very popular. Almost every single issue of the early English newspapers, corantos, printed in 1621–4, has an account of Gabor's recent actions.

69 Goff, *Woman of the Tudor Age*, p. 241.

70 It was of course forbidden to discuss religious matters on stage, but playwrights always could present Catholics as villains.

71 It has been suggested by J.D. Spikes that the extant 'biographical' plays of the period share a common pattern: 'the use of the Acts as primary source; a single, unified dramatic action centering in the mortal conflict between the Protestant protagonist and a Catholic antagonist; adjunct episodic material designed to locate the protagonist's story in the context of universal history; and an appeal to the audience, often direct, to behold this exemplum of God's great plan for the English people, and to carry it forward with all dispatch. Such a formulation would comfortably embrace most of the extant examples of the type – *Oldcastle, Cromwell, If You Know Not Me*, and *Duchess*' – quoted from 'Jacobean History Play', p. 147. J.D. Spike's essay, however, concentrates on the myth of 'the 'Elect Nation' and tends to underestimate

the immediate political significance of the plays in question. And the fact that Drue based his plot on Foxe does not automatically make him a propagator of the myth. To locate the protagonist's story in the context of universal history in the case of *The Duchess of Suffolk* is simply reading into the text features that do not exist there.

3. The matter of war

1 J.Q. Adams, *The Dramatic Records of Sir Henry Herbert, Master of the Revels, 1623–1673* (New Haven and London, 1917), p. 26.
2 Ibid., p. 51.
3 *The Plays and Poems of Philip Massinger*, ed. by Philip Edwards and Colin Gibson (Oxford, 1976), vol. I.
4 *The Letters of John Chamberlain*, ed. by N.E. McClure (Philadelphia, 1939), vol. II, p. 523.
5 P. Edwards, Introduction to *The Bondman* in *Plays and Poems of Philip Massinger*, vol. I, pp. 304–7.
6 P. Edwards, 'The Sources of Massinger's *The Bondman*', *Review of English Studies*, 15 (1964), p. 21.
7 Ibid., pp. 22–5.
8 Ibid., p. 25.
9 With the possible exception of scene ii; but this, in turn, is only forty-one lines long! This is less than 10 per cent of Act I. See T.A. Dunn, *Philip Massinger*, pp. 57–8.
10 Edwards, 'Sources of *The Bondman*', p. 26.
11 Edward Arber, *A Transcript of the Registers of the Company of Stationers of London; 1554–1640 A.D.* (London, 1877), vol. IV, p. 113.
12 *The Contemporary Review*, XXVIII (August 1876), pp. 495–507.
13 Ibid., p. 496.
14 In the Introduction to his edition of *The Bondman* (Princeton, 1932), pp. 28–43.
15 Edwards, *Plays and Poems of Philip Massinger*, p. 303; see also Allen Gross, 'Contemporary Politics in Massinger', *Studies in English Literature 1500–1900*, vol. VI (1966), pp. 279–290; and also Philip Edwards, 'The Royal Pretenders in Massinger and Ford', *Essays and Studies*, N.S. 27(1974), p. 31.
16 As was the fate of John Reynolds who in spring 1624 published *Votiuae Angliae, or the desires of England, to persuade his Majesty to draw his sword for the restoring of the Palatinate to Prince Frederick*; Reynolds was arrested in July, fined and served a prison sentence. See *A Companion to Arber*, ed. by W.W. Greg, (Oxford, 1967), pp. 225–6.
17 See R.E. Ruigh, *The Parliament of 1624* (Cambridge, Mass., 1971), pp. 34–5.
18 C. Russell, *Parliament and English Politics 1621–1629* (Oxford, 1979), pp. 175–6.
19 *The Somers Collection of Tracts*, ed. by Walter Scott (London, 1809), pp. 602–3.
20 Quoted from the original, p.*xv*.
21 See R. Lockyer, *Buckingham. The Life and Political Career of George Villiers, First Duke of Buckingham, 1592–1628* (London and New York, 1981), p. 208.
22 For evidence that the Pope, Catholicism and – at times – Spain were associated with the Antichrist see Christopher Hill, *Antichrist in Seventeenth-Century England* (London, 1971), pp. 1–40.
23 [Numero 21] *The Newes of Europe, with all such particular accidents, as haue chanced in seuerall Prouinces ...* (London, 1624), p. 20.
24 This book was printed in Heidelberg.

25 See L. Hanson, 'English Newsbooks, 1620–1641', *The Library*, 4th series, XVIII (1938), p. 367.

26 Lockyer, *Buckingham*, p. 208.

27 *An Experimentall Discoverie of Spanish Practices. Or the Covnselle of a well-wishing Souldier, for the good of his Prince and State, Wherein is Manifested From Known experience, both the Cruelty, and Policy of the Spaniard, to effect his own ends* (n.p., 1623), pp. 22–3.

28 Russell, *Parliament and English Politics*, p. 86.

29 In *Works*, (Utrecht, 1624), p. 5.

30 Russell, *Parliament and English Politics*, p. 177.

31 *CSP, Domestic*, James I, 1623–5, (London, 1859), vol. CLX (77), p. 188.

32 See M.A. Breslow, *A Mirror of England. English Puritan Views of Foreign Nations, 1618–1640* (Cambridge, Mass., 1970), pp. 45–73.

33 Quoted from S.R. Gardiner, *A History of England Under the Duke of Buckingham and Charles I 1624–1628* (London, 1875), vol. I, p. 38.

34 Ibid., p. 39.

35 Ibid., p. 50; see also pp. 48–51.

36 Lockyer, *Buckingham*, p. 208.

37 Ibid., p. 193.

38 Ibid., p. 185.

39 *CSP, Venetian*, vol. XVIII (1623–1625), p. 233. The original is in fact dated 8 March, but this was equivalent to 27 February in English terms.

40 Ibid., p. 244.

41 Ibid., p. 257.

42 Ibid., p. 268.

43 Ibid., pp. 280–1.

44 *CSP, Domestic*, CLXIII (16), p. 219.

45 See Edwards's Introduction to his edition of *Renegado*, in *Plays and Poems of Philip Massinger*, p. 5.

46 Gardiner, *A History of England*, pp. 9–10.

47 *A Sermon Preached Befor the Honourable Assembly; of Knights, Citizens, and Burgesses, of the lower House of Parliament: February the last, 1623* [= 1624], by Isaac Bargrave: Doctor in Divinitie; Chaplayne to the Prince's Heghness (London, 1624), p. F₂.

48 *Somers Collection of Tracts*, p. 602.

49 *Vox Coeli, or News from Heaven Wherein Spaines ambition and treacheries to most Kingdomes and Free Estates in Europe, are unmasked and truly represented, but most particularly towards England, and now more especially under the pretended match of Prince Charles with the Infanta Donna Maria*, Written by S.R.S.N. [i.e. Thomas Scott]. Printed in Elisium, 1624; *Somers Collection of Tracts*, p. 582.

50 Ibid., p. 585.

51 Ibid., p. 594.

52 Ibid., p. 603.

53 (Argument 10), p. B₄ᵛ.

54 'War only', cried Eliot, 'will secure and repair us.' The fleet, he added, might be fitted out by the help of 'those penalties the Papists have already incurred' – quoted from Gardiner, *A History of England*, p. 23.

55 *CSP, Domestic*, CLXI (4), pp. 193–4.

56 Lockyer, *Buckingham*, p. 189.

57 See Spencer, Introduction to *The Bondman*, pp. 192–3.
58 Ibid., p. 193. It may be added that Thomas Scott's *A Post-Script, Or, A Second Part of Robert Earle of Essex His Ghost* (1624) mentions that in 1588 the Spaniards carried with them 'butcherly kniues, iron ghiues, shackles, wire-whipps, whips with spurre-rowels, and other torturing instruments, intended to torment vs, old and young' (p. 7).
59 Quoted from *Somers Collection of Tracts*, p. 592.
60 Ibid., p. 595.
61 Ibid., p. 602.
62 Ibid.
63 Ibid., pp. 595–6.
64 This view is shared, among others, by Ruigh, *Parliament of 1624*, p. 37, n.78.
65 See Louis B. Wright, 'Propaganda against James I's "Appeasement" of Spain', *The Huntington Library Quarterly*, vol. VI, no. 2 (1942–3), p. 151.
66 *CSP, Domestic*, CLXIV (8), p. 231.
67 Gardiner, *A History of England*, p. 60.
68 Ibid., p. 57.
69 Ibid.
70 See, for instance, *CSP, Domestic*, CLXII (56) and CLXIII (1), (16), (48), (50), (74).
71 *CSP, Domestic*, CLXIII (16), p. 219.
72 Ibid.
73 Gardiner, *A History of England*, p. 57.
74 *CSP, Domestic*, CLIII (16), p. 219.
75 *CSP, Domestic*, CLXII, pp. 205, 212–13.
76 *CSP, Venetian*, vol. XVIII (1623–5) (London, 1912) (365), pp. 293–4.
77 Gardiner, *A History of England*, p. 58.
78 For details of Mansfeld's winter expedition see ibid., pp. 112–34.
79 J.Q. Adams (ed.), *The Dramatic Records of Sir Henry Herbert, Master of the Revels, 1623–1673* (New Haven and London, 1917), p. 28.
80 H.K. Russell, 'Tudor and Stuart Dramatisation of the Doctrine of Natural and Moral Philosophy', *Studies in Philology*, XXXI (1934), pp. 18–19.
81 G.E. Bentley, *The Jacobean and Caroline Stage* (Oxford, 1956), vol. III, pp. 460–1.
82 F. Bowers (ed.), *The Dramatic Works of Thomas Dekker* (Cambridge, 1961), vol. IV, p. 12.
83 C. Hoy, *Introduction, Notes, and Commentaries to texts in 'The Dramatic Works of Thomas Dekker' edited by Fredson Bowers* (Cambridge, 1980), p. 2.
84 All the quotations used in this chapter come from Bowers's edition of *The Sun's Darling, Dramatic Works of Thomas Dekker*, vol. IV, pp. 15–67.
85 Ibid., p. 17.
86 The text is not very clear at this point:
   [RAYBRIGHT:] I am grand child to the Sun (I.i.147)
   [WINTER:] Bright son of Phebus! (v.i.108).
87 See quotation above, p. 47.

4. The matter of Spain

1 In other words, the created world is not mimetic: it does not 'pretend' to mirror 'real life'.
2 This is not intended to belittle the importance of such significant studies as those by E.C. Morris ('The Allegory in Middleton's *A Game at Chesse*', *Englische Studien*, 38 (1907), pp. 39–52), J.R. Moore ('The Contemporary Significance of Middleton's

Game at Chesse', *PMLA*, 50 (1935), pp. 761–8), J. Sherman ('The Pawns' Allegory in Middleton's *A Game at Chesse'*, *Review of English Studies* XXIX (1978), pp. 147–59), R. Sargent ('Theme and Structure in Middleton's "A Game at Chess"', *Modern Languages Review*, 66 (1971), pp. 721–30), or P. Yachnin ('*A Game at Chess* and Chess Allegory', *Studies in English Literature*, 22 (1982), pp. 317–30), to mention only a few. Because in a number of essays the stress is put on establishing 'who represents whom' in the allegory, the critical dispute is often relegated to a position outside the play proper, and it becomes an object in itself for a critic to convince his readers that, say, the White Queen's Pawn stands for 'Elizabeth of Bohemia', or for 'common people', or for 'England', or for 'Prince Charles' etc. This is, of course, an accepted critical procedure, but it often leads to reading into the text meanings that are corroborated by a critic's conviction only. The play creates a political world of itself and a critic's task should be to analyse this world first, before relating it to a historical context.

3 What I am trying to say here is that the play does not have to be interpreted only in its relationship to Anglo-Spanish affairs in the 1620s.

4 I have used R.C. Bald's edition of *A Game at Chesse* (Cambridge, 1929).

5 When Ignatius expresses his resentment against some of the chessmen he is reminded by Error:

> Why would you have 'em playe agaynst themselues?
> Thats quite agaynst the Rule of Game, Ignatius.   (74–5)

6 R. Sargent ('Theme and Structure') has remarked that 'since the play proper is presented entirely in terms of a game of chess ... Middleton needs to avoid initial confusion as the action starts by providing some sort of introduction that will prepare the audience for what they are to see' (p. 722).

7 J. Sherman ('The Pawns' Allegory') attaches 'symbolic' importance to the scenes in which full houses appear: 'The second "full-house" represents, as completely, the Parliament of 1624. Here the liberties of people are restored by the recall of Parliament, and the black intentions of Spain (the Black Bishop's Pawn) are at last recognized' (p. 156).

8 This applies both the chess and generic rules. Their relationship is actually reminiscent of a vicious circle: consistent employment of one set of rules leads to the violation of the rules belonging to the other set. Simply speaking, the more 'chess' we have, the less drama remains.

9 N. Taylor and B. Loughrey, 'Middleton's Chess Strategies in *Women Beware Women'*, *Studies in English Literature*, 24 (1984), p. 342.

10 Ibid., p. 344.

11 Yachnin, '*A Game at Chess* and Chess Allegory', p. 318.

12 The 'chess blunders' serve the function of the initial signal to readers or spectators that this is not 'true chess', but a pretext to talk about matters external to the game.

13 See note 8 above.

14 Which is negated by the dramatic action.

15 Sargent, 'Theme and Structure', p. 721.

16 Moore, 'Contemporary Significance', p. 763.

17 Yachnin, '*A Game at Chess* and Chess Allegory', pp. 329–30.

18 The most controversial theory was presented by E.C. Morris ('Allegory of Middleton's *A Game at Chesse'*), who claimed that, for instance, the White Bishop's Pawn 'stands' for Frederick, the Elector Palatine, the White Queen's Pawn for Elizabeth of Bohemia, the Black Bishop's Pawn for the Duke of Bavaria, the Black Queen's Pawn for the Archduchess Isabella and the Black Knight's Pawn for the

Emperor. As noted by M. Heinemann, 'Some of the subtler allegorical meanings critics have seen in the play seem too strained to be convincing: notably the identification of attempts to seduce the White Queen's Pawn with attacks on the Palatinate. Allegory and symbolism had to be of a kind that could be easily picked up in the theatre by a popular audience' (*Puritanism and Theatre* (Cambridge, 1980) p. 160).

19 Ibid.

20 In 'political' terms, 'Middleton has shown an England on the whole appallingly susceptible to appearances, and to professions of good faith' (Sherman, 'The Pawns' Allegory', p. 159). And R. Sargent had observed that 'this pattern of aggressive evil attacking guileless innocence and yet suffering defeat is emphasized by its occurrence twice in the sub-plot' ('Theme and Structure', p. 729).

21 Warnings against traitors at court were common in the political literature of the period. For instance, in *Tom Tell-Troath*, a warning of that kind is addressed directly to King James: 'They that fly higher, and fixe their speculations upon the mysteries of the court, doe apparently perceive that the count of Gondemar hath taught some of your actiue ministers to juggle, onely to make them passively capable of his owne conjuringe; and that, by the penetratinge faculty of a yelowe Indian demon hee hath at his command, and is master of your cabinet, without a key, and knowes your secrets before the greatest part, and most faithful of your councel' (*Somers Collection of Tracts*, p. 473).

22 Sargent, 'Theme and Structure', pp. 726–7.

23 R. Sargent has observed that 'on one level this checkmate is operating as a pun. The Black House is rendered harmless, its designs checkmated, it cannot hope now to outwit them. At the level of a game of chess, however, there is also an appropriateness in the choice of this particular checkmate. For "checkmate by discovery" necessitates the co-operation of two pieces of the same colour. One piece is moved to reveal that the second is holding the King in check' (ibid. p. 726). The latter claim raised objections of another critic: 'The emphasis in this scene [i.e. 'checkmate by discovery'] ... is on the "literary" sense of the chess term; Middleton has no regard for its technical significance' (Yachnin, '*A Game at Chess* and Chess Allegory', p. 328).

24 See note 21 above.

25 As many of the Black Knight's speeches, this one, too, alludes to the popular anti-Spanish bias of political pamphleteers. As R. Sargent put it: 'Middleton demonstrates the narrow dogmatism, the irrational bias, and the extravagant oversimplifications likely to arise at a time of national crisis and excitement' ('Theme and Structure', p. 721). In point of fact, Middleton closely follows a number of contemporary tracts, as the affinity of the Black Knight's speech to a corresponding passage in *Vox Coeli* will illustrate:

> Q.M: ... Gondomar ... is exceeding great and familiar with King James.
> Q.E.   Else he could never have gotten open the prison dores for the Romane priests and Jesuites.
>
> ...
>
> E6   ... Nor have procured a gallant fleete to secure the coast of Spaine ...
> PH.   Gondomar ... hath now brought matters to this passe, that no sincere advice, honest letter, religious sermon, or true picture, can point at the King of Spaine'   (pp. 586–8).

An impressive number of Middleton's sources are reproduced in R.C. Bald's edition of *A Game of Chesse* (Notes, pp. 137–58).

26 The Black Knight betrays the military plans of the Black House against the White. It is worth pointing out here that the particular houses are described as 'human' countries separated by the sea, and the 'chess' convention disappears here completely. Middleton, it seems, wanted to be sure that the association of the houses with Spain and England would be obvious even to less intelligent readers or spectators. By doing so, he destroys the artistic consistency of the text.

27 The same characterization of Spain's ambition to conquer the world through cunning policy rather than military action is to be found in contemporary English political pamphlets. For instance, Thomas Scott in his *Vox Populi* (1620) makes Gondomar reveal that to achieve his goal he 'beheld the endeauours of our Kings of happie memorie, how they haue achieued Kingdomes and conquests by this policie, rather then by open hostilitie' (p. 9), and for the same reason the Spaniards 'had secret and sure plots and proiects on foot in all those places, and good intelligence in all Courts' (p. 31).

28 The Black Knight's 'galician brain' is referred to by the Black Bishop (in II.ii.271), which echoes Thomas Scott's *Vox Coeli* (1624), in which Queen Elizabeth talks about Gondomar's 'Castillian, or rather Galician braine' (p. 588), and Queen Anne of his 'perfumed braine' (ibid.). In Scott's *Second Part of Vox Populi*, Gondomar himself talks about the 'proiects' in his 'braine' (p. 20).

29 Sherman, 'The Pawns' Allegory', p. 150. One cannot agree with the opinion, recently expressed, that 'Middleton departs from tradition in his play by fusing the contrasting connotations of the metaphor in such a way as to create moral ambiguity and satiric irony' and that the play forms a 'concealed presentation of the corruption in the White House' and of the 'affinities' between both Black and White Houses (R.A. Davies, A.R. Young, '"Strange Cunning" in Thomas Middleton's *A Game at Chess*', *University of Toronto Quarterly*, XLV (1976), p. 239). In point of fact, the conflict is not as much between the White and the Black Houses as between true and 'false' religion.

30 Ibid., p. 238.

31 Ibid., p. 242. It may be pointed out that it is not the white pieces' characters who appear 'devilish', but only those who pretend to be white, yet in their nature are truly black.

32 Loyola appears in hell in Phineas Fletcher's *Appollyonists*, where a council of fiends is in session, and the Spirit of Ignatius expresses his desires:

> That blessed Isle, so often curst in vaine,
> Triumphing in our losse and idle spight,
> Of force shall shortly stoop to Rome and Spayne:
> I'le take a way ne're knowe to man or spright.

(*The Poetical Works of Giles and Phineas Fletcher*, ed. F.S. Boas (Cambridge, 1900), vol. I, pp. 171–3).

33 E.M. Wilson, O. Turner, 'The Spanish Protest Against "A Game at Chess"', *Modern Languages Review* XLIV (1949), p. 480.

34 Ibid. In a contemporary letter, written in verse, in which Middleton's play is described, we read that the Fat Bishop was damned to 'ye Fire' (line 48), that is, to the 'bag' or hell (G. Bullough, '"The Game at Chesse". How it Struck a Contemporary', *Modern Languages Review* XLIX (1954), p. 157).

35 That as the founder of the Society of Jesus, Loyola was frequently associated by Protestants with the devil, may be illustrated by a passage in *State Mysteries of the Jesuites* (1623), in which a novice complains that a 'Hereticke' dared to claim that Ignatius should be 'most properly compared to a Montigibel, the very tunnel of Hell'

(quoted from R.C. Bald's edition of *A Game at Chesse*, note to 1.i.265–9, p. 140).

36 Sherman, 'The Pawns' Allegory', p. 151.

37 The 'flames' seem to echo the 'fire of purgatory', mentioned by the Black Knight earlier in the play, when he receives intelligence from various countries and comments on the news from Spain:

> Hispanica!, blind worke tis,
> The Jesuite has writ this wth Juice of lemmans sure
> It must bee held close to the fire of Purgatorie
> Er't can be read   (1.i.334–7)

The 'altar in flames' – not an attribute of Catholicism in itself – could certainly provide a theatrical symbol for the 'hellish' nature of the Church of Rome. However, the 'fire' and the 'images' of the altar are also reminiscent of theological imagery. It was believed that Antichrist or his ministers would make 'fire come downe from heauen', and that he (i.e. Antichrist) would put life into 'the image of the beast' (Richard Bernard, *Looke Beyond Luther* (London, 1623), pp. 115, 161–2).

38 See Heinemann, *Puritanism and Theatre*, p. 162.

39 The use of the 'Bag' as a contemporary hell-mouth was noted by M.C. Bradbrook in *English Dramatic Form* (London, 1965), pp. 46–7.

40 I am not the first, of course, to elaborate on the black chessmen's 'devillish character'. As rightly observed by R. Sargent, 'that the Spaniards are really to be thought of as creatures of Antichrist is additionally reinforced in *A Game at Chess* by imagery that connects them with Satan, the Serpent. They are actually called devils a number of times, though so common an epithet of disapproval would mean little on its own. But more convincing imagery associates the Black House with snakes, and attributes to its members venom and poison, broadening out into more general images of disease and corruption' ('Theme and Structure', p. 730).

41 We cannot accept the view that 'the whole board is possessed by the forces of Blackness' (Davies, Young, '"Strange Cunning"', p. 243).

42 D.M. Holmes, *The Art of Thomas Middleton. A Critical Study* (Oxford, 1970), p. 186.

43 As J. Sherman noted, Middleton has shown us England under two sorts of attack: religious pressure, which turns out to be merely a preliminary to, and cover for, threats of rape and murder 'which must stand as metaphors of territorial invasion' ('The Pawns' Allegory', p. 155).

44 Because Loyola is obviously 'blinded' by the light, the implication is that he had come from 'darkness', which corroborates our opinion, expressed above, that he is to be considered as arriving from hell.

45 In Daniel Featly's *An Appendix to the Fisher's Net* (1624) we find an illustration of 'The Popish Wheele, or Romish Circle' (p. 177), which is described in the following way: 'therefore obserue that the verses written in the vttermost and largest circles, one ouer against the other, meete in the word Error, to signifie that though the common Papists, and the Iesuites walke in diuers circles. Yet that the *terminus ad quem*, in which they both meete, is error' (p. 178).

46 As noted by D.M. Holmes, 'the polished poetic idiom makes the Black Bishop's Pawn eminently plausible, and eminently dangerous. The insinuation of fleshy allusions into a sacred context, reminiscent of the secretive . . . looks forward to the attempted rape that the Black Bishop's Pawn resorts to in II.i.' (*Art of Thomas Middleton*, p. 188).

47 R.C. Bald explains: 'The pictures referred to here were actually by the artist Giulio Romano. They were a series of scandalous illustrations to some equally scandalous

verses by Pietro Aretino' (*A Game at Chesse*, p. 146).

48 The only direct dramatization of historical events connected with the Spanish match is the visit paid to the Black House by the White Knight and the White Duke. However, if we were to treat the play as a dramatic version the visit made by Prince Charles and the Duke of Buckingham to Madrid, we would immediately discover that the play is highly inaccurate and incomplete. For instance, there is no mention of the Infanta, of marriage negotiations, or of the contract. In much of the play, Middleton deals with matters only loosely connected with the match, or totally unrelated to it. Even as an allegory, the play does not 'cover' any consistent historical sequence of events, and remains a conglomerate recollection of Gondomar's activities in London, the fortunes of de Dominis, and the treacherous activities of Spanish and English Catholics.

49 Taylor's sermons were entered in the Stationer's Register on 24 May 1624, that is, a couple of weeks before Middleton's play was licensed, and over two months before it was staged.

50 This was also published in London.

51 As, for instance, Samson Lennard's translation of Parrin's *Luthers Fore-Runners* (London, 1624).

52 William Haller, *Foxe's Book of Martyrs and the Elect Nation* (London, 1963), p. 125.

53 Ibid., p. 165.

54 In *The Sermons of* ... (London, 1624), p. 560.

55 In *The Works* (Utrecht, 1624), p. 2.

56 *Vox Coeli*, in *Somers Collection of Tracts* (London, 1809), p. 581.

57 Ibid.

58 Ibid.

59 Ibid., p. 585.

60 Ibid., p. 581.

61 Ibid., p. 593.

62 *Robert Earl of Essex His Ghost*, in *Somers Collection of Tracts*, p. 598.

63 Hieron, *Sermons* (London, 1624), Book II, pp. 317–18.

64 See Christopher Hill, *Antichrist in Seventeenth-Century England* (London, 1971), p. 14.

65 Ibid., p. 15.

66 Ibid., p. 25.

67 M.A. Breslow, *A Mirror of England. English Puritan Views of Foreign Nations, 1618–1640* (Cambridge, Mass., 1970), p. 55.

68 Quoted in ibid., p. 59.

69 See, for instance, *Troubles in Bohemia and other kingdomes procured by Jesuites* (n.p., 1619), and *The English Spanish Pilgrime, Or, A New Discoverie of Spanish Popery and Jesuitical Stratagems* ... (London, 1630).

70 *Vox Coeli*, p. 594.

71 *The Treatise Concerning Antichrist* (London, 1603), p. 3.

72 *The Discovery of the Man of Sinne* (London, 1614), p. 10.

73 *Babels Balm* (London, 1624), p. 4.

74 *Runne From Rome* (London, 1624), p. 79.

75 *Two Sermons* (London, 1624), p. 16.

76 *Catalogus Protestantium*, (London, 1624), p. 53.

77 For other examples see Hill, *Antichrist*, passim.

78 (London, 1624), pp. 47–50.

79 In *Works*, pp. 1–2.

80 *Two Sermons*, sig. A3ᵛ.
81 This work was also published in London.
82 *Christ's Victorie Over the Dragon: Or Satan's Downfall* (London, 1633), p. 697.
83 Taylor, *Two Sermons*, p. 8.
84 In *Luther's Fore-Runners*, Pt III, sig. Iiii3ᵛ.
85 Cf. numerous references in the play to the Black Knight's fistula. Another satirical comment of this kind made by Middleton (and presumably understood by contemporary audiences) is the reference to a Jesuit made by the Black Bishop's Pawn:

> And here comes hee whose Sanctimonious breath
> Can make that Sparke a Flame ...   (1.i.34–5)

No editor of the play had anything to say on the above lines, but in John Gee's *The Foot Out of the Snare* (1624) we find an account of a Catholic priest's powerful breath:

> But to acquaint you with the strange power of a Catholique Priest's breath ... the company of Priests, for potency of breath, doo put downe Leno, Hell, the Diuell and all: for, the Diuell, who can well enough indure the lothsome odors and euaporations of Hell, is not able to endure the vapour issuing from the mouth of a Priest, but had rather go to Hell, than abide his smell.   (pp. 52–3)

86 sig. Bᵛ.
87 *Works*, p. 8.
88 Beard, *Antichrist the Pope of Rome*, p. 300.
89 *Two Sermons*, p. 22.
90 *The Sermons*, p. 566.
91 (London, 1625), pp. 3, 8.
92 *The Discovery of the Man of Sinne*, p. 21.
93 *The Isle of Man: Or, The Legall Proceeding in Man-shire against Sinne* (London, 1627), pp. 301–2.
94 Parrin, *Luther's Fore-Runners*, sig. K_{kkk}.
95 Ibid., sig. L_{lll}ᵛ.
96 *The Isle of Man*, pp. 26–7.
97 Abbott, *Danger of Popery*, p. 42.
98 Taylor, *Christ's Victorie*, pp. 700–1.
99 Goodwin, *Babels Balm*, pp. 34, 42.
100 Mason, *New Art of Lying*, p. 2.
101 *A Treatise Concerning Antichrist*, p. 92.
102 Ibid., pp. 92–5.
103 Scott, *Inglands Ioy*, p. 8.
104 *The Sermons*, p. 575.
105 Ibid.
106 Goodwin, *Babels Balm*, p. 77.
107 Abbott, *Hand of Fellowship*, Book I, p. 45.
108 Wadsworth, *English Spanish Pilgrime*, p. 28.
109 *A Treatise Concerning Antichrist*, p. 100.
110 Abbott, *Dangers of Popery*, p. 17.
111 (London, 1624), p. 17.
112 *Two Sermons*, p. 7.
113 *Luther's Fore-Runners*, Pt III, p. 70.
114 *Babels Balm*, p. 46.
115 *The Danger of Popery*, p. 8.

Bibliography

A Hand of Fellowship, To Help Keepe ovt Sinne and Antichrist (London, 1623).

Abbott, R., *The Danger of Popery* (London, 1625).

Adams, J.Q. (ed.), *The Dramatic Records of Sir Henry Herbert, Master of the Revels, 1623–1673* (New Haven and London, 1917).

'The Office-Book, 1622–1642, of Sir Henry Herbert, Master of the Revels', in *To Doctor R. Essays ... Collected and Published in Honor of the Seventieth Birthday of Dr. A.S.W. Rosenbach* (Philadelphia, 1946), pp. 1–9.

An Answer to the Question: Whether the Emperour that now is, can bee the Judge on the Bohemian Controuersie or no? (n.p., 1620).

The Appollogie of the Illustrous Prince Ernestus, Earle of Mansfield, &c (n.p., 1622).

Arber, F., *Transcript of the Registers of the Company of Stationers of London; 1554–1640 A.D.* (London, 1877).

A.W., *The Court and Character of King James* (London, 1650).

Baliński, M., Lipiński, T., *Starożytna Polska pod względem Historycznym, jeograficznym i statystycznym opisana* (Warsaw, 1846).

Bargrave, J., *A Sermon Preached Befor the Honorable Assembly; of Knights, Cittizens, and Burgesses, of the lower House of Parliament* (London, 1624).

Bawcutt, N.W., 'New Revels Documents of Sir George Buck and Sir Henry Herbert, 1619–1622', *Review of English Studies*, XXXV (1984), pp. 316–31.

Beard, Th., *Antichrist the Pope of Rome, Or the Pope of Rome Antichrist* (London, 1624).

Bentley, G.E., *The Jacobean and Caroline Stage* (Oxford, 1941–1968).

Bernard, R., *The Isle of Man: Or, the Legall Proceeding in Man-shire against Sinne* (London, 1627).

Bertie, G., *Five Generations of a Loyal House* (London, 1845).

Bevington, D., *Tudor Drama and Politics. A Critical Approach to Topical Meaning* (Cambridge, Mass., 1968).

Boas, F.S. (ed.), *The Poetical Works of Giles and Phineas Fletcher* (Cambridge, 1900).

Bowers, F. (ed.), *The Dramatic Works of Thomas Dekker* (Cambridge, 1961).

Bradbrook, M.C., *English Dramatic Form* (London, 1965).

Breslow, M.A., *A Mirror of England. English Puritan Views of Foreign Nations, 1618–1640* (Cambridge, Mass., 1970).

Bullough, G., '"The Game at Chesse". How it Struck a Contemporary', *Modern Languages Review* 49 (1954), pp. 156–8.

Burgess, J., *Certaine letters declaring in part the passage of affairs in the Palatinate* (Amsterdam, 1620).

Burton, H., *Censure of Simonie* (London, 1624).

Butler, M., *Theatre and Crisis 1632–1642* (Cambridge, 1984).

Calendar of the Clarendon State Papers Preserved in the Bodleian Library, ed. by the Revd O. Ogle and W.H. Bliss (Oxford, 1872).

Calendar of State Papers, Domestic, (1623–25) and *Venetian*, (1619–21, 1623–25).

Carter, C.H., *The Secret Diplomacy of the Habsburgs, 1598–1625* (New York and London, 1964).

Chamberlain, J., *Letters*, ed. by N.E. McClure (Philadelphia, 1939).

Dahl, F., *A Bibliography of English Corantos and Periodical Newsbooks 1620–1642* (London, 1952).

Davies, G., 'English Political Sermons, 1603–1640', *The Huntington Library Quarterly*, vol. III, no. 1 (October 1939), pp. 1–22.

Davies, R.A., Young, A.R., '"Strange Cunning" in Thomas Middleton's *A Game at Chess*', *University of Toronto Quarterly*, XLV (1976), pp. 236–45.

Dekker, Th., Ford, J., *The Sun's Darling*, in F. Bowers (ed.), *The Dramatic Works of Thomas Dekker*, IV (Cambridge, 1961).

D.M. [a note on the Duchess of Suffolk], *The Gentleman's Magazine*, vol. 77 (March 1807), pp. 209–10.

Downame, G., *A Treatise Concerning Antichrist* (London, 1603).

Drue, Th., *The Life of the Duchess of Suffolk* (London, 1631).

Dunn, T.A., *Philip Massinger* (London, 1957).

Edwards, Ph., 'The Sources of Massinger's *The Bondman*', *Review of English Studies*, 15 (1964), pp. 21–6.

'The Royal Pretenders in Massinger and Ford', *Essays and Studies*, N.S. 27 (1974), pp. 18–36.

and Colin Gibson (eds.), *The Plays and Poems of Philip Massinger* (Oxford, 1976).

Englisham, G., *The Forerunners of Revenge*, in *Harleian Miscellany*, II (London, 1809).

Featly, D., *The Romish Fisher Caught and Held in His Owne Net* (London, 1624).

An Appendix to the Fisher's Net (London, 1624).

Finett, A., *Finetti Philoxenis* (London, 1656).

Firth, C.H., *The Ballad History of the Reign of James I*, *Transactions of the Royal Historical Society*, 3rd ser. (London, 1911).

Foakes, R.A., Introduction, in William Shakespeare, *King Henry VIII*, The Arden Edition (London, 1968).

Foulkes, A.P., *Literature and Propaganda* (London and New York, 1983)

Foxe, J., *Acts and Monuments*, ed. by J. Pratt (Oxford, 1877).

Fraser, A., *King James* (London, 1974).

Frijlinck, W.P. (ed.), *The Tragedy of Sir John Olden Barnavelt* (Amsterdam, 1922).

Gardiner, S.R., *Prince Charles and The Spanish Marriage: 1617–1623. A Chapter in English History* (London, 1869).

A History of England Under the Duke of Buckingham and Charles I 1624–1628 (London, 1875).

'The Political Element in Massinger', *The Contemporary Review*, XXVIII (August 1876), pp. 495–507.

Gee, J., *The Foot Out of the Snare: With a Detection of Sundry Late Practices and impostures of the Priests and Iesuites in England* (London, 1624).

New Shreds of the Old Snare (London, 1624).

Goff, Lady Cecilie, *A Woman of the Tudor Age* (London, 1930).

Goldberg, J., *James I and the Politics of Literature* (Baltimore and London, 1983).

Goodwin, G., *Babels Balm: Or the Honey-Combe of Romes Religion* (London, 1624).

Green, M. [an account of the Duchess of Suffolk's fortunes], *The Gentleman's Magazine*, vol. 76 (August 1806), pp. 691–2.

Greg, W.W., *A Companion to Arber* (Oxford, 1967).

Gross, A., 'Contemporary Politics in Massinger', *Studies in English Literature*, VI (1966), pp. 279–90.

Gurnay, E., *The Romish Chaine* (London, 1624).

Haller, W., *Foxe's Book of Martyrs and the Elect Nation* (London, 1963).

Halliwell, J.O., *The Autobiography and Correspondence of Sir Simond D'Ewes, Bart., During the Reigns of James I and Charles I* (London, 1845).

BIBLIOGRAPHY

Hanson, L., 'English Newsbooks, 1620–1641', *The Library*, 4th ser., XVIII (1938), pp. 355–84.

Harleian Miscellany (London, 1809).

Harrison, J., *A Short Relation of the departure of the high and mightie Prince Frederick King Elect of Bohemia; with his royal vertuos Ladie Elizabeth* (Dort, 1619).

Heinemann, M., *Puritanism and Theatre* (Cambridge, 1980).

Henslowe's Diary, ed. by R.A. Foakes and R.T. Rickert (Cambridge, 1961).

Herford, C.H., Simpson, P. and E. (eds), *Ben Jonson* (Oxford, 1925–1952).

Heywood, Th., *A Marriage Triumph Solemnized* (London, 1613).

Hieron, S., *Sermons* (London, 1624).

Hill, Ch., *Antichrist in Seventeenth-Century England* (London, 1971).

Hockham, W., *Prince Charles his Welcome to the Court, or a true subjects love for his happy returne frome Spaine* (London, 1623).

Holinshed, R., *Chronicles of England, Scotland, and Ireland* (London, 1587).

Holmes, D.M., *The Art of Thomas Middleton. A Critical Study* (Oxford, 1970).

Howard-Hill, T.H., 'Stage Directions in Middleton's *Game at Chess*', paper presented at the annual meeting of the SAA at Cambridge, Mass., 1984.

Hoy, C., *Introduction, Notes, and Commentaries to texts in 'The Dramatic Works of Thomas Dekker' edited by Fredson Bowers* (Cambridge, 1980).

Hume, M., *The Court of Philip IV. Spain in decadence* (London, 1907).

Jonson, B., *Neptune's Triumph for the Return of Albion*, in Herford, C.H., *et al.*, *Ben Jonson*, VII (Oxford, 1941), pp. 681–700.

Limon, J., *Gentlemen of a Company. English Players in Central and Eastern Europe* (Cambridge, 1985).

Lockyer, R., *Buckingham. The Life and Political Career of George Villiers, First Duke of Buckingham, 1592–1628* (London and New York, 1981).

Marcus, L.S., 'The Occasion of Ben Jonson's *Pleasure Reconciled to Virtue*', *Studies in English Literature*, 19 (1979), pp. 271–93.

Mason, H., *The New Art of Lying, Covered by Iesuites under the Vaile of Equivocation* (London, 1624).

Massinger, Ph., *The Plays and Poems, see under Edwards, Ph*

Middleton, Th., *A Game at Chesse* (London, n.d., = 1624).

   A Game at Chesse, ed. by R.C. Bald (Cambridge, 1929).

   The Works of, ed. by A.H. Bullen (London, 1886).

Moore, J.R., 'The Contemporary Significance of Middleton's *Game at Chesse*', *PMLA*, 50 (1935), pp. 761–8.

Morris, E.C., 'The Allegory in Middleton's *A Game at Chesse*', *Englische Studien*, 38 (1907), pp. 39–52.

Murray, J.T., *English Dramatic Companies, 1558–1642* (London, 1910).

The Newes of Europe, with all such particular accidents, as haue chanced in seuerall Prouinces, no. 21 (London, 1624).

Nixon, A., *Great Brittaines Generall Ioyes* (London, 1613).

Oman, C., *Elizabeth of Bohemia* (London, 1964).

Orgel, S., *The Jonsonian Masque* (Cambridge, Mass., 1965).

Orrell, J., 'The London Stage in the Florentine Correspondence, 1604–1618', *Theatre Research International*, vol. III, no. 3 (1978), pp. 157–76.

   'Buckingham's Patronage of the Dramatic Arts: The Crowe Accounts', *Records of Early English Drama* (1980:2), pp. 8–17.

Parrin, J.P., *Luthers Fore-Runners* (London, 1624).

Payne, L.W., *The Hector of Germanie*, Publications of the University of Pennsylvania, Series in Philology and Literature, vol. XI (Philadelphia, 1906).

The Present State of affaires betwixt the Emperor and the King of Bohemia (n.p., 1620).

Rainolds, J., *The Discovery of the Man of Sinne* (London, 1614).

The reasons which compelled the states of Bohemia to reject the archduke Ferdinand (Dort, 1619).

Reynolds, J., *Votiuae Angliae* (London, 1624).

Ribner, I., *The English History Play in the Age of Shakespeare* (Princeton, N.J., 1957).

Ruigh, R.E., *The Parliament of 1624. Politics and Foreign Policy* (Cambridge, Mass., 1971).

Russell, C., *Parliament and English Politics 1621–1629* (Oxford, 1979).

Russell, H.K., 'Tudor and Stuart Dramatisation of the Doctrine of Natural and Moral Philosophy', *Studies in Philology*, XXXI (1934), pp. 1–27.

Sargent, R., 'Theme and Structure in Middleton's "A Game at Chess"', *Modern Languages Review*, 66 (1971), pp. 721–30.

Schreiber, R.E., *The Political Career of Sir Robert Naunton 1589–1635* (London, 1981).

Scott, Th., *A Briefe Information of the Affaires of the Palatinate* (n.p., 1624).

    Certain Reasons and Argvments of Polecei, Why the King of England should hereafter give over all further Treatie, and enter into warre with the Spaniard (n.p., 1624).

    An Experimental Discoverie of Spanish Practices (n.p., 1624).

    A Post-Script, Or, A Second Part of Robert Earle of Essex His Ghost (n.p., 1624).

    Robert Earl of Essex His Ghost (n.p., 1624).

    A Second Part of Spanish Practices (n.p., 1624).

    The Spaniards Perpetuall Designes to an Vniversall Monarchie (n.p., 1624).

    A Speech Made in the Lower House of Parliament, By Sir Edward Cicell, Colonel (Utrecht, 1624).

    Symmachia: Or, A True-Loves Knot. Tyed Betwixt Great Britaine and the Vnited Prouinces, by the wisdom of King Iames (n.p., 1624).

    Vox Coeli, or News from Heaven (Paradise, 1624).

    The Works (Utrecht, 1624).

Scott, W. (ed.), *Somers Collection of Tracts* (London, 1809).

Sherman, J., 'The Pawns' Allegory in Middleton's *A Game at Chesse*', *Review of English Studies* XXIX (1978), pp. 147–59.

Sienkiewicz, K., *Dziennik z podróży do Anglii 1820–21* (Warsaw, 1953).

Sisson, C.J., *Lost Plays of Shakespeare's Age* (Cambridge, 1936).

Smith, Wentworth, *The Hector of Germanie, or the Palsgrave, Prince Elector* (London, 1615).

Spencer, B.T., Introduction to his edition of Massinger's *The Bondman* (Princeton, 1932).

Spikes, J.D., 'The Jacobean History Play and the Myth of the Elect Nation', *Renaissance Drama*, N.S., VIII (1977), pp. 117–49.

Sulimierski, F. (*et al.*) (eds.), *Słownik geograficzny Królestwa Polskiego i innych krajów słowiańskich* (Warsaw, 1883).

Taylor, N., Loughrey, B., 'Middleton's Chess Strategies in *Women Beware Women*', *Studies in English Literature*, 24 (1984), pp. 341–54.

Taylor, J., *English-Mans Love to Bohemia* (Dort, 1620).

    Taylor his Trauels: From the Citty of London in England, to the Citty of Prague in Bohemia (London, 1620).

    Prince Charles his welcome frome Spaine (London, 1623).

Taylor, Th., *Two Sermons: The One a Heavenly Voice, Calling All God's People Out of Romish Babylon. The Other An Everlasting Record of the Utter Ruine or Romish Amalek* (London, 1624).

    Christ's Victorie Over the Dragon: Or Satan's Downfall (London, 1633).

    Tom Tell-Troath: Or, A free Discourse touching the Manners of the Time. Directed to his Majestie by Waye of humble Advertisement (n.p., n.d.; c. 1623).

Trevelyan, G.M., *England Under the Stuarts* (London and New York, 1965).

Troubles in Bohemia and other Kingdomes procured by Jesuites (n.p., 1619).

Wadsworth, J., *The English Spanish Pilgrime, Or, A New Discovery of Spanish Popery and Jesuitical Stratagems* (London, 1629).

Webbe, G., *Catalogus Protestantium: Or, The Protestants Kalendar Containing A Surview of the Protestants Religion long before Luthers daies, euen to the time of the Apostles, and in the primitive Church* (London, 1624).

Wedgwood, C.V., *The Thirty Years War* (New York, 1961).

Wilson, E.M., Turner, O., 'The Spanish Protest Against "A Game at Chess"' *Modern Languages Review*, XLIV (1949), pp. 477–82.

Wood, Th., *An Oration or speech appropriated unto the princes of Christendom* (London, 1624).

Wotton, Anthony, *Runne From Rome, Or A Treatise Shewing the necessitie of Separating from the Church of Rome* (London, 1624).

Wright, L.B., 'Propaganda against James I's "Appeasement" of Spain', *The Huntington Library Quarterly*, vol. VI, No. 2 (1942–3), pp. 149–72.

Yachnin, P., 'A Game at Chess and Chess Allegory', *Studies in English Literature*, 22 (1982), pp. 317–30.

Zins, H., *Polska w oczach Anglików XIV–XVI w.* (Warsaw, n.d. = 1965).

Index

INDEX